Mary S. Lovell has been a biographer for twenty-five years, during which time she has written a number of bestsellers, including *Straight on Till Morning: The Biography of Beryl Markham* and *Amelia Earhart: The Sound of Wings*, which was made into a film in 2009. More recent subjects have been the Victorian adventuress Jane Digby (*A Scandalous Life*); the six Mitford sisters (*The Mitford Girls*); and the Tudor entrepreneur, Countess of Shrewsbury (*Bess of Hardwick*).

THE
RIVIERA SET

1920–1960: The golden years
of glamour and excess

MARY S. LOVELL

ABACUS

First published in Great Britain in 2016 by Little, Brown
This paperback edition published in 2017 by Abacus

3 5 7 9 10 8 6 4 2

A CIP catalogue record for this book
is available from the British Library.

ISBN 978-0-349-13989-0

Typeset in Garamond by M Rules
Printed and bound in Great Britain by
Clays Ltd, St Ives plc

Papers used by Abacus are from well-managed forests
and other responsible sources.

Abacus
An imprint of
Little, Brown Book Group
Carmelite House
50 Victoria Embankment
London EC4Y 0DZ

An Hachette UK Company
www.hachette.co.uk

www.littlebrown.co.uk

This book is dedicated to
my granddaughters Robyn and Imogen
to thank them for bringing
much joy into my life.

Contents

PART THREE

Introduction

The Château de l'Horizon

I have been a biographer for over thirty years, but this book is less a biography of a person, more the story of a house and those who peopled it between the years 1930 and 1960.

It was beautifully proportioned, an exquisite white art deco villa on the French Riviera which acted as a collecting point for a group of people who were often world-famous celebrities, many of whom were able to enjoy a lifestyle of almost unrelenting pleasure.

First, it was the stylish brainchild of the American actress, society hostess, possibly royal mistress and certainly hugely successful investor Maxine Elliott. In 1930 she bought a piece of seaside real estate between Cannes and Juan-les-Pins, consisting of a narrow stretch of rocks with a small promontory. It was less expensive than many pieces of building land in this idyllic location, because there was no sandy beach. Indeed at first there seemed no obvious site for a house of any significant size since it was hemmed in by the parallel features of the

1

main road between Cannes and Antibes and the main railway line between Marseilles and Nice.

By 1932 a stunning dwelling had been constructed on the unpromising site by dynamiting the rocks to provide a flat foundation platform for a villa, as well as a deep depression to house a swimming pool.

The villa was the Château de l'Horizon. Designed by a young American, Barry Dierks, who was to become one of the most famous architects of the art deco period on the Riviera, it would provide a secluded backdrop during the next three decades for an indulgent, glamorous, even decadent lifestyle which is arguably unsurpassed, and where one guest thought nothing of filling a bath with dozens of bottles of iced champagne to refresh her aching feet after an evening's dancing in Cannes.

Since the last decades of the nineteenth century, Cannes had been famous as a winter resort for British and Russian royalty and aristocracy, but it was considered far too hot in the summer months for civilised living. The area was only discovered as a summer holiday location in 1926, by New Yorkers Gerald and Sara Murphy – the inspiration for Dick and Nicole Diver in Scott Fitzgerald's *Tender is the Night*. The Murphys attracted to their ménage an eclectic group of artists, writers and performers, the most famous of whom were Pablo Picasso, Paul Robeson, Cole Porter, Dorothy Parker, Jean Cocteau and Scott and Zelda Fitzgerald. Those on the periphery of the Murphy set included Maxine Elliott, introduced by her friend Elsa Maxwell, and they were able to monopolise beaches empty of tourists before the secret leaked out and the Côte d'Azur became an all-year-round haven for the richest people on the planet, a place away from 'home' where hardly any whim or eccentricity was too outrageous to be acceptable. Maxine Elliott quickly spotted the trend – she was good at that – and she moved in ahead of the advancing tide of the Riviera's burgeoning popularity.

That popularity has never faded. While I was writing this Introduction, I happened to see a headline in a daily newspaper: 'Average price of a five-bedroom house in the Côte d'Azur reaches £18 million . . .'[1] Today the newly super-rich – mainly Russian oligarchs, oil-rich Arabs and Chinese super-entrepreneurs – are busy making the Riviera their own, a place where money is everything, and in order to be accepted into the inner circle it seems imperative to own the largest yacht in marinas already crammed with what look like mini cruise-liners each with their own pools, helicopters and submarines.

In the Thirties the richest residents were mainly British, and in order to belong to the charmed circle social position, style and elegance were considered to be of equal importance to money. In the post-war years a new set took over – Americans and Europeans mostly, and then it was fame and glamour that counted. This book covers that earlier, more glamorous time on the Riviera when entry into the charmed circle required either money beyond the dreams of the average human, breeding, or talent and the ability to entertain one's fellow guests. And quite often then, as now, outstanding physical beauty, especially when exquisitely dressed, trumped everything else.

Initially, I was inclined to write off these gatherings as nothing more than a coming-together of frivolous rich people to eat lotus and drink champagne, and some of it was just that. However, I came to realise that in some ways this lifestyle had its own place in history too. For it was here that the badly bruised Churchill came to recover from his battering during his wilderness years in British politics; he found a different audience prepared to listen to him and admire him as he formulated his policies. He loved luxury and wallowed unashamedly whenever it was on offer, but in the Thirties such spoiling was beyond his own pocket. He had known Maxine Elliott since he was a stripling, for she had been a friend of his beloved mother. He amply repaid his hostess with wit and conversation, and his mere presence at the villa hiked Maxine's house parties to an altitude where an invitation to dine while Churchill was in residence at the Château de l'Horizon was virtually a royal command, and this included royalty, former royalty and heads of state. It also brought intellectuals willingly to the table. Maxine never capitalised on this: she sensed Winston was restoring himself, and took great care only to invite people whom Winston liked and would entertain him, or were useful to him. Equally, the Côte d'Azur provided a sanctuary for the Duke and Duchess of Windsor, who were also emotionally battered by the world. They too found a balm of sorts among this shimmering crowd.

I felt I could not write the story of the château and its glittering inhabitants without first telling Maxine Elliott's own story, for how else could one explain the extraordinary mix of world-famous people that this elderly matron in the last decade of her life managed to attract, so that an invitation from her to stay at the Château de l'Horizon was one of the most sought after on the French Riviera, and the Riviera Set drifted towards her house as filings to a magnet.

PART ONE

I

In the Beginning ... Jessie Dermot

Jessica Dermot was born in Rockland, Maine on 5 February 1868,[1] during an ice storm which froze the normally busy harbour into inactivity for six weeks. Her father, Tom Dermot, was a New England sea captain of Irish descent; her mother, Adelaide, came from older pioneering stock – early Protestant immigrants from Bohemia. The family was God-fearing, respectable and hard-working.

Little Jessie – or 'Dettie', as the child pronounced it, which became a lifelong nickname – was reared and educated along with her siblings in a strict, no-frills ethos, in a white clapperboard cottage on State Street. Rockland, which had been settled a century earlier, and developed around its shipbuilding industry and lime quarries, was still a very small town, where everyone knew everyone else's business. Who among the respectable New Englanders who dutifully trudged through the snow to attend little Jessie's baptism could have possibly predicted that this baby, born into such an ordinary family, would one day be the toast of two continents, be described by an English king as the most beautiful woman in the world, integrate with scarcely a ripple into the normally impenetrable English upper classes to be regarded as a hostess of international renown, and become the intimate and trusted friend of world leaders?

She was not an outstandingly beautiful child, but she was striking and different, olive-skinned and black-haired like her maternal grandmother. But it was her eyes that people most remembered; they were unusual, the colour of alexandrite, whose chief feature is that it appears to change colour with the light – one minute dark brown, the next pale amber, and sometimes a deep mossy green. Her childhood contemporaries recalled her as someone who always knew what she wanted and went for it. She was neither noticeably popular nor unpopular at school, not a girly girl but a slightly chubby tomboy, always willing to involve herself in anything that was fun or exciting.

Her father's career had moved on an upward curve. The rewards of hard work and thrift had enabled him to move his wife and five children (one child had died in infancy) from the little cottage to a substantial brick family house on Main Street. The house was mortgaged and registered in his wife's name against the possibility of him suffering a fatal accident at sea, which would at least provide her with the equity. At the same time he had commissioned and built a new ship, the *Will C. Case*, a 141ft three-masted ocean-going barque in which he invested every cent he could claw together. On 10 January 1878 the new ship was fully rigged, loaded with cargo (mostly lime), and victualled to leave with the morning tide on a transatlantic crossing. A massive storm struck Maine in the early hours of the morning and Rockland took the brunt of it. Captain Dermot raced to the harbour and in an almost heroic feat managed to cut his ship loose from the old timber wharf which was breaking up. Somehow he steered her safely through the churning seas littered with damaged boats and storm debris, and drove her ashore on a sandy beach south of the town. His ship was repairable – just, but the cost was beyond him. There was no insurance, and to raise enough money Captain Dermot had to sell shares in his ship, leaving him with only a minority holding.

After that life changed for the family. From being a successful ship owner-master with a future, Captain Dermot was now merely an employee of his shareholders. There was no shame in it, of course; neighbours and townsfolk understood and sympathised. But the family's standing in the community had altered and they felt the difference keenly. Life was that little bit harder for them all and, worst of all, Adelaide Dermot developed severe migraines and periods of chronic depression. She began to spend weeks and then months locked away in her bedroom. Her husband was away at sea for months at a time, in a triangular trading pattern of New York to South America, thence to Spanish ports, on to Liverpool and back to Rockland, loaded on all sailing legs with any profitable cargo. Relatives in Rockland helped out, but inevitably a good deal of the running of the house and care of the younger children fell upon Dettie's shoulders.

She was up to it because there was much of her father's strength and energy in her. Tom Dermot had been born in County Galway in 1837, but at about ten years old was found living rough among a gang of boys in the docks of Liverpool, surviving on nothing but his wits. He was a child victim of the Great Famine, his parents probably part of the diaspora, but whether he had run away from them or been orphaned no one knew. He was informally adopted by a kindly American skipper whose own son had died, taken to the United States and there given a home and an education, but there was always a rough heartiness and a vigorous strength about Tom, coupled with a severity which became increasingly intimidating to his emotionally sensitive wife.

By the time she was fourteen Dettie was showing elements of the beauty for which she was to become famous, and thereby attracting far too much attention from the opposite sex for her parents' comfort, especially from one Arthur Hall, the son of a rich local family. Ten years older than Dettie, he rode fast thoroughbred horses and drove the latest-model carriages. So the worried Dermots were pleased when Dettie developed a solid friendship with a girl from school and often stayed overnight at her home. One day Captain Dermot bumped into this girl's father and thanked him for all the hospitality afforded to Dettie, only to be told they hadn't set eyes on her in months. The game was up. Once they began asking around, her stunned parents found a body of evidence about the relationship between Dettie and Arthur Hall that was enough to ruin Dettie's reputation.

There was always a strong suspicion that Dettie was pregnant by Arthur Hall when, shortly after the liaison became known about, she sailed with her father for South America. She was away for about five months and it was given out in Rockland that Dettie was unwell and was accompanying her father for her health. But the glowing, confident – even defiant – girl who returned, looking far more mature than her fifteen years, wearing gold earrings and carrying a parrot on her shoulder, showed no signs of illness, and she was certainly not pregnant. She never forgave those who were responsible for separating her from Arthur Hall: even in her last years she still made bitter remarks about the matter, and once, when she had become a famous actress, she rudely snubbed some Rockford matrons who had travelled to New York to see her perform and then called on her. They had been part of the clique she considered responsible for the ending of her teen-age romance.

Having seen New York and Rio, several Spanish ports (where members of the crew reported that her dark beauty had almost stopped the traffic), and Liverpool, Dettie felt she had outgrown her home town and was outspoken in her opinions. No doubt the good folk of Rockland shook their heads, drew their own conclusions and went about their own business. But Captain Dermot quickly realised that Dettie could not return to school in Rockland; somehow he raised the money to send her away to a reputable Boston boarding school for her final year of education.

By now Adelaide Dermot's mental condition had become so serious that her husband was forced to retire from the sea in order to care for her and his younger children. He traded his shares in the ship for shares in a jeweller's business belonging to a relative and reluctantly went to work in the shop.

Dettie spent part of her long school vacation that summer of 1883 in New York with the family of a school friend (undoubtedly adequately vetted by Captain Dermot this time) who ran a respectable boarding house for professional men. Dettie quickly fell under the spell of New York in the mid-eighties. It was modern, cosmopolitan and exciting – some buildings even had electric lighting. She also fell under the spell of one of the residents of the boarding house, George McDermott, a thirty-year-old lawyer and First Marshal of the city, who dressed well, had a commanding presence and was a lavish spender. In 1884, as soon as she turned sixteen, the couple applied to Captain Dermot for permission to marry. This was readily given; Dettie would be safe with this ambitious young man (he was already earning $2500 a year) who would be able to care for her and give her the sort of life and lifestyle that she had glimpsed during her relationship with Arthur Hall, and to which she now aspired.

A happy family wedding followed and Dettie was provided with forty dresses for her trousseau by female relatives, friends and neighbours before she left in triumph for a new life in New York. There was one subsequent visit by the newlyweds to Rockland and after that little, other than an occasional letter, was heard of Dettie for three years. By then she had left George, who had resigned his job with the City of New York to go into private practice and at which he proved singularly unsuccessful. He began to drink heavily, and when drunk became physically violent. Dettie came from a seafaring community and would have been no stranger to a man in drink; her own father liked a drink. But she would not tolerate a wife-beater, and soon found herself a protector in the shape of John Montgomery Ward, a Major League baseball star.[*] The last Dettie saw of George was his drunken body lying in the gutter, where Ward had knocked him after George, affecting the part of an outraged husband, had tackled him.

When Dettie turned up in Rockland soon afterwards with Ward at her side the townspeople were shocked. She had fled

---

[*] Ward was playing shortstop for the New York Giants at this time.

to her parents' home to explain her position and tell them she was suing for a divorce, without thinking how it would look. To her dismay she found her family in a worse situation than her own. Her mother's condition was now so severe that for her own safety, and that of her younger children, Tom, Grace (who died in infancy), Lew, May Gertrude (always called Gertrude) and Sam, Adelaide had been committed to the State Asylum in Augusta, where she died soon afterwards.

With the death of his wife, Tom Dermot's life in Rockland came to an end. He was desperate to get back to sea, but sail was giving way to steam in the east coast ports and commands requiring his skills were becoming scarce. He sold his share in the jeweller's business, persuaded the owners of his former ship to sell her to a buyer in San Francisco and left his younger children with relatives until he could send for them. He then sailed the *Will C. Case* around Cape Horn and delivered her to California, where he intended to begin a new life. In California he met forty-two-year-old schoolteacher Isabella 'Belle' Paine, a Rockland girl who had been a childhood sweetheart. Isabella was also recently widowed and within a year the pair were married.

Tom bought a small house in Oakland overlooking San Francisco Bay and his children came out to live with them. He was offered command of the sailing ship *Portland*, trading between California and Alaska. In his absences the childless Isabella became a loving stepmother to Tom's family, and this now included Dettie. Dettie had been badly affected by the failure of her marriage – heartbroken, it was said – despite her baseball-player follower. She was still only nineteen, and her teenage years had been peppered with incident and tragedy – her father's financial losses and (equally important) his loss of

13

face in that tight community, her mother's mental illness and eventual death, her own extraordinary burgeoning beauty, the ill-fated affair with Arthur Hall, and now her failed marriage to George whom, for all his faults, she claimed to have loved deeply. John Ward faded from the picture and shortly afterwards married the Broadway actress Helen Dauvray. All this had taken a toll on Dettie and for a short time she was content to rest and let her stepmother care for her while she considered her options.

In 1890, the choices which offered any degree of independence to a respectable young woman, even a reasonably well-educated one, were limited. She could aspire to become a teacher, governess or seamstress. She could learn to operate a typewriter and perhaps obtain work in an office, though all of these options were low paid and Dettie wondered how much independence she would have working for someone else and living at home. The alternative would be to remarry, but this was a long way down her list of ambitions; she had been burnt by her experience with George. She had lost her puppy fat, had grown tall and stately, with a luscious dark beauty so striking that she really stood out in any crowd, and drew admiring looks wherever she went. Only a decade earlier her walk would have made her crinolines sway, but fashion now decreed more natural skirts, and with her full bust, wide hips and tiny waist (helped by tight lacing), Dettie was what men of her era termed a fine woman. One acquaintance described how her small head was crowned with great braids of coal-black hair while her eyes 'were a sort of violet, and I have never seen such big ones, or with such a soft and tender look'.[2]

In an era when actresses were more famous for their appearance than their acting ability, Dettie lost count of the number of times people told her she ought to go on the stage. She had never acted, but she had certainly entertained her relatives at family parties with recitations and droll performances. The drawback was that she knew her family, and especially her father and her aunts, would be appalled since actresses at that time did not enjoy a reputation for morality. However, ignoring the negative aspects, and despite her father's words – 'You're a damned fool!' – ringing in her ears, twenty-one-year-old Dettie headed back to New York, where she still had a few friends and knew her way around, now determined to get herself a job on the stage.

Calling herself Jessica Dermot she enrolled in a drama school at a theatre in Madison Square, and found herself an inexpensive room in a boarding house. Luckily her looks, her pure speaking voice with hardly any accent (her father had always insisted his children speak properly, without any 'Yankee slang') and her pretended sophistication caught the eye of the elderly acting coach who ran the school. There was no physical intimacy between them but Dettie was seen everywhere on his arm – he enjoyed showing her off in top restaurants and taught her much from his own fifty years in the theatre: how to project her voice, how to memorise scripts, how to move on the stage so as to command attention. As for losing her self-consciousness in front of an audience, he told all his pupils that the only way was to keep doing it until it became second nature. Dettie learned fast from her elderly mentor and placed her hopes in his plans for his star pupil, but that September he had a heart attack and died suddenly. Not, however, before he had advised her to change her name to something more striking – more in keeping with her spectacular looks.

They took time over this, experimenting with names that sounded grand and had a ring to them. Eventually Dettie said the grandest name she knew was Maximilius – the name of the father of a rich school friend. They toyed with Maxime, but then hit on the idea of a subtle alteration and Dettie became Maxine; this pleased her because if the 'x' was omitted it spelled Maine, which she felt was lucky. She always claimed she had invented this forename, and so was the first to bear it. For a surname she chose her grandmother's maiden name, Elliott.

Albert Marshman Palmer was one of the leading impresarios of the day; he owned several theatres, staged numerous productions and had enjoyed a string of successes. Hearing that Palmer was about to cast bit-part roles in a new production of *The Middleman*, which had enjoyed success in England, Dettie did not wait for auditions but applied directly as Miss Maxine Elliott for a private interview, citing the name of her late mentor. She had no acting experience to offer, and knew that if she was to get a job she would have to promote herself as she was. So she dressed carefully and rehearsed her interview. Her plan worked and Palmer later admitted he chose her because she was stunning, had stage presence and could pass – at a pinch – as an English lady. He offered her a small role and Dettie was on the bottom rung of the ladder, with a salary of twenty-five dollars a week.

Over the next five years Maxine – as she was now known to everyone other than her family and childhood friends – worked hard and gradually landed bigger and better parts. It was grinding work, travelling huge distances across the United States by train as part of a touring theatre company.

There was never enough time to rest properly between the small towns where they would put on a week's performance and move on, always staying in third-rate boarding houses. Fortunately, Maxine had boundless energy and youth on her side, and eventually she climbed a few more rungs of the ladder and took lead roles in minor productions.

In those days before television and movies, the theatre was the only available public entertainment. Popular actors had the status of A-list celebrities and those at the top, such as Henry Irving and Sarah Bernhardt, were as iconic to late Victorians as Elvis Presley or Marilyn Monroe would be in the following century. Maxine was yet to reach the top of this greasy pole, with the celebrity status that meant she had arrived, but she was on her way.

2

Miss Maxine Elliott

In 1893 Maxine landed the female lead in a spectacular new play, *The Prodigal Daughter*, which included as its final scene the finish of the Grand National. With ten real racehorses and jockeys racing round a huge revolving stage, this production opened to huge success in New York and Maxine's salary was raised. One of the first things she did was to send for her younger sister to live with her in larger rooms in a better boarding house. She believed that after seventeen-year-old Gertrude had been given some singing lessons she might get work as an extra in productions of which Maxine was the star. Maxine's name began to appear in gossip columns, and job offers trickled in. One was for a touring production and she made her acceptance conditional: her younger sister must have a part. So Gertrude played the ingénue in a number of productions that followed; in Oscar Wilde's *A Woman of No Importance*, for example, Gertrude played Lady Stutfield, a naive character desperate for male attention.

The two sisters did not work together for long, because Maxine soon received an offer from Augustin Daly, whose company was famous for its lavish musicals, Shakespearean productions which attracted the top names in the classical acting profession, and also dashing dramas.* Although she would not be able to bring Gertrude in with her, Maxine could not turn Daly's offer down and soon she was playing Silvia in *Two Gentlemen of Verona*, Hermia in *A Midsummer Night's Dream* and the lead in *The Heart of Ruby* – a romantic comedy-drama set in Japan, featuring an oriental heroine with a wisp of gauze as a yashmak. She worked indefatigably in those years and earned the respect of her acting colleagues. She was especially pleased that her acting ability in the Shakespeare productions was reviewed favourably because previously it had been her beauty that had been regarded as her chief asset. On the back of these reviews Daly took his company to London in 1895, where Maxine was quoted in the English press, saying that this was her second trip to England – she did not feel it necessary to explain that on her previous visit she had been a schoolgirl in disgrace.

That summer at Daly's Theatre, Leicester Square, playing Hermia and Silvia, she took London by storm. Interviewed extensively, Maxine graced the covers of three women's magazines, and she was showered with invitations by hostesses happy to welcome a beautiful and talented Shakespearean actress at their parties. Her manners were faultless and her pleasant deep voice was apparently almost without an accent. The Daly Company's leading lady, Ada Rehan, was slated by

---

* It was Daly who first introduced the idea of the villain tying someone to railroad tracks to be saved by the hero or heroine. The device became so beloved by silent-picture directors that it eventually became something of a cliché.

critics such as George Bernard Shaw and Max Beerbohm, but Maxine was described as having 'rare beauty ... a handsome Hermia, playing the part with care and good judgment'. Another stated, 'Miss Maxine Elliott, who is remarkably handsome, was graceful, courteous and unaffected as Silvia.'[1] Fortunately, the company regarded this as good for their reputation and Ada Rehan took no umbrage. Meanwhile, Maxine enjoyed what was to be her first London season of many. She was too late that year for the Derby and Chelsea, but there were many other attractions for her to attend between performances, and these included racing at Royal Ascot and Goodwood, boating at Henley, cricket at Lord's, polo at Windsor Great Park, joining the crowds for Trooping the Colour, and daily carriage rides in Rotten Row. She listened and learned as she met many famous people, and some would become lifelong friends, including Lord Randolph Churchill and his American wife Jennie. Elsie de Wolfe, whom Maxine had met briefly in New York, was in London too. Elsie had begun her own outstanding career as an actress and enjoyed some success, but her chief ability was to wear clothes really well and strut about. Within ten years Elsie would quit the stage to become the leading interior decorator of her day, a profession which she claimed to have invented – there were plenty of architects, she said, but no decorators.

Although not short on invitations in New York, Maxine was far removed in status from the American aristocratic families such as the Astors and Vanderbilts. But she found to her surprise that in England her profession, added to her looks, far from being a hindrance, was instead a passport to the exclusive gatherings of the upper classes. Indeed, there was great excitement that summer when, in the Birthday

Honours, Queen Victoria bestowed a knighthood on Henry Irving. It was the first time anyone in the theatre had been so honoured and did much to make the acting profession socially acceptable. At a party at the Lyceum to honour Sir Henry, Maxine met the great man, as well as theatrical luminaries Ellen Terry, Max Beerbohm and a leading actor who would figure largely in her future, Johnston Forbes-Robertson, known as Forbie, with whom Elsie de Wolfe was discussing a new play.

When she returned to New York that autumn, to open there and later to tour for six weeks as Olivia in *Twelfth Night*, Maxine's friends noted that her accent was now more English than American. Despite her success in her chosen career, her time in England had changed her horizons. The old days of cheap boarding houses, trying to grab a space in a crowded dressing room to apply make-up, and sitting up all night on trains were already long behind her: she was a leading lady, and she had been content with this achievement until she glimpsed in England a milieu that greatly appealed to her. How to make herself part of that way of life taxed her mind considerably in the year that followed, and while it was a dream presently out of her grasp, it remained a lodestar to her and coloured her plans.

A year later Maxine and the leading man, Frank Worthing, left the Daly Company when they were bypassed for leading roles. They decided to strike out together, and take their talent to the west coast. Maxine had an additional agenda. Gertrude, towards whom Maxine felt fiercely maternal, was back living with the Dermots in Oakland and had written to say she longed to return to Maxine and the stage. Furthermore, it was easier to get a divorce in California than

New York and Maxine hoped that a suit filed on the west coast by a Mrs Jessica McDermott would go unnoticed in New York and not create adverse publicity. Initially, Maxine's plan worked well. She starred in several productions in San Francisco that summer of 1896, and at a party she met Nat Goodwin, one of the most famous comedians of the day.

Nat was thirty-nine years old and a fellow New Englander (born in Boston). Like Maxine he was at the tail-end of divorce proceedings and was open to change. Although he was only 5′ 7″, had thin red hair, pallid skin and pale eyes, he countered these physical deficiencies by a super-confident air and his unique style of dressing. He wore beautifully tailored clothes, pale kid gloves, a top hat and hand-made shoes, and carried a gold-topped cane. Nor was he afraid of jewellery; signet rings and flashing diamond studs in his shirt front completed his fashionable ensembles. When Nat Goodwin was in the room he was always the centre of attention. A comic genius, he had a huge number of adoring fans in the USA who slavishly followed his rackety personal life in gossip columns and magazines without his misdemeanours affecting his career; rather, his transgressions seemed to make him all the more interesting and lovable. He made things happen wherever he went, a clown, certainly, but one with style and presence. On stage he could bring an audience to tears of laughter by an elegant wrist movement, a slight turn of the head or eyebrows raised at precisely the right moment. His public never realised that Nat's delivery – his 'just being himself' and throwing in off-the-cuff lines – was the result of many hours a day, rehearsing, studying lines, changing scripts to capitalise on audience reaction during the previous performance, an insistence that all the other actors must, like himself, know their parts and stage placements inside out, and be capable of split-second timing.

In his autobiography Nat recorded his first impressions of Maxine, who was twenty-eight at the time they met. He noted that, although stunning, she was not dressed by a couturier, and she was 'with' Frank Worthing, who was evidently in love with her, but she was not in love with Frank. She was, Nat wrote,

> one of the most beautiful women whom I had ever seen, her raven black hair and eyes in delightful contrast to the red hues that formed an aureole, as it were, above her head. There she sat, totally unconscious of the appetites she was destroying, absorbing the delicate little compliments paid her by that prince of good fellows, John Drew. How I chafed at the etiquette which prohibited my being at her side![2]

Next morning he called on Maxine and Gertrude in their rooms, and offered Maxine a contract to star in his new production in Australia, adding that he was sailing the following day and required an answer on the spot. Maxine was already under contract to a rival producer at seventy-five dollars a week and coolly explained she could not get out of it in under two weeks in order to allow her understudy to rehearse adequately. However, she said, if he would increase his offer to $150 a week, and find parts for Gertrude at half that, they would follow him out on the next sailing. Nat not only accepted her terms but offered them both three-year contracts and a guaranteed tour of the USA on their return from Australia. He was slightly annoyed that he would have to open in Melbourne with Blanche Walsh, his existing leading lady; however they decided that in the interlude before sailing Maxine would be able to make the most of the agreement in terms of publicity stories about the forthcoming tour and she could use the voyage via Honolulu to learn her lines. On being told this news Frank Worthing fainted.

Shortly after the sisters arrived in Melbourne Blanche Walsh saw how the land lay and flounced off back to America, leaving the field clear for Maxine to shine. At the same time the gossip columns became aware of Nat's impending divorce. He claimed that his wife was frequently so drunk she could not fulfil her matrimonial obligations. Mrs Goodwin was not too drunk, however, to employ a top divorce lawyer, who soon discovered that Maxine's divorce had quietly passed through the courts, and she threatened in a newspaper interview to counter-sue Nat, naming Maxine as co-respondent (along with several other beauties whom Nat had courted during the previous two years). At this, the discomfited Blanche Walsh came forward, saying she was also happy to give evidence for she recalled that Nat and Maxine's adjoining hotel suites in Australia had connecting doors.

Nat's autobiography, written two decades later, reveals the injured self-justification he suffered when this news broke in the press. Maxine had wept uncontrollably, believing her career to be over, and it was so unfair, he wrote, because they were totally innocent. It was Gertrude's suggestion that they counter the adverse publicity by issuing an announcement that, since her arrival in Australia, Maxine's divorce had been granted, and that subsequently she and Nat had become engaged to be married. In the event, the publicity surrounding their respective divorces, Nat's philandering and their betrothal provided the couple with acres of media coverage and, rather than harming their reputations, increased their popularity. When they returned to the United States their productions played to packed houses and were advertised as standing room only for weeks in advance.

They married in February 1898, and among some diamonds and a percentage in the theatre company profits, Nat's wedding gifts to Maxine included a handsomely decorated private railcar so that in future they could go on tour in absolute comfort. It was the equivalent of owning a private jet today.

Neither pretended it was a love match. They liked each other, and they rubbed along comfortably enough, and there were compensations. Nat was proud of Maxine's talent and beauty, and she was quick to realise that Nat could give her a better life than she could provide for herself, and she was now able to bank all her earnings. True he drank rather too much – but unlike her first husband Nat was a happy drunk. Also, Maxine had a tendency to depression, and Nat could always cheer her up when she started to worry.

Within a few months of their marriage Nat and Maxine, along with Gertrude, were on their way to England to enjoy the delights of another English summer season. While Maxine was busy buying a new wardrobe Nat went out and bought them a house – in a day. Maxine had said they should have a country house within easy reach of London, but Nat said he bought it chiefly because he was amused by the seller's name – Lord Penzance, which he thought sounded like a character from an Oscar Wilde play. To be fair, it *was* a country house, although it was only thirty years old and came complete with a large staff and market garden. Set in extensive grounds with an oak wood, meadows and winding stream as well as formal gardens, Jackwood was perched on the summit of Shooters Hill* and enjoyed extensive views over Eltham and beyond to Kent. A mock-Tudor mansion built in 1874, it was everything an American might expect from an English country house, from its large bedchambers with dressing rooms, servants' quarters, library, drawing room, dining room, morning room, study, lofty great hall and magnificent grand staircase to its stabling and lodge at the bottom of the long wooded drive. At Jackwood Nat dressed in tweeds and startled the local gentry with his fast riding and driving high-perch carriages more suitable for cutting a dash in Park Avenue than English country lanes.

As the couple entertained lavishly, Maxine watched and learned from her guests; abandoning dramatic colours she began to dress in filmy pastel gowns. Initially it was mainly big theatrical names who accepted the enjoyable 'Saturday to Monday' invitations. These included Sir Henry Irving, Max Beerbohm, W.S. Gilbert, Nellie Melba and visiting Americans such as Ethel Barrymore and Elsie de Wolfe. Nat and Maxine also accepted invitations, and before they returned to America in the autumn of 1898 Maxine had seen enough to realise that if she were to be accepted into English society, Jackwood was not the right setting. It was too new.

In 1899 Nat and Maxine were among the top ten theatrical performers in the USA. As nationally recognised personalities they appeared in advertisements, their opinions were canvassed, their names on a billboard guaranteed packed houses and curtain

---

* Shooters Hill is now part of Greater London, but in 1898 it was still a rural suburb, if only eight miles from London Bridge.

calls of up to thirty were noted in reviews. Newspapers regularly carried stories about their progress and revealed the minutiae of their personal lives. Nat relished the notoriety; Maxine was less enchanted but recognised it was necessary. By now she was active in selecting the new productions and she also recruited cast members. Nat had branched out into occasional straight dramatic roles with notable success, and Maxine could play anything from Shakespeare to farce to emotional drama. It was probably an initiative of Maxine's to take their company to London after their production of *Nathan Hale** was a smash hit in New York. They added *The Cowboy and the Lady* and *An American Citizen* to their repertoire as a deliberate policy not to try to compete with English drawing-room plays.

Their reviews in London were mixed for the first two productions were simply too American for British tastes; however, they fared better with *An American Citizen*. But it was a busy, fulfilling season and they made some useful contacts. Maxine was thrilled when Gertrude was courted by William Montagu, the twenty-two-year-old 9th Duke of Manchester, and she promoted the relationship with alacrity. Although people who knew her well later in life would never know it, Maxine never forgot those hard years of cheap boarding houses and scrimping, making her own clothes, sleeping upright on trains while she travelled across America, and just how difficult life was without money. It is tempting to wonder whether, had she not been married to Nat, Maxine would have set her own cap at the young duke. However, she had not far to look in the duke's family

---

* Nathan Hale was a hero of the American Revolution, who was executed as a spy by the British.

to know that if Gertrude married him her younger sister would never want for anything, so she pushed the relationship whenever possible. Duke William's own mother was the Cuban-American beauty Consuelo Iznaga. His father, the 8th Duke, had married her in 1876 and, unwittingly, had begun an avalanche of marriages among land-rich, cash-poor members of the British aristocracy to American heiresses and beauties, including Jennie Churchill, who was unfailingly kind to Maxine.*

As they were about to leave for New York Gertrude was offered a good part, as a beautiful young princess, in a new production called *The Royal Family*. It was agreed that Gertrude could not afford to turn down the offer of a lead role and so – suitably chaperoned – she remained in England to further her career. It was a great shock to Maxine when, a few months later, a letter from Gertrude advised that she had married Johnston Forbes-Robertson, who had stepped into the shoes of Sir Henry Irving to play the lead in the latest production of *Hamlet*, to rave reviews. He was twenty years older than Gertrude.

Having set her heart on Gertrude becoming a duchess, Maxine was truly hurt because the marriage to 'Forbie' had happened behind her back, but she was also furious at what she saw as Gertrude's betrayal. She took her anger out on Nat and on other members of the cast, acting like a diva, and the marriage began to suffer as a result. Nat wrote that a cruel and hard look appeared in the eyes that had previously been warm and dreaming. He reacted by seeing other women and

---

* Another of Gertrude's court of followers was the son of Chulalongkorn of Siam (better known as the King in *The King and I*) but a mixed marriage – even to a prince – was a step too far for Maxine, so she put a stop to it.

drinking heavily, which by some miracle was not picked up by newspapers. Maxine decided to ignore his behaviour, at least in public, even though on one occasion Nat was so drunk he could not perform and the audience had to be refunded $1400. It was a significant sum and a story was concocted that he had mistakenly taken an overdose of the medication he used for first-night nerves.

More and more Maxine found that the people Nat invited home for drinks were those she would rather not meet – horse-racing acquaintances and gambling men. For the sake of publicity she pretended deep concern for her 'sick' husband, but in fact she was growing further away from Nat and had already started to imagine a life in England without him. She now regarded him as holding her back and when they quarrelled she told him that his friends were vulgar.

Despite the difficulties in their personal life, the couple's professional life was phenomenally successful. They toured in *The Merchant of Venice* with Nat playing Shylock and Maxine as Portia. It was not well reviewed in New York but played to good, profitable houses across the country as they travelled back and forth in their luxurious private railcar. They did not take the production to England, but spent the summer at Jackwood. Other triumphant tours followed throughout 1900 and 1901 and Maxine invariably banked her share of the takings. A good manager of her money (unlike Nat, who spent open-handedly), Maxine was quietly building a substantial fortune.

They were in England in October 1901 for the birth of Gertrude's baby, with Maxine still behaving more like a bossy mother than an elder sister. While Forbie was performing in Scotland, Maxine ignored the well-laid plans that he had made at his London family home for the birth of his child. Instead, she whisked Gertrude to Jackwood and it was there that the first of Maxine's much-beloved nieces, Maxine Frances Mary – but always called Blossom – was born.

Early that summer a well-placed friend* to whom Maxine had confided about Nat's transgressions introduced Maxine to a man of the 'right sort' with the aim of cheering her up, and making her life more bearable. The person selected to bridge the chasm between Maxine's life as a popular American actress and her emerging social aspirations in England was George Keppel.

The Honourable George Keppel, youngest son of the 7th Earl of Albemarle, was a personal friend of the new king, Edward VII. He lived at the heart of the royal set and was not only physically handsome, but a man of impeccable charm and good manners; indeed, his only problem in life was a scarcity of money. It was in June 1901 that Maxine received a note from him asking if he might call on her. She knew perfectly well who he was – few people who cared about such things did not. His wife Alice, who was the same age as Maxine, was not only the foremost hostess in England but the favourite mistress of the King. 'I do not mind what she does,' George Keppel famously remarked, 'as long as she comes back to me in the end.' It is safe to say that the Keppel marriage was an open one, and each behaved with discretion.

Maxine was well aware how such matters were conducted back home, where, if a married man belonging to

---

* Believed to be Jennie Cornwallis-West (formerly Lady Randolph Churchill). Lord Randolph died in 1895 and in 1900 Jennie remarried. Her second husband was George Cornwallis-West, who was the same age as Winston.

the Four Hundred* called on a beautiful actress without a chaperone, there was only one outcome. Furthermore, an actress who became the mistress of such a man expected to be treated liberally, but this did not include being received in the same social circles as his wife. Yet Maxine recognised that if she handled the matter carefully, here was a man who could give her an *entrée* into the brilliant English society she had glimpsed during her first visit with the Daly Company six years earlier, and which had since eluded her. She needed to convince him that she was more than just a pretty actress.

She received him alone and George was bowled over by Maxine's beauty, decorous charm and witty conversation. His reaction was that this woman would be a considerable asset to his wife's house parties, at which one of the prime responsibilities was to amuse the King. The next time they met, Maxine went on his arm to meet Mrs Keppel, who agreed with her husband that Miss Elliott was a find. Maxine was invited to call on Mrs Keppel at her next At Home.

It was at the Keppels' home in Portman Square that Maxine began to meet some of the personalities who peopled her later life: Lady Colebrooke; Mrs Ronnie Greville; Lord and Lady Alington; the fabulously rich, widowed 5th Earl of Rosebery; and Muriel Wilson, who had a loose understanding with young Winston Churchill, penniless but recently elected as Member of Parliament for Oldham and at the very beginning of his political career. Earlier that year Winston's first love, Pamela Plowden, had broken off their

---

* The cream of New York society. So called because Mrs Astor's ballroom could only accommodate four hundred guests. Anyone not on Mrs Astor's list was considered an arriviste, and was unlikely to be invited to the places that mattered.

engagement and married Lord Lytton. Since then Winston had courted other eligible young women; Muriel Wilson was one of two to whom he proposed a lasting relationship, the other was the actress Ethel Barrymore, an acquaintance of Maxine's in New York. Both women turned Winston down, Muriel because she thought Winston would never amount to anything.

Invitations began to flood in for the vivacious and beautiful Miss Elliott, now viewed as an asset at any party, but she reached the summit of her present ambitions when she called on Mrs Keppel before sailing for New York. Mrs Keppel appeared, explained that the King was paying an unexpected visit, and on hearing of Maxine's arrival had expressed a wish to meet her. This was a woman whom he had heard was as beautiful as Helen of Troy; small wonder, then, that this serial womaniser wanted to meet her – and as she was an actress that it was perhaps better done in private. Mrs Keppel did not need to blush for Maxine: she already knew that; and, down to her perfect curtsey, Maxine played the part of a duchess again. The King was captivated, and when bidding her goodbye said he would make sure not to miss her next London show.

In the USA again, Maxine secretly initiated plans to separate her life from that of Nat. She arranged with a leading playwright* to have a play written for her, with no part in it for her husband. News had leaked out (she blamed Nat) of Maxine's meeting with the King and she was badgered by reporters. Knowing only too well that her campaign for acceptance by the British upper classes required absolute discretion,

---

* Charles B. Dillingham.

Maxine resolutely played down the incident, merely confirming that she had met the King at the home of a friend, whom she refused to name. But Nat would not let a good opportunity go and the result was a flush of stories that Maxine had been to the palace for lunch in the presence of Queen Alexandra, and would be attending the forthcoming coronation. Despite Maxine's annoyance about this, she continued to appear with her husband in stock productions. They were always well received by theatre audiences, who adored seeing this romantic golden pair on stage together, but perhaps their very best acting was reserved for convincing their fans that they were still the couple who had everything, including a happy marriage.

The summer of 1903 was a difficult time for the Goodwins. Back in England, Maxine was invited everywhere and as a consequence was never available to host parties for Nat's theatre friends. He accompanied her to a house party on only one occasion and immediately realised that he was out of his depth: in his autobiography he stated that he felt he had more in common with the butler, and while walking past an open window had overheard a guest ask Maxine how she came to marry such a vulgar little man. Such rudeness to Maxine seems unlikely, and the truth of the episode doubtful, but Nat railed against the high living and low morals he claims to have witnessed. He did not name names, but gave sufficient hints to identify some of those present.

One was patently Archibald Primrose, the 5th Earl of Rosebery. Later that summer, somewhat astonishingly, Rosebery suggested to Maxine that she divorce Nat and marry him, evidence of which was found among Maxine's papers.[3]

More than twenty years earlier Rosebery had fallen in love with and married the highly intelligent, though plain, Hannah Rothschild, the wealthiest heiress in Britain. At Oxford, the young and handsome student, already land-rich in his own right, openly declared three ambitions: to marry an heiress, to win the Derby and to become Prime Minister.* He was introduced to Hannah by Benjamin Disraeli (by now Earl of Beaconsfield) and his wife, and while Rosebery's subsequent pursuit of Hannah was regarded as a solecism by a largely anti-Semitic society (indeed, both families heartily disapproved), it was a genuine love match and the couple's wish to marry overcame all obstacles. Disraeli himself gave Hannah away at their wedding in 1878 and the London home of the newlyweds was the palatial Lansdowne House on the corner of Curzon Street near Berkeley Square, while incomparable Mentmore in Buckinghamshire was their country residence. There were four children from the marriage, and Hannah, an indefatigable hostess, proved to be a tremendous asset to Rosebery. When she died at the early age of thirty-nine, he was truly heartbroken and retired from society and politics for almost a decade. By the time he met Maxine he had been a widower for more than nine years and it was said that he had never looked at another woman in that time. It is fair to say he was astonished when Maxine turned him down, and one has to wonder why she did so when she had been so anxious for her sister to marry the Duke of Manchester. She hankered after Rosebery's life-style and position in society, but it seems she had decided that she wished to keep her independence and make her entry into society on her own terms.

---

* All of which he would eventually achieve.

Soon after the Goodwins returned to America in 1903 they agreed to an amicable separation, each settling by contract to share a percentage from the other's future works. To the press they stated that the split was a professional one only, and indeed Nat remained part of Maxine's life for some years, although he was generally kept busy with his own productions.

The play Maxine had commissioned from Dillingham was aptly named *In Her Own Way*. She lived in the New York house she had shared with Nat at 326 West End Avenue while she started rehearsals and coped with costume fittings and photography sessions for publicity shots. Having slimmed down to her lowest weight, and with a new wardrobe from Paris, Maxine was, at the age of thirty-five, at the very height of her luscious beauty. When she appeared in drawing-room scenes there was little play-acting needed – she knew how a great society lady *really* behaved and she played the part subtly, with authority, with dignity, but also with a true glamour. She made every woman want to imitate her hairstyle, her dress, even the way she used her eyes. Theatre critics were stunned and she carried the show almost alone; it was the greatest hit of her career. Previously she had been the other half of the Nat Goodwin duo, but from this point Maxine Elliott was a solo star. Her dressing room was filled nightly with roses from admirers, babies were named after her, she was mobbed after every performance by autograph hunters and press photographers, hundreds of letters and packages from well-wishers arrived at her home daily, and she could have lived comfortably just off the income from products she endorsed in the papers. She was, in a word, bankable to those who invest in theatre productions.

Dillingham claimed to have earned a hundred thousand dollars in his percentage of returns from *In Her Own Way*, so Maxine's take was probably three times that amount in the two-year run, which included a hugely successful national tour. No one in the theatre worked harder than Maxine, and there was hardly a city in which she did not perform. The price she paid was a loss of enjoyment in her work. In later life she would inform her niece's husband that after she had said 'I love you' at precisely 10.28 every evening – plus matinees, she found nothing very interesting in the theatre.[4] Her ambition now was to acquire and accumulate money. She began investing her savings, and it has long been accepted that her legendary knowledge of the stock market stemmed from a friendship, which was rather more than platonic, with the financier John Pierpont 'J.P.' Morgan. Be that as it may, from this point in her life Maxine seldom made an investment that did not pay off.*

In summer 1905 she decided to take *In Her Own Way* to London, where the King fulfilled his promise and not only attended a performance, but ostentatiously stood to lead the applause. Following this triumph Maxine was lionised: her surviving appointments diary reveals what her life was like. Among the invitations (and return invitations) for tea, dinner, Saturday-to-Monday house parties,† boxes at the races, Henley, drives in Rotten Row with existing acquaintances such as Mrs Keppel, Mrs Ronnie Greville, Mrs George

---

* In her later years, Maxine controlled every investment herself, and when her executors examined her records they were amazed at her business acumen. It was said that she understood financial investment and re-investment so well she could have run a broker's office perfectly competently.

† The term 'weekend' was not then in common use.

Cornwallis-West (formerly Jennie Churchill) and Lady Alington, one also finds the names of other leading members of society such as Lord Sandwich, Lady Caernarvon of Highclere Castle,* Lady Gordon-Lennox, Lady Jersey, Lady Daisy Warwick, Baroness D'Erlanger, the Paget sisters, Lady Molesworth, Prince Francis of Teck (brother to Princess Mary – who would become Queen Mary), the Marquess of Granby (later Duke of Rutland), Sir Ernest Cassell and Alfred de Rothschild. She went cruising with J.P. Morgan on his yacht in the Mediterranean, during which trip she was introduced to the Kaiser. Winston Churchill often took her to tea at the House of Commons and they sometimes played golf together, making up a foursome with Winston's brother John and his wife Gwendoline. Considering that this strata of society was notably a 'closed shop', it is extraordinary that Maxine was able to infiltrate it in the way she did.

But it was not only society that drew Maxine to England; Gertrude and Forbie now had a second daughter and this little family had pride of place in Maxine's heart. They *were* her family, and though they had busy and very successful careers of their own as Shakespearean actors, Maxine tried to see them whenever possible. She was such a powerful force that only Forbie's strength of character prevented Maxine from taking them over, and it became a family joke with Maxine's nieces that of Captain Thomas Dermot's six children, Maxine was the best son he had.

In 1906 Maxine was the first actor of note to appear in San Francisco following the big earthquake of April that year.

---

* Maxine was a frequent guest at Highclere Castle (the setting for the fictional *Downton Abbey* television series).

She perhaps accepted because of her remaining family links there, but apart from the occasional visit when she appeared on stage in the city, she more or less lost touch with her father and stepmother after this date and they became part of a life which held little relevance to her. Two of her brothers were dead* and the youngest, Sam, was a drunk whom Maxine tried to help but eventually gave up on. She never could stand drunks.

By this time she had played many roles but was at her best playing upper-class Englishwomen, parts she frequently reprised because they were what her fans wanted. But Maxine was becoming bored with it all and a failed production of *Under the Greenwood Tree* in both New York and London seemed to provide the impetus she needed to move on. She wrote to a contemporary, the distinguished British actress Constance Collier, that while she admired people who had a conscience about their art, the only thing that appealed to her was 'great big receipts' – large enough for her to think of retiring from the stage. 'This is the worst tour we have ever had or will ever have,' she continued, 'but we shall make fourteen thousand pounds in the twenty weeks so we just shut our teeth and say "Wot t'hell!" and wait for June . . . '5

In August 1907 there was a half-hearted attempt at reconciliation with her husband in Trouville, but this came to an end when Nat picked up and read a letter she was writing, in which she stated that she was bored with him, and that she was now only ever happy when in England. He pocketed the letter, and when he subsequently divorced her on grounds of

---

* Tom, the eldest, shot himself in 1902; Lew, a seaman, drowned in the Indian Ocean in 1905.

desertion he used it in his evidence. It had been his original intention to cite J.P. Morgan, Alfred de Rothschild and Lord Rosebery, among others, in a charge of multiple infidelities, and he was only persuaded with difficulty by his attorney that it was unnecessary to be so vindictive. Instead, he divorced Maxine for desertion and the uncontested case in Reno took only seven minutes of the court's time.

Jackwood was leased to Max Beerbohm and later sold for half what Nat originally paid for it. Maxine rented a small country house, Coombe Cottage, from another friend, Lord Charles Beresford. She still had many commitments in America, and it was where she made her money, but she was free now to go her own way, and she regarded England as 'home'.

In April 1908 she bought a piece of land on West 39th Street in New York, set up a corporation called Elliott Theatre Company and proceeded to build her own theatre. The capital was three hundred thousand dollars and three thousand hundred-dollar shares were traded. It seems very likely that the hand of J.P. Morgan was in this scheme. Overriding her co-investors who wished it to be called the Maxine Elliott Theatre, she insisted on Maxine Elliott's Theatre, and of course she got her way, as she inevitably did when dealing with men. To be doubly sure there was no mistake the name was not merely painted, but carved into the marble façade with its Corinthian columns. When the first production opened that December,* Nellie Melba was in the audience along with a good representation of the Four Hundred. Six months later, when the theatre was well established with new productions

---

* *The Chaperon* by Marion Fairfax.

booked for seasons ahead Maxine left it in the hands of good managers and went to London to appear in a play there. She only played once more in her own theatre and she was content to let its profits add to her growing fortune. Meanwhile she still had another ambition to achieve, for while her fortune was growing, her social ambitions were yet to take off.

Although she did not lack for invitations, and notably despite the King's signal approval when he attended her show in 1905 and reportedly told an aide that he thought Miss Elliott the most beautiful woman in the world, Maxine noted that she was never included in the lists of guests who were invited to events attended by the King. Whether this was self-preservation on the part of the King's posse of mistresses who controlled Edwardian Society, is open to debate. Maxine decided to do something about it, and laid her plans accordingly.

She learned that the King was to spend a few weeks at a spa in Marienbad, and though he would inevitably be surrounded by his usual hostesses Maxine knew that the rules were more relaxed in an overseas venue compared with London drawing rooms. Taking with her as companion and chaperone Mrs Lee Eleanor Graham, another American beauty and society hostess who was kept on the perimeter of the inner circle of the King's set, Maxine made her way to Paris, where she purchased an entire new wardrobe by Worth, all in white or pastels. Then she announced that she was travelling to Marienbad for her health.

The two women took suites in a hotel directly across a large courtyard from the Weimar Hotel, where the royal party was staying, and from there Maxine was able to take note of the time of the King's daily perambulations. One morning

Maxine, dressed in a filmy gown, was sitting reading on a bench along the route taken by the King. Surrounded by a number of gentlemen, most of whom Maxine knew well, the King passed her, as she knew he must. The effect on the King as she lifted her huge lambent eyes, smiled at the party, bowed her head slightly and then lowered her eyes again to her book, was immediate. He spoke quietly to his gentlemen and as the party continued down the path to the Weimar an equerry returned to speak to Maxine. He told her that the King had recognised her and had invited her to join his party that evening at a dinner being given by Mrs Arthur James. An invitation would be delivered during the afternoon.

Maxine was acquainted with Mrs Arthur James; realised, too, what was likely to happen and suspected that no such invitation would be forthcoming. Nevertheless, she prepared herself carefully for the dinner, and watched from behind the curtains of her suite as carriages arrived at the Weimar and the beautifully dressed guests went in. Eventually Mrs Graham said, 'Well, Max. That's that, then.' But Maxine, who was a great judge of character, simply smiled and told her to wait a little longer.

When the dinner was due to begin Mrs James asked the King to choose a partner to take in to dinner, only to be told that he had already decided to take in Miss Elliott. Within minutes a footman was despatched across the courtyard, offering an explanation that Maxine's invitation had, inexplicably, fallen behind the desk. She was handed an envelope in which there was a card, bearing the engraved inscription: 'The Equerry is commanded by the Duke of Lancaster* to

---

* The alias used by King Edward when travelling.

invite Mrs Goodwin to dinner at 7.30 Tuesday, August 18th'. Attached to this was a handwritten note from Mrs James: 'Will you dine with us tonight ... at 7.30?'

Taking her time, Maxine put on her white fur stole and walked slowly across to the Weimar. It was impossible for a hostess to refuse to invite a guest nominated by the King, and Maxine – well aware of how Mrs James had attempted to cut her out – smiled innocently as she accepted her apology. Maxine was now given the sole attention of the King, and all the other guests were made to wait for fifteen minutes while she had a pre-dinner cocktail at the King's insistence. Again, Maxine made no attempt to hurry, totally at ease while she chatted with His Majesty. Noticeably, she made him laugh. After that evening she was included in *all* the activities of the royal party – drives in the forest, promenades in the parks and the dinners, smart little levees thrown for the King by local aristocracy. In the following year Maxine went to Marienbad again, staying in the same hotel as the royal party, and was named in the press as 'one of the King's constant companions and often was his preferred dinner companion'.[6] Whether these outings and her intimacy with the King involved sleeping with him will probably never be known, although in biographies Maxine is often referred to as one of the ageing King's mistresses.

It was at this point, having rented Combe Cottage for a year, that Maxine purchased a country estate from Lord Poltimore. Named Hartsbourne, it was at Bushey in Hertfordshire, less than an hour by carriage from London. As soon as the contracts were signed she brought in architects and ordered a complete redecoration, which included central heating, large built-in wardrobes and a bathroom in every guest room (an unheard-of luxury in England). There was also a beautifully appointed nursery for her sister's children when they came to stay, and a new modern kitchen with another innovation: refrigeration.

Overlooking the park, two large and luxurious suites were constructed. One was to be Maxine's own suite on the ground floor; the other, on the first floor, was always known as the King's Room. From Maxine's suite, which consisted of a bedroom, boudoir and bathroom and had doors which opened onto the drawing room, a door led to a small hallway and the private staircase to her maid's room above, and also – conveniently, some might say – to the King's Room.

Maxine had learned a thing or two while staying at some of England's grandest houses. As a result, no guest of hers would ever complain of the cold, be expected to trot along a chilly corridor at night to visit the bathroom, or wait for a poor maidservant to struggle upstairs with boiling water for a hip bath. Hartsbourne boasted hot water on tap and good-sized baths. The theme throughout Hartsbourne was carefully directed by Maxine – white and gold, bright and airy. A light-coloured balance of comfortable and luxurious modern furnishings mingled with grand and exquisite Louis Quinze antiques. This style bore the hallmark of Elsie de Wolfe, and although she is not on record as having a hand in the decor at Hartsbourne, de Wolfe was a frequent visitor and one of Maxine's best friends. While the work was being carried out Maxine returned to New York and made a successful tour of the United States in a play called *The Inferior Sex*.

When she returned to an almost completed Hartsbourne late in 1909, a note from the King was waiting for her. It suggested he visit her for a quiet weekend with just his valet and an equerry. Maxine was sure-footed enough to be alert to the implications of this; a clandestine relationship was not part of her plan. The King had to accept her as any other woman in society, and visit her openly with some companions or not at all. She despatched a polite note begging the favour of some names she might invite to amuse His Majesty during his stay. No reply came for many weeks and Maxine thought she had burnt her bridges by making her position abundantly clear. But eventually, in April, without any comment about her note, she received a list of suitable names along with a date for early May. Hartsbourne was thrown into an orgy of preparation and plans for a royal visit that would include the equerries, a detective, plus valets and maids, as well as the other guests. In the few days leading up to the royal visit the house was filled with exquisite flower arrangements, all the guest rooms were made ready, menus and wines chosen, and Maxine's wardrobe freshened up as she fussed over every detail.

The news on 6 May 1910 fell like a guillotine blade; the King was dead of bronchitis. He never occupied the King's Room at Hartsbourne, but it had been designed for him and the King's Room it would always remain.

3

Hartsbourne

During his lifetime, both as Prince of Wales and as King, Edward VII had totally dominated society, and the habits and mores of the Edwardian era did not end with his death. They continued, almost unchanged, in a sort of golden epilogue.* Those who mattered in British politics, in finance and in the military, still ran the country and life went on as before as they swirled between endless house-parties, the summer season, Cowes and shooting in Scotland in the autumn. And as before, much of the machinery that made the country work operated outside the formality of Westminster.

Perhaps the person in society who was most affected by the old King's death was his favourite mistress, Alice Keppel, whose immense power in society vanished. The quiet and

---

* This would end only with the diplomatic crisis of July 1914, following the assassination in Sarajevo of Archduke Franz Ferdinand.

shy new monarch, George V, would not play the same role in society as his father, and never lent his name to an era, but he was still the arbiter of who was acceptable in royal circles. Immediately, he and Queen Mary, plus his mother, let it be known that it would be more comfortable for everyone if Mrs Keppel was not invited to any of the events they attended. Alice and her complaisant husband George – who was briefly Maxine's lover – remained friends with Maxine and although the Keppels moved to Italy to save face soon after the old King's death, they were occasional guests of Maxine's for the remainder of her life.

With the Keppels out of favour, Maxine might well have found difficulties – after all, they had introduced her. But she seems to have had no difficulties with the transition. Maxine was born to be hostess at Hartsbourne. To her gratification, the house was not merely a fashionable venue for the *haut monde* to gather but, without a conscious effort by her, it also became a leading political salon in the four years prior to the outbreak of war. Maxine lived life to the full, savouring the fact that it was a life she had made for herself, containing everything she had ever wanted or aspired to – including, unexpectedly, the love of her life.

Having attended many 'Saturday to Mondays' at country houses, she knew how often the women guests were cold and bored during the daytime while the men went shooting or hunting. Although some women hunted, the main occupations for those who did not were – all too often – reading and gossip. So Maxine provided a luxurious, restful atmosphere where guests were all entertained in lavish style and in the greatest comfort. The Hartsbourne visitors' book shows that the first guests were Winston Churchill and his wife

Clementine, and that they were regular visitors thereafter. Clementine, whom Winston had married in 1908, was a competitive tennis player and at Hartsbourne she not only had a choice of grass or hard courts but invariably found that good players had been invited to give her a match. Winston's greatest friend, the brilliant F.E. Smith (later Earl of Birkenhead), was also often invited, together with his intellectual wife Margaret Furneaux. Winston's formidable aunt Lady Sarah Wilson, who had inadvertently become the first woman war correspondent after being captured during the Boer War, was another favourite visitor, along with Winston's mother Jennie, and her youthful second husband George Cornwallis-West, who was widely acknowledged as the handsomest man in England. The Cornwallis-Wests struggled to make ends meet, thanks to their extravagant lifestyle, and were always happy to accept such invitations. It was not, however, an entirely one-way arrangement: Jennie's fabled wit, sparkling manner and knowledge of everyone who mattered, not to mention her concert-standard piano playing, made her a distinct asset at any gathering.

The Churchill family were part of a social group who represented soft power in Edwardian England, and which included politicians from all parties as well as powerful landowners. All came to Hartsbourne to mingle with their friends. Among the regular visitors were the Duke of Rutland, with his artist wife and three daughters, including the lovely Lady Diana Manners,* who would be a lifelong friend to Maxine, and the Earl of Drogheda and his wife

---

* Lady Diana Manners was not actually the Duke's daughter. Her father was the writer Henry Cust, but the Duke accepted her as his own child because 'it would be bad-manners not to do so'.

Kathleen who was, like Winston, interested in the new science of aviation, and who was to become Maxine's best woman friend. Lord Rosebery also came often: Maxine's refusal of his proposal had made no difference to their friendship and she was glad to be able to offer him hospitality. Other names in the Hartsbourne visitors' book include Lord Curzon, the former and, arguably greatest, Viceroy of India, who had been recently widowed. He courted Maxine and even proposed to her; during a subsequent visit to New York the papers somehow heard about this and trumpeted that Maxine was about to become Lady Curzon. When an editor wired her and asked her directly, 'Are you going to marry Lord Curzon?' she responded robustly: 'I would not marry God.'*

Anyone who was anyone went gladly to Hartsbourne. Maxine was nicknamed the Queen of Harts and her invitations were rarely declined. When she was not filling Hartsbourne with guests she was a guest herself, driven around the country to great houses by her chauffeur, Hoath, in her white De Dion-Bouton (known as the White Incomparable).

She worried when in 1911 Nat Goodwin, from whom she had been divorced two years earlier, published his memoirs. Naturally he was not especially flattering of Maxine, though he praised her physical beauty and acting ability. He was bitter about the way she had treated him and hinted pointedly about her relationships with J.P. Morgan and other men. However, the book was poorly written; his attempts at

---

* A niece wondered whether Lord Curzon's forenames had put Maxine off him: George and Nathaniel were the names of her two former husbands.

humour signally failed, and it was soon out of print. There was no aftermath for Maxine, other than a few splashy newspaper articles in America that were not repeated in England – and to Maxine England was what mattered. Her visits to the USA were now only to oversee business matters concerning her theatre and her investments, which had made her a rich woman.

In June that year, a few days after the coronation of King George V, which Maxine attended, Winston stayed at Hartsbourne for a few days along with his mother, his old love Muriel Wilson, and J.M. Barrie. Clementine had been able to attend the coronation but felt unable to accompany him to Hartsbourne since she was nursing their four-week-old son, Randolph. Winston wrote to tell Clementine how Maxine was being 'so nice', and described how she had tamed a bullfinch so that after only twenty-four hours it sat on her shoulder and ate seeds from her mouth. 'See how much these innocent birds know,' he wrote.[1] Although she enjoyed the tennis, there was something a touch too flamboyant about Hartsbourne for Clementine, and though Winston enjoyed it hugely, she faintly disapproved.

That July Maxine was at Wimbledon for the final of the men's singles. She was there to support the clear favourite, the fair-haired, blue-eyed Tony Wilding, a handsome open-faced New Zealander who had won both the men's singles and doubles trophies the previous year, and was now defending his singles title against the Englishman Herbert Roper Barrett.* Tony had been a guest at Hartsbourne on

---

* After a hard-fought game, with the score 6–4, 4–6, 2–6, 6–2, Barrett retired, conceding the match to Wilding. Wilding could not, however, repeat his success of 1910 as he and his English partner Josiah Ritchie lost the doubles final.

several occasions and Maxine had sometimes partnered him in matches against Gerald du Maurier and Clementine Churchill on her occasional visits, as well as other equally distinguished guests. Maxine, now forty-two (though she admitted to thirty-seven), was probably already in love with Wilding, but there was a fifteen-year age gap between them. Jennie Churchill had shrugged at this older woman convention when she married George Cornwallis-West who was more than twenty years her junior – indeed, he was just a couple of weeks older than her son Winston – and she paid for it in hurtful comments and ridicule. A music-hall joke of the time was that Jennie had been seen walking in Hyde Park and peering into perambulators. When asked what she was doing she replied that she was looking for her next husband. Jennie wisely laughed this off in public, but it caused her hurt and Maxine knew it. However, Jennie had been the daughter-in-law of a duke, was well established in English society and her social position was unassailable. Maxine felt she was still on probation and could not afford to take any chances with her reputation – her new life was far too important.

Tony Wilding was born and raised in Christchurch, New Zealand, and although he studied law at Cambridge and was a clever man, he was not a scholar per se. His two loves, at which he excelled, were sport and 'mechanics'. He began playing cricket at school and in his teens had reached county level, but at Cambridge was recognised as a tennis player of quite exceptional brilliance. In 1905 he made his international debut as part of the Australasian Davis Cup team before returning to New Zealand to work in his father's law practice. In 1906 he took Australian Open singles and doubles titles, and was also called to the Bar in London at the Inner Temple. During the following two years he not only qualified as a barrister at the New Zealand Supreme Court, but helped the Australasian team to victory in the Davis Cup as well as winning his second Australian Open and two doubles titles at Wimbledon.

Although he had taken some doubles titles there, it was in 1910 that he really burst onto the English tennis scene, when he became the singles champion and the golden boy of tennis. But it was his personality and enormous charisma which earned him real and lasting friends among royalty and in English society. An online article would later claim that he combined the looks and charm of Leslie Howard and Cary Grant with the flamboyant daring of Errol Flynn, yet he was totally without any self-importance or side and had the innocent morality of a boy.[2] Important men such as King Gustav of Sweden and the former Prime Minister Arthur Balfour were proud to call Tony their friend.

He was happy to spend time with Maxine on the Hartsbourne courts, knocking balls against the wire-netting perimeter fence and demonstrating how she could greatly improve her game by simply changing the way she held her racquet, or twisting her wrist on the backhand. He was always happy to play against beginners and never patronised anyone by allowing them to win, but instead showed them how to improve their game.[*] In those days, when house-guests were expected to contribute to the entertainment, just

---

[*] One tennis umpire who later on in their relationship saw Tony and Maxine play in a doubles tournament thought they were probably good enough to compete at county standard and wrote that he always regretted that the pair had not 'had a go at the mixed handicap championship at Surbiton in 1914', which he felt they could have won.

as Jennie Churchill played the piano, Winston performed his impression of a bear under a shaggy rug or recited a lengthy poem from memory, and Maxine acted out a sketch or did an impression, Tony Wilding earned his invitations to Blenheim, Hartsbourne, Eaton Hall, Kingsclere Castle, Mentmore and Charlton (F.E. Smith's house) with the fresh and generous spirit of giving of himself. At the same time, he did not suffer fools, whatever their status. Once at Blenheim, when there was an informal tennis tournament among the male guests, he was asked by the Duke to play in an exhibition match against the winner for the visiting King and Queen. Since it was known that on the following day he would be playing in an important tournament he was angry, and critical of the thoughtlessness of his host in expecting him to jeopardise an important game for the amusement of royalty.

Equally, he was kind to a fault and would happily spend an evening missing a good dinner or a party to work into the early hours on the broken-down car of a fellow guest. Everyone who wrote of him portrayed him as one of the most attractive and fine men they had ever met.

When Maxine cheered Tony on at Wimbledon in 1911, she was cheering a good friend, with whom she was also in love. The next few years were the happiest of Maxine's life: she and Tony were close companions, and became lovers. Tony occupied rooms next to the King's Room, with access to the private staircase. Hartsbourne became his pied-à-terre in England, and he left clothes there when he was not travelling to tournaments around the world. When he played in European matches, or was in the South of France during the winter months to play in the major tournaments, Maxine was inevitably there too, to cheer him from the front row. On the few occasions when Maxine gave in to persuasion and made an appearance in the theatre in London, if Tony was in the country he would attend every performance. He was immensely proud of her, and this was evident in his letters home to his parents.[3] Maxine's appearances on the stage were never regarded as infra dig by her society friends; on the contrary, hostesses would book two or three rows of seats in the stalls for their dinner guests and the cream of London society, including the Royal Family, flocked to watch her.

Tony was Wimbledon champion again in 1912 and 1913, and in the euphoria of the 1913 victory he and Maxine announced their engagement. No date was set for the wedding, but they were now able to be open about their affection for each other and this full-blown love was for Maxine something entirely new to her. Her marriage to George when she was sixteen had been for what she had then regarded as love. In retrospect, she realised it was a teenage crush on an older man whom she believed could give her a good life until, unfortunately, he turned out to have feet of clay. She always regarded the marriage to Nat as a *mariage de convenance* with no great spark of romance, at least on her part, but they had developed an amicable relationship which had worked reasonably well for many years, and to the advantage of both partners. What she felt for Tony was something very different. She already knew what it was like to be regarded as half of a golden team, but this was a different experience entirely; this time there was no need for pretence at being a loving couple. It was all real.

At last Maxine had everything she ever yearned for:

financial stability thanks to J.P. Morgan's guidance; a beautiful home; a circle of friends whom she admired and enjoyed, and who in turn respected her; and Tony – who made her feel truly alive and fulfilled for the first time in her life. During her young adulthood she had worked hard and missed out on the untroubled enjoyments of her peers, but dancing in Tony's arms during those rapturous pre-war years she enjoyed the feeling of carefree youth. Newspaper articles gushed about how her lavish parties for distinguished guests were 'famous. The popular hostess provides her guests with golf, tennis and motoring, and regales them with enthusiastic descriptions of her experiences as an amateur farmer. She maintains a herd of nearly seventy cows.'[4]

This golden period slid to an end in 1914. The year began well enough, with Tony playing on the circuit in France from January to April. The couple spent several months in Cannes and then went on to Paris, where Tony won the World Hard Court Championships in June. So close were they that several reports appeared in the press that they had secretly married, but the couple denied this.

Although life appeared to be normal, nobody who knew Winston Churchill, then First Lord of the Admiralty, could have remained ignorant of the possibility of a European war. Certainly not those connected with Hartsbourne, where the diplomatic situation in Europe was a major topic of discussion at every weekend gathering that spring. In Cannes Maxine and Tony had heard constantly how the German General Staff were baying for war with France and Russia. During Wimbledon, Archduke Franz Ferdinand was assassinated in Sarajevo, which precipitated Austria's declaration of war against Serbia. Since Tony had already made it clear that if war came he intended to fight for the British Commonwealth, he was now uncertain about whether to make forward travel reservations to compete in the Davis Cup tie which followed in late July. On the advice of Winston and F.E. Smith he went ahead and booked his ticket to New York.

Maxine was in the Family Box for the Wimbledon singles final, alongside Kathleen Drogheda. They hoped to see Tony take the title for the fifth successive year, which was an unheard-of record. But Tony unexpectedly lost his Wimbledon crown to his close friend Norman Brookes, in partnership with whom he had won two Wimbledon doubles titles. On the previous day Tony had partnered the French women's champion Marguerite Broquedis in the mixed doubles final. Marguerite was having an off-day and Tony had had to do all the work. They lost 4–6, 6–4, 6–2, and the match left Tony exhausted going into the men's singles final on 4 July.

Maxine sat with tears streaming down her face, her shoulders shaking with sobs, a hand across her mouth with dismay as Tony dropped points. Norman Brookes, who knew Tony's game well, could hardly believe what was happening, and he said later that during the last set Tony's hand was shaking badly. *The Times* picked this up, to report that 'his racquet shook like a butterfly net'. Brookes won the last point with a mis-hit when the ball hit the wood of his racquet and jinked over the net. Tony was not the man to begrudge the title to one of his best friends and he openly celebrated with Brookes, placing an arm around him as they walked off court together laughing.

In the first three days of August Germany declared war on Russia and France. On the fourth it was Belgium's turn, and German troops invaded the neutral country to attack Liège. Britain, committed to help the Belgians, declared war on Germany the same day. With the army in full retreat, the Belgian government abandoned Brussels on 17 August. By then Tony was in the USA and preparing for the Davis Cup final, held on 6–8 August.* The Australasian team took the title convincingly, in no small part due to Tony's matches – he was described in the press as 'invincible' – but his overriding concern was that because transatlantic sailing schedules were already affected by the war he might get stuck in America and not be able to make a contribution himself.

By the time Tony reached Southampton at the end of August the Germans were in control of most of Belgium and were advancing rapidly. Britain was mobilising as fast as it could. Tony had spoken with Winston before he sailed to New York in July, and made clear his wish to 'get in first' in the coming war, in some way connected with motorised transport. Winston had long recognised that mechanisation was going to take over from the horse in modern warfare, and he had – in the teeth of opposition by naval chiefs – overseen the formation of the new Naval Brigade, which was equipped with vehicles. Now, at Winston's suggestion, Tony obtained a temporary commission in the Royal Marines, was gazetted second lieutenant and in early October left for France to find that the Naval Brigade had been moved to Antwerp. Within a few days, however, he was seconded to the Intelligence Corps and work that suited his skills admirably. He was a driver and a superb mechanic who, because of his frequent travels to France, knew the country well and spoke fluent colloquial

* This would be his last tournament.

French. Tony wrote to his family and to Maxine describing how he would motor in his Alda car as close to the enemy lines as possible, obtain as much information as he could collect, and report back to his chiefs. He enjoyed the work, and as he did not spare himself was immensely popular. Those early cars were very unpredictable and needed someone like Tony looking after them since a breakdown close to the front meant almost inevitable capture. 'This is a motor war,' he wrote home. 'Horses are more or less useless. Shrapnel fire is bad; it whistles and shrieks ... a bad business, war ... It is gradually getting cold. Too awful to think of the poor devils in trenches while we have a roof over our heads and some degree of comfort.'[5]

At the end of October Tony transferred to the RN Armoured Division, which often took him to the Front. Unlike many pundits he saw at once that they were in for a long war and that there was no possibility of it being over by Christmas. In February 1915 he was given some leave, which he spent with Maxine, returning to duty on 16 March to learn he had been promoted to lieutenant and posted to a new squadron of armoured Rolls-Royce cars which was commanded by his friend the Duke of Westminster. He shared the naval flying officers' mess and was given command of thirty men, a junior officer, three guns and a number of armoured cars that covered the area between La Bassée and Dunkirk. Before long they were moved up to the Western Front and on 2 May, based on several glowing commendations, Tony Wilding was gazetted captain.

On 8 May Tony wrote to a friend that, for the first time, he had been given a job which he thought was likely to end in him and his unit being 'blown to hell. However, if we succeed we will help our infantry no end.'[6] His mission was to destroy the enemy guns at Port Arthur and already he had considerable success with fast in-and-out attacks on enemy sites. On the following day, covered in mud and exhausted after a twelve-hour attack on the enemy at Aubers Ridge, he was resting in a dug-out next to a gun placement on the front line. With him were a lieutenant and two private soldiers. Men in a nearby trench reported hearing a great gust of laughter from the dug-out, quenched suddenly by a direct hit by a shell which exploded on impact. The two privates, and Tony, were killed instantly; the lieutenant was badly injured but survived.

Tony was buried the following day in a nearby orchard.*

* Captain Anthony Wilding was later re-interred at the Rue-des-Berceaux Military Cemetery in Richebourg-l'Avoué, Pas de Calais. Maxine paid for the headstone.

4

Maxine's War

Maxine was not the sort of woman to sit at home and knit scarves while the men went off to fight. Despite her affection for Winston she disagreed violently with him about women's suffrage,* and had she been able to join the fight conventionally she probably would have done so. Instead, as men began to leave for France she quietly did some research, looking for a way in which she could help, without getting in anyone's way.

Initially she got together with one of her closest friends – Millicent, the Duchess of Sutherland – and together they provided a large motorised van, fitted out as an ambulance and staffed with a nurse, which could transport four wounded men to a field hospital. Maxine was keen to drive or accompany a driver in this vehicle and she soon found there was nothing to stop her. Other women were running similar

---

* Churchill was opposed to women having the vote.

projects, allowed to choose their own field of operations and operating under licence by the Red Cross. Maxine arrived in France in October 1914, in the same week as Tony, bringing her De Dion-Bouton car and her chauffeur. It was just after Antwerp had been abandoned and the Allied forces withdrawn to West Flanders. Maxine chose to base herself in Boulogne-sur-Mer, an hour's drive from the fighting, from where she could easily provide some help where it was most needed, and see Tony on a regular basis.

There was plenty of scope for relief ambulance drivers and, recognising that need, Maxine would eventually provide twelve ambulances, but within weeks she hit on an alternative way of providing assistance. German fear of Belgian resistance after the invasion caused them to implement a policy of *Schrecklichkeit* ('terror') against civilians. This included massacres, executions, hostage-taking and the burning of villages, which became known as the Rape of Belgium. Tens of thousands of Belgians fled their homes for the countryside, to take what shelter they could find in barns, chicken houses and ruined buildings, and during that intensely cold first winter of the war they had little shelter, little or no means of heating, and hardly any food. Effectively caught between the two fighting armies, these refugees died in vast numbers of preventable causes: hunger, illness, childbirth, childhood illnesses, small injuries which turned septic, cold and general neglect. The chiefs of the armies had their own men to worry about; no one seemed to care about the Belgian civilians. Except Maxine.

She wanted to alleviate the terrible suffering, but soon met her first obstacle. Maxine realised that she would not be allowed to drive around a war zone in a vehicle dispensing aid, but then the extensive canal network linked to the

Yser River came to her notice – almost certainly pointed out by Tony – and she worked out that with the necessary permissions she could use these canals to reach distressed communities over a wide area and bring aid to people who had no one else to help them.

After some further research she instructed her stockbroker to sell stock to enable her to purchase the 150ft, three-hundred-ton barge *Julia*, which was lying more or less abandoned at Calais. She arranged for the barge to be gutted and fitted out to her own specification with utmost speed. She redesigned the vessel to have three sections; aft was a basic first-aid clinic as well as comfortable, heated accommodation for herself and a small team. The team would assist her in distributing supplies of food, clothing, blankets and medicines that were to be stored forward, in the largest section of the barge, which was a vast ship's hold. Amidships was a soup kitchen capable of feeding hundreds of people a day. This work was speeded along with the help of a team of soldiers that she had somehow managed to 'borrow' with Tony's help, for they were able to see each other every week. In mid-December Maxine went back to London to harry her Hartsbourne friends for financial support.

Lord Northcliffe placed an appeal in his newspapers for funds to enable Maxine to buy supplies for the barge and the appeal was answered generously by the British public, who were horrified at the stories coming out of Belgium. To Maxine's chagrin a similar appeal in the American newspapers brought almost no reaction, although later on she was given a big consignment of American grain. Winston guaranteed space for her stores and supplies in the navy freighters plying between Dover and Calais; Kathleen Drogheda agreed to work on the barge alongside Maxine whenever she could get away. It was not a large crew – a Belgian skipper who knew the waterways, along with Maxine's old butler and her maid, who was half-Belgian (both of these members of staff were longing to serve in some capacity and needed no urging). While spending Christmas with her sister Gertrude* in London, Maxine also recruited Gertrude's elderly chauffeur, and an experienced nurse, a Miss Close, to run the clinic. She hoped to round up a few civilian volunteers to help with the heavy work of distributing aid while she ran around London obtaining passes, carnets, permits and letters of reference from important men, so that she would not be hindered in her work by unnecessary officialdom.

Duly equipped, Maxine returned to Calais in early January and set up her headquarters at the Grand Hotel there. She gained a letter of approval from the King of Belgium, and with Tony's help she was given a car and driver by his CO, which helped her to get everything in place. Not everyone was in favour of her scheme: Lord Kitchener and Sir John French were deeply opposed, and were choleric when, on 7 February, she set off, boldly flying an American ensign from the stern. Tony had wangled some leave and travelled with her for the first part of her mission along with a junior officer and three Belgian soldiers who slept in the blanket store.

When they reached an area which was requesting aid either Maxine or Kathleen would scrounge a wagon if necessary to transport provisions from the barge to starving

---

* Gertrude was now Lady Forbes-Robertson, since her husband had been knighted in 1913. Gertrude gave birth to a fourth daughter while Maxine was in England that Christmas: Diana, but always called Dinah in the family because it was the name of a barge dog Maxine had just acquired for the *Julia*.

villagers. They supplied grain and paid local bakers to provide hundreds of loaves a day for free distribution. Maxine somehow obtained a large army truck to run back and forth to Calais in order to keep the *Julia* stocked. She found an abandoned school and commandeered it for the storage of supplies, paying a local man to act as a caretaker. On one occasion her team relieved a typhoid hospital staffed by nuns that had completely run out of food. The nuns were on their knees praying for divine intervention at the exact moment that Maxine arrived at the convent. Within six weeks the towns of Ypres, Furnes and Poperinge, and some sixty villages in West Flanders, were all aware of Maxine's barge and army truck full of supplies, and relied on her to keep them alive that bitter winter of 1914–15. No one who sought assistance was ever turned away. When they came across serious injury the *Julia*'s crew used the truck, or any transport they could find and commandeer, to get the victim to the nearest field hospital. Maxine brooked no hindrance: these people were too needy for officialdom.

Meanwhile, the *Julia* had become a floating mini-Hartsbourne. Many former friends or their sons were by now serving on the Western Front; the Dukes of Sutherland and Westminster popped aboard for tea, while Lady Sarah Wilson, who couldn't miss reporting on a war, was glad to rest in fairly civilised surroundings. Archibald Sinclair, Lord Wodehouse, Lord De La Warr, Lady Dorothie Feilding – all came calling and were sure of a welcome and decent food. Maxine felt that the serious aspect of the *Julia*'s work did not mean there could not be plenty of laughter in off-duty times, with games of bridge and other card games to pass the time and relax, drinks and gossip about people they knew.

Tony reported back to his unit on 15 March and Maxine went on with her work. She was thrilled when he received his promotion to captain in early May, and on 8 May he managed to get to the *Julia* for the day. Kathleen had returned to England for a spell, so they were able to spend the time alone. In the afternoon they argued about something – Maxine never said what it was and probably it was nothing very serious, but they disagreed – and parted in annoyance with each other some hours earlier than he had planned to leave.

Two days later she was given the news of Tony's death. That disagreement would haunt her until her own death twenty-five years later.

Maxine was never the same again after May 1915. Photographs show that she aged noticeably. Of course, women all over Europe who lost their loved ones suffered the same anguish, and it would be simplistic to write that she was heartbroken; that goes without saying, but she was careful to erase all trace of her bereavement, so there is no surviving evidence of what she felt. Following her own death all of Tony's letters were burned without being read, on her specific instruction. She never spoke of her feelings for Tony afterwards but she was so withdrawn and silent from that date onwards that her nieces would recall how they hated being taken to Hartsbourne, which never regained the sparkle of the pre-war years.

Initially Maxine transmuted her grief into an Amazonian determination to avenge the death of the only man she had ever wholly loved. She carried on, silent and grim-faced, running the *Julia*, feeding the multitudes, until a year later her mission was finally recognised as essential war relief and an official aid agency was created to take over the work. She wrote regular dispatches and letters to American newspapers describing the horrors she saw on a daily basis, and how the *Julia* was literally keeping thousands of people alive. She hoped for more funding but America was still isolationist, and contributions slow to trickle in.

During the winter of 1915–16 an old friend called at the *Julia* several times. It was Winston, accompanied by Archibald Sinclair[*] on one occasion, and on another by Edward Louis Spears.[†] All three were serving on the front, and Winston, still psychologically affected by the effects of the disastrous Dardanelles campaign, welcomed the physical occupation of the trenches rather than an HQ post.[‡] He was in good spirits when, on a teeming wet day, Maxine took two photographs of Winston and Sinclair in their trench outfits when they visited her: one of only two known photographic images of Winston's period of service on the Western Front. Winston – who served as a colonel – had supplemented his own uniform to deal with weather contingencies: an extra-long trench coat, a riding stock and a blue French helmet instead of his regimental bonnet. Spears wrote of his visit with Winston in his diary in December 1915: 'tea with Maxine

---

[*] Sir Archibald Sinclair, Bt (Archie Sinclair) was a politician and, later, leader of the Liberal Party. He served in the army during the First World War, rising to the rank of major in a Guards machine-gun regiment. He was second in command to Churchill when the latter commanded the 6th Battalion of the Royal Scots Fusiliers at Ploegsteert Wood (known as 'Plugstreet') on the Western Front in 1916. They formed a lasting friendship, which would become a significant political alliance in later decades.

[†] The much-decorated Major-General Sir Edward Louis Spears, Bt. Senior liaison officer between the British and French armies in the First World War, he and Churchill were firm friends. Churchill trusted Spears and would rely heavily on him in the Second World War. Born in Passy, France to a British father, Charles Spiers, and an Irish mother, he grew up bilingual. He changed the spelling of his surname by deed poll in 1918 as he claimed it was always being mispronounced, but more probably it was regarded as too Germanic.

[‡] Churchill liked to disparage this service by claiming he preferred to serve with his men because the officers' mess at HQ was teetotal.

Elliott on her barge. Nice, clever woman. Must have been v. beautiful'.[1] Winston and Maxine both returned to London in May 1916, in Winston's case to report first-hand on trench warfare to Parliament. With the help of Lloyd George, who on becoming Prime Minister in December that year insisted on having Winston in the Cabinet, he began a two-decade climb back to the political heights he had lost. Maxine returned to the theatre to recoup her financial position.

During the time the *Julia* was operational Maxine effectively fed, clothed and treated an estimated three hundred and fifty thousand people who had no other place to turn for sustenance and medical aid. It is impossible to estimate how many lives Maxine helped to save.* Although she had received many welcome donations in supplies and money, mostly from Britain, by the time she was relieved of this vital aid work in 1916 she had used up a good part of her personal fortune. She had funded the *Julia* mission by steadily selling shares in a dismal market; at the time, in her desperation to do something for the thousands of unfortunate displaced people, expediency was everything and she had not worried about the cost. But after it was over, when she examined her financial circumstances and discovered how far short she was of her minimum objective of a million dollars in capital, she knew that however much she disliked the idea she had to return to the stage to refill her depleted coffers.

Curiously, because it seems out of character, almost the first thing Maxine did on reaching London was to ask Constance

---

* Maxine's relief work was never forgotten by the Belgian people, and after the war the King of the Belgians appointed her a Knight of the Order of the Crown. Also, at Maxine's urging, the King rewarded Kathleen Drogheda with a sapphire ring, and in England Kathleen was invested with the CMG.

Collier to arrange for her to see a psychic to try to get in touch with Tony.[2] Their quarrel had been playing on her mind. Although she had a number of sessions, there is no knowing whether she believed she had any success, for she never spoke of it afterwards.

As part of an incisive self-assessment, she accepted that at forty-eight her looks were fading and that she must trade on past successes. Overweight from her time on the barge eating the wrong foods, she dieted and lost thirty pounds, had a small facelift and dyed her hair, but despite her need for maximum publicity she resolutely refused to allow any mileage to be made of her war work, saying that it was 'the most sacred thing' in her life and was not to be capitalised upon. In the event, she had no trouble restarting her career and between 1917 and 1920 appeared in two profitable Broadway shows and made a lengthy tour of the USA. As she no longer had the luxury of her own railcar she was often to be found snoozing in the sleeper car on a mound of mink coats.

In California she made two silent films for Sam Goldwyn (*Fighting Odds* and *The Eternal Magdalene*), during the course of which she met and became friends with Charlie Chaplin. As with most things that Maxine tackled head on, her film career was a success, and by February 1920 she had reached her goal of a million dollars in stocks. She made her last appearance at her own theatre, in a play called *Trimmed in Scarlet*. It only ran for two weeks and when the final curtain came down Maxine ended her stage career.

Following the Armistice she had re-opened Hartsbourne between engagements, but she was a different Maxine and Hartsbourne was different, too. So many faces were missing that gatherings were sometimes painful. When there were guests Hartsbourne was still run on lavish lines but the hostess was quieter and often withdrawn.

There is a story that Maxine had a brief affair with Oswald Mosley at this time. Universally known as Tom, he had served as an eighteen-year-old on the Western Front as an observer in the Flying Corps, and it is likely that he met Tony Wilding there in 1915. An air crash, sustained while he was showing off to his family, left Mosley badly injured and caused what was to become a permanent limp; although he returned to fight in the trenches and fought bravely, he ended the war behind a desk in the Foreign Office, which possibly saved his life since the casualty rate of young pilots was very high. In 1918 he decided to go into politics and his self-confident manner made him an attractive prospect (he had not, at that time, developed the extreme convictions for which he is now known). His motivation was a determination to prevent any further European wars and he was unexpectedly returned as Conservative MP for Harrow, at twenty-two the youngest member to take a seat. He was soon known for his articulate speeches in the House, delivered without the need to refer to notes.

Maxine was always looking for interesting new talent to introduce into her house parties, and Tom Mosley came with a personal introduction from Elsie de Wolfe, with whom he had stayed in Paris when he attended the Versailles Peace Treaty meetings.

At the time Mosley was courting Lord Curzon's daughter Cynthia ('Cimmie'), and Curzon was still a devoted friend of Maxine's. It was certainly at Hartsbourne that Mosley met some of the giants on the political scene such as Winston Churchill, F.E. Smith and Lloyd George. It seems somehow unlikely that Maxine indulged in an affair with Mosley, a man almost thirty years her junior, at a time when her family and friends reported her general depression. She had never recovered from Tony's death, and as she was working in the USA for a great deal of the time prior to Mosley's marriage to Cimmie Curzon in May 1920 there hardly seems sufficient time for them to have come together. One of Mosley's sons and several biographers assert (offering no evidence) that there was a brief affair, and although it is a fact that Mosley was known for his womanising before, during and after his marriage, it feels hard to reconcile this gossip with Maxine's theatrical commitments and her demeanour.

Despite her unhappiness Maxine still entertained occasionally, and when pressed. For instance, she threw a glittering ball for the two young princes, Edward, Prince of Wales, and Henry, inviting at the request of the Prince of Wales his mistress Freda Dudley Ward.

In the summer of 1921 there was a new tragedy. While staying with friends, wearing brand new very high-heel shoes bought on a recent trip to Italy, Winston's mother Jennie* tripped on a wooden staircase and broke her ankle as she fell. Gangrene set in, and she died of a haemorrhage following amputation surgery. Maxine was deeply upset by this, and six weeks later, when Winston and Clementine's three-year-old

---

* Following her divorce from George Cornwallis-West at the start of the war, Jennie reverted to her former title, Lady Randolph Churchill, which she used even after she married for a third time. Jennie had divorced Cornwallis-West for his adultery with the infamous Mrs Patrick Campbell ('Mrs Pat'), a leading actress of the day who had a number of adulterous affairs (including, before Gertrude married him, Forbie – who was almost suicidal when Mrs Pat terminated the affair). Her most famous relationship was with George Bernard Shaw, who was obsessed and wrote *Pygmalion* for her. She was known for her wit, and is credited with the remark, on hearing that two male friends were lovers: 'My dear, I don't care what they do, so long as they don't do it in the street and frighten the horses.' Mrs Pat married Cornwallis-West, but the marriage was not a success.

daughter Marigold also died suddenly from complications following a childhood infection, she found it difficult to know what to say to offer him comfort when they met at a mutual friend's house party in the north, where Winston was staying in order to give an important speech.

Gradually, it was borne in on Maxine that she had lost interest in Hartsbourne. Despite the somewhat frenetic gaiety of post-war society, without Tony nothing was the same and she recognised that those golden pre-war years could never be regained: there were too many absent friends. Her eldest niece, Blossom, visited Maxine regularly at Hartsbourne in the early Twenties and testified that her formerly vivacious aunt seemed to have tired of organising her famous Saturday-to-Monday parties. Mostly, when Blossom stayed there she found Maxine with only her closest female friends as guests: Lady Portarlington, Kathleen Drogheda (who was in the throes of a bitter divorce), Millicent, Duchess of Sutherland,* Muriel Wilson (who had once refused Winston's proposal of marriage), Olive Winn,† and Elsie de Wolfe. If any of them suggested driving into London for the evening Maxine would invariably look up from a card game and say disparagingly, 'Oh we don't want to go to the theatre tonight, do we?' Blossom recalled only one incident when a glimpse of the old Maxine appeared. By request she threw a party for 'the young', including Lady Diana Cooper, and Lord Rosebery's son; musicians were hired and the carpets were taken up for some modern, energetic dancing of the new flapper dances such as the Black Bottom. Maxine appeared to take part in everything with

---

* Like many of Maxine's friends, Millicent, Kathleen and Olive had all driven ambulances in the First World War.
† Olive Winn, better known as Lady Baillie, the millionaire owner of Leeds Castle in Kent.

tremendous enthusiasm, but when it was all over, and the guests had departed, she sighed deeply and remarked to her breathless young niece that it had all been 'such a bore'.

In 1922 Maxine bought a substantial mansion in Abbey Road, Maida Vale, which had some tennis courts behind it, and the following year she sold Hartsbourne. For some time, with the advice of Elsie de Wolfe, she threw herself into renovating the new London property, convinced that she could persuade Forbie and Gertrude, with their daughters, to come and live with her. But Forbie wasn't having it, and Maxine was hurt by what she saw as a rejection of her affections by her only family. Increasingly lonely in what was a very large house, she joined a bridge club where she played against experts and became so obsessed that she would play until 5 a.m. and refused invitations to other entertainments. On the few occasions she accepted and joined a house party she was always to be found in a foursome playing bridge. 'Heaviness' was what her nieces recall of those years. 'Heaviness of body, movement and spirit,' wrote one. 'I remember sighs of Aunt Dettie's, deeper and heavier than any have ever heard.'[3] Maxine had always been inclined to depression, and her bereavement and lifestyle led her into a cycle of misery in which she gained weight again and aged considerably. It took her two years to work through this episode, and when it was over she realised that she had lost touch with her old Hartsbourne friends and was missing good conversation.

It was at this point that the irrepressible Elsa Maxwell, whom Maxine had known since before the war, came back into her life. Elsa had been a guest at a number of Maxine's soirees and was always happy to entertain her fellow guests with her own brand of piano music and singing. Not only did she compose songs which were taken up and used by Cole Porter and other famous names, but she could play any type of music – classical, jazz, popular ballads – with great confidence and élan – and accompanied singers, who included Noël Coward, Cole Porter and – later on – Maria Callas. She was an asset as a guest and no one ever had anything but praise as Elsa's pudgy fingers galloped over the keyboard, yet she had never received any formal teaching (which caused her to harbour a deep resentment against her mother, who had refused her request for piano lessons). Elsa wrote in her memoir of staying at Hartsbourne where it seemed to her that there was 'a Princess or an Earl on every landing'.[4] Untidy in her appearance and overweight though Elsa was, she hardly sat still and was filled with an exuberance which seemed not to irritate but spread joy. She wrote that she quickly realised the futility of attempting to compete on equal terms with the hordes of naturally slim 'stick insects' in society, so she decided in her twenties not to let it worry her. People accepted her for what she was, or not. And if they didn't the loss was theirs.

Born in Iowa and raised in San Francisco, Elsa had made her way to Europe in 1909, where she met Dorothy Fellowes-Gordon – always known as Dickie – who became her lifelong friend.* Dickie was rich enough to fund even

---

* These two women were so discreet that even Elsa's biographer found it impossible to say for sure that they were actually lovers. If so, Dickie was bisexual for she also had a number of liaisons with men, including an eight-year affair with the Duke of Elba, which she discussed with the biographer Hugo Vickers in hours of interviews, yet never spoke of any sexual element in her relationship with Elsa. Furthermore, Elsa swore to Lady Colebrooke that she and Dickie were not lesbians. Elsa appeared to accept Dickie's heterosexual relationships with equanimity, though there is no ambivalence about Elsa's sexual orientation: in her autobiography she wrote how she knew in her teens, when kissed by her fiancé, that she could never make love to a man.

Elsa's idea of a good party, and the two set about having a life of fun, Elsa throwing lavish parties, playing and singing in the theatre, in top nightclubs, or at other people's parties and simply enjoying life. She had first made her name as a big-time party thrower in Paris in 1919, when she met Maxine's friend Elsie de Wolfe. Elsa was then thirty-eight and according to her memoir had still not decided what she wanted to be when she grew up. She boasted that she owned nothing; no property, no furniture. She travelled light. Of course she stayed in the world's top hotels while travelling light, and she was leaving the Ritz one day when a woman tapped her on the shoulder and asked, 'Aren't you the woman who sings those risqué songs?' She then proceeded to ask if Elsa was available on the following day to help her entertain some important delegates to the Versailles Peace Conference, including Arthur Balfour, the dour former British Prime Minister who was now Foreign Secretary.

Elsa initially described her accoster as 'chic and elderly', but the impression of age was one soon lost. Elsie de Wolfe was a fifty-four-year-old human dynamo; an aesthete who exercised slavishly, standing on her head for thirty minutes a day, turning cartwheels and walking on her hands until the day she died aged eighty-five. She was probably the only woman who could match Elsa for boundless energy. American by birth but raised and educated in Scotland, she had started in the theatre, in a similar, though not so successful, way as Maxine Elliott. She gave up the stage in 1904 to take up interior design at the suggestion of her long-term partner and lover Elisabeth 'Bessy' Marbury, a theatrical agent – possibly the first woman theatre agent – whose portfolio of famous clients included Oscar Wilde,

George Bernard Shaw and other Victorian notables. In 1905 Elsie secured a commission to decorate the Colony Club (of which Bessy Marbury was a founder), a leading women's club in New York, and when it opened in 1907 her design, incorporating freshness, light pastel colours, delicate writing desks, English chintz and French *toiles*,[5] launched her career. The club proved a shop window for her designs and the rich society women who patronised the club were Elsie's target market.

After a series of prestigious projects upon which she had worked were featured in contemporary magazines her order books were always filled. Within five years an entire floor of a Fifth Avenue office building was needed to house her staff of assistants, secretaries, artists and accountants. She not only charged fees, but earned commission on every piece of furniture she purchased to fill the rooms she designed, so that by the time the First World War broke out she had become a very rich and successful woman, and was an international celebrity in her field. Following voluntary service as an auxiliary nurse during the war, she transferred the main sphere of her interior design operations to Paris, where she bought the Villa Trianon at Versailles, which had formerly been a royal residence.

Elsa Maxwell wrote that it was difficult to describe the exhilarating atmosphere of post-war Paris, when 'Every day was like a sparkling holiday . . . The city echoed to the music of bands welcoming returning soldiers. Shops, theatres and cafés were jammed . . . ' Because of its location the Villa Trianon's neighbours included many English diplomats based at the Paris Embassy and Elsie soon became a leading socialite, being described by newspapers as the best-dressed woman in the world, and even began to appear in popular songs.*

Elsa Maxwell undoubtedly knew exactly who Elsie de Wolfe was when she introduced herself on the steps of the Ritz in 1919 and asked Elsie to sing and play at Villa Trianon. They may not have met, but they were both friends of Maxine Elliott.

For Elsa Maxwell the occasion would prove to be her spring-board to international fame, just as the Colony Club had been Elsie's. Elsie de Wolfe's parties were formal, amusing, chic and discreet – an extension of herself. Elsa Maxwell's parties were also an extension of herself, but were more like romps that often seemed to have just happened. In fact, Elsa had a for-mula; she claimed that no one ever remembered her parties for what they ate and drank but for the fun they had, and that it had been the monotony of other people's parties which led her to invent her own unique style of entertainment.

Those who dined with Elsie and Elsa that evening in June 1919 never forgot it. Elsa was already acquainted with the guest of honour, Arthur Balfour, for they had met once at Hartsbourne before the war. Other notable guests were Sir Ian Hamilton, Commander-in-Chief of the Army at Gallipoli; Consuelo, the Duchess of Marlborough; and Oswald Mosley. It was 'a trifle stifled', Elsa recalled, 'until I played and sang some of Cole Porters "secret" songs'.[6] Elsa and Cole Porter were good friends (she always called him Coley, and was the

---

* In 'Harlem On My Mind' by Irving Berlin the lyrics mention the 'high-falutin' flat that Lady Mendl designed'. (Elsie had married Sir Charles Mendl in 1926.) Cole Porter's song 'That Black and White Baby of Mine' includes the lines 'All she thinks is black and white / She even drinks black and white') about her black and white decor phase. In 'Anything Goes', he wrote the lines 'When you hear that Lady Mendl, stand-ing up / Now turns a handspring, landing up / On her toes / Anything goes!'

only person allowed to do so) and Balfour's eyebrows met his hairline when Elsa began singing the irreverent 'private' lyrics. Soon, though, he was roaring with laughter along with the others and afterwards he complimented Elsa, saying it had been a first-rate evening and that he would enjoy seeing her again. 'How about dinner a week tonight at the Ritz?' she asked, surprising even herself. And through something of a haze she heard him say 'I should be charmed.'

Elsa's heart dropped because, as she wrote in her autobiography, she could not even afford an omelette at the Ritz, let alone host and pay for a dinner party there. Over breakfast next day she explained the matter to Lady Colebrooke, another Hartsbourne contact, with whom Elsa was staying. Alex Colebrooke was amused and told her not to worry about the expense; she would cover it. She also laughed off the problem of whom to invite to keep the great man entertained, jotting down a list of names she would rope in: Mrs George Keppel; the Princess Edmond de Polignac;* Lord D'Abernon;† Grand Duke Alexander of Russia; and Sir Ronald Storrs. 'That,' she told Elsa kindly, 'should balance your table quite nicely.' The guests enjoyed the dinner so much that nobody wanted to leave and Balfour, having confided that he hated the thought of going back to his miserable hotel room, happily accepted Elsa's suggestion that she take them all on to

---

* Formerly Winnaretta 'Winnie' Singer, a daughter of the American sewing machine magnate. A well-known lesbian and famous patron of the arts, 'Princess Winnie' became one of Elsa's best friends. She married the homosexual Prince Edmond de Polignac in 1893 in a 'lavender marriage', for the title, but they hated each other and had long ago separated. Fully aware that she was regarded as *nouveau riche* by the Parisian *gratin* (the top people in Paris), Winnie nevertheless had the confidence of the super-rich. When a duchess attempted to squash her by saying haughtily 'My name is better than yours,' Winnie retorted, 'Not at the bottom of a cheque it's not.'
† British ambassador to Germany, 1920–5.

a Parisian nightclub. After four hours Balfour chuckled like a schoolboy as he told Elsa it was the 'most delightful and degrading evening' he had ever spent.

News of this party with the social lion Balfour, reputedly so difficult to entertain, spread like wildfire in Paris and soon Elsa was deluged with requests to organise parties and with invitations to play at other parties, not as a paid entertainer but as a guest who played and sang simply because she enjoyed it. She had no competition because once she heard a song she could play it by ear – all the latest jazz songs that people wanted to dance to, some of which were simply not available yet as phonograph recordings or even sheet music.

After that Elsa's parties became internationally famous: in Paris, in London, in Cannes, in Venice. It was she who began the craze for scavenger hunts, which stopped traffic as guests raced each other in automobiles around the city in search of items with which they must return to base: in London it might be a policeman's helmet, in Paris the list included 'a slipper taken from Mistinguett on the stage of the Casino de Paris; a black swan from the lake in the Bois de Boulogne . . . three hairs plucked from a redheaded woman . . . a pompon off the cap of a French sailor; a work animal; and a handkerchief from the Baron Maurice de Rothschild's house.'[7] By the end of the evening Elsa's apartment building was inundated with a donkey, chickens, several crabs, a bucket of fish, and a baby crocodile. No one managed to capture a black swan, for the swans attacked violently in self-defence. The landlady was outraged and took a great deal of pacifying.

Another huge success which had the whole of Paris and London talking was a murder party in which only two of the guests at a large dinner were in on the scheme. One was the 'victim', who played dead, and the other was an accomplice to help things along, calling for the police and so forth and advising the guests that they must stay put. Eventually, a 'detective' arrived and sifted through the evidence – all planted well in advance, including advertisements placed in the personal columns of newspapers for several days with the initial 'M'. It all pointed at the Duke of Marlborough being the killer, and the other guests, especially the Duke, were genuinely horrified, having no idea that the police were actors and that the whole thing was not really happening.

A year or more passed before Elsa next saw Maxine Elliott, in 1922 at Abbey Road. She saw at once that Maxine was depressed and was shocked to see the difference in her friend's demeanour. She bullied Maxine into making several trips to Paris, but it took her another two years to lure Maxine to Paris to live.

If ever the Twenties really 'roared' it was in Paris in the middle years of the decade. The horror of the Great War had waned and as young people were released from the hardship and sacrifice of five years (including the months after the Armistice when the Spanish Flu epidemic killed more than in the slaughterhouse of the trenches), old class barriers tumbled. Jazz music mirrored a new age; art deco triumphed aesthetically, and newly enfranchised womanhood shingled its hair, raised its skirts and discarded chaperones. Paris in 1924 was the Paris of Cole Porter, Noël Coward, Isadora Duncan, Somerset Maugham, Scott and Zelda Fitzgerald, Gerald and Sara Murphy, Ernest Hemingway, Pablo Picasso and the fashion designer Jean Patou. Not all were rich: young Hemingway's success as a writer lay in the future and he and his wife Hadley lived on fresh air and the kind invitations of well-off friends enthralled by his promise. Elsa Maxwell was friends with them all, of course. She had chummed up with Patou to their mutual advantage: his signature perfume Joy – discovered while he was visiting a *parfumerie* in Grasse with Elsa – was marketed at her suggestion, and with huge success, as 'the costliest perfume in the world'.*

Maxine came back to life in Paris. With the encouragement of Elsa and Elsie de Wolfe, she joined in what was on offer, knowing that when she got tired of being cheerful there was bridge, for Noël Coward, the actor Clifton Webb and Elsa Maxwell could always be relied upon to make up a congenial foursome. So she bought a luxurious apartment in Avenue Saint-Honoré-d'Eylau and enjoyed the task of decorating it with Elsie's helpful contributions. Even so, as Gertrude told her daughters, Aunt Maxine in Paris during those days was just 'a ghost compared to the old Dettie . . . if only you'd seen her then – the sparkle, the gaiety'.[8] Only once Maxine showed something of her old self when, on a visit to London, she met the world heavyweight champion boxer Gene Tunney. Gertrude went home thrilled because she had watched her older sister revert to her youth, and exert herself to charm and captivate this shy man of the hour in order to persuade him to give a demonstration of his training exercises for dinner guests. But at least Maxine's life was cheerful again. She spent her winters in Paris and St Moritz, summers in Cannes and

---

* Distilled from ten thousand jasmine flowers and around four hundred roses, as well as small amounts of tuberose, ylang-ylang and michelia per ounce, when launched in the mid-Twenties it sold for forty dollars an ounce, and it was indeed the world's most expensive perfume. In 2000 it was voted the perfume of the century, beating Chanel No. 5 into second place, and it has not lost its allure. A modern variation, Joy Forever, costs about a hundred pounds for an ounce of eau de parfum.

Antibes, and travelled almost annually to New York, usually in the autumn, to review her investments.

She spent a year in 1928–9 in Cannes, sharing with a friend* the massive pink Villa Corne d'Or, which overlooks the Croisette. Here, on one of the earliest and best courts on the Riviera, she played tennis, and golf on the nearby links. She did not lack companionship: half of English society spent some part of the winter in the South of France and more and more of them were beginning to spend time there during the summer months. Winston always loved the Riviera, and in the winter of 1922–3 had rented a similar property, the Villa Rêve d'Or, when the Coalition collapsed and he came round after emergency surgery to find himself out of Parliament without, he famously quipped, 'office, seat, party or appendix'. Clementine enjoyed the climate and the competitive tennis, but more and more she came to consider the company too raffish. She also disliked the fact that Winston enjoyed gambling at the Casino and it was not unknown for him to lose more than she felt they could afford. Increasingly Winston travelled to the Côte d'Azur alone, but his friend Consuelo – having divorced the Duke of Marlborough and been happily remarried to Jacques Balsan – was often there, and there were others of the old Hartsbourne set for company.

The new people that Maxine met in post-war Paris with Elsa Maxwell were also on hand when they visited the tiny seaside village of Antibes. There in 1922 Gerald and Sara Murphy had prevailed upon the owners of the small Hôtel Cap d'Antibes to remain open through the summer. This

---

* Ethyl Cox, Mrs George Esslemont Gordon Leith. Leith was a prize-winning South African architect who had worked with Edwin Lutyens in the design of New Delhi.

was essentially the world of Scott and Zelda Fitzgerald, the backdrop to *Tender is the Night*, and the family-orientated but champagne-fuelled beach parties of the Murphys where anyone from Pablo Picasso, to Charlie Chaplin, or Coco Chanel and the Duke of Westminster was likely to turn up.

Initially introduced to the Murphys' circle of friends by Elsa, Maxine discovered in Antibes during the summer months a different, more carefree Riviera lifestyle than the one she had found living in the Cannes mansion, and she liked it. She enjoyed the eclectic conversation and gossip. That year the gossip was all about Hugh Grosvenor and Coco Chanel.

In 1923 Hugh Grosvenor, the 2nd Duke of Westminster, widely described in newspapers as 'the richest man in the world' and known as Bendor* to everyone who knew him, was introduced to Gabrielle 'Coco' Chanel at a party on the Riviera. He was coming to the end of his second marriage; the first (to Jennie Churchill's sister-in-law Shelagh Cornwallis-West) had ended when he sent his wife a curt note telling her he could no longer live with her and she must leave the house. His second wife, Violet Nelson, could not take her husband's marital infidelities and had begun divorce proceedings.

Coco Chanel, then aged forty, was a successful businesswoman† and had expanded her already thriving fashion house when she launched her signature perfume

---

* Bendor, from the family armorial 'azure with a bend d'or'. His grandfather, the first Duke, owned the 1880 Derby winner Bend Or, and Hugh's red hair was a similar colour.
† In this incestuous society Coco had been assisted in starting her company by her lover Étienne Balsan, the playboy brother-in-law of Consuelo Balsan.

Chanel No. 5. The forty-four-year-old Duke fell hard for Coco, but he had a rival. Another man also desired Coco, and not even the Duke could ignore him, for it was Edward, the Prince of Wales. For the next year Coco was involved with both of them, and there is nothing like a bit of honest rivalry to stimulate desire, especially to a man who had never been denied anything in his life. The Prince visited Coco's Paris apartment a few times, allowed her to call him David, a name reserved for his closest intimates, and, according to *Vogue*, a passionate affair took place. Bendor tried harder: he pursued her constantly and showered her with gifts, including a huge uncut emerald concealed within a crate of vegetables that he had delivered to her apartment (though it is hard to envisage Coco Chanel unpacking her own vegetables). On another occasion he pretended to be a member of staff from a famous florist, delivering a gigantic bouquet. He was evidently fairly successful since Chanel's secretary offered him a tip. Among the many gifts Bendor gave Coco was a parcel of land at Roquebrune-Cap-Martin, where she would build an exquisite white marble villa called La Pausa. The pair were lovers for over a decade, during which time the Duke remarried. When asked about this Coco shrugged insouciantly; 'There are many Duchesses of Westminster,' she replied, 'but there is only one Coco Chanel.'

In those early days of Riviera summer holidays it was still fashionable to be pale and interesting. Women still sat in deep shadow, protecting their white skins with parasols or by covering up when in the sun. But after Bendor and Coco returned from a cruise of the Adriatic on the Duke's yacht in 1924, tongues began to wag furiously, and it was not because the pair could hardly keep their hands off each other – that was fairly normal behaviour on the Riviera – but because Coco was as 'brown as a sailor'. She had allowed herself to tan all over, and Coco was nothing if not a trend setter. A new fashion sprang up which – like Chanel No. 5 – has prevailed ever since.

Gradually Maxine Elliott found that the time she spent on the Riviera during the Twenties rejuvenated her. Feeling younger and fitter at every visit, she came to the decision to move there permanently. Unlike many of her friends the terrible financial crash of 1929 did not hurt her greatly; she was such a smart and shrewd investor that although some of her stocks temporarily reduced in value she was hardly damaged. She looked at the villas that were for sale but nothing suited her. She missed her old friends of the English house-party scene – and those who survived were, like her, growing noticeably older now – and she had the urge and the means to entertain them again. She hankered to recreate something of those heady pre-war days at Hartsbourne on the Riviera. Maybe a little less formal than Hartsbourne, but where she could choose her company and recreate a similar tone.

After a year of searching along the coast, failing to find the right house in the right location, Maxine came to the conclusion that there was only one solution. She would have to build a villa to her own requirements. Her chief priority was that the site must be directly on the sea. There were plenty of beautiful houses in the sunny hills behind Cannes where Picasso built his villa Californie – a name which has since lent itself to the entire area – but that was not what she wanted. Having lived for a year in the Villa Corne d'Or, she discounted Cannes too. It was too busy; she wanted tranquillity, preferably in the Golfe Juan, the huge bay which lies between Antibes and Cannes. None of the available properties suited her, and because the main road ran – and still runs – along the seafront for most of the eight miles of the gulf, sites for a villa were extremely limited. She was offered a long twenty-metre-wide strip of rocks lying between the sea and a stretch where the railway line and main highway ran next to each other. It looked unpromising, yet on the credit side it was halfway between Antibes and Cannes, the sea lapped the rocks, and as there was no appreciable beach it was unlikely to be bothered with uninvited trippers. But even if a villa could be built on the rocks there, how would she gain access from the road across the railway line? A level crossing, perhaps?

A quite exceptional architect was required, but Maxine had already met the right man. One of the houses she had often visited during the year she lived in Cannes was the Villa Mauresque, which was some miles to the east on Cap Ferrat and belonged to Willie Somerset Maugham. He had bought this property cheaply because the pseudo-Moorish and Renaissance extensions installed by the previous owner* were considered ugly, and the very large garden was derelict, so it had been assumed that anyone who bought it would knock it down and rebuild. Maugham purchased the villa in 1926 when he was among the top-earning writers in the world and though he disliked the original architecture he did not demolish it. Instead he employed a young American architect, Barry Dierks, who was part of Maugham's intimate circle of gay men, to change the façade and modernise the interior. Lawns were laid in the gardens, and other areas were planted

---

* A Catholic bishop, and personal confessor to King Leopold II of Belgium.

with pines, mimosas, aloes, oleanders and camellias – almost anything that flowered found a home there, as well as the native hillside plants of thyme and rosemary. A swimming pool was added, near a natural rock cave in the hillside which would provide shade for bathers. Maugham would spend the following forty years there, and the Villa Mauresque became known for its lavish hospitality, an obligatory stop for visiting celebrities, as well as attracting numerous artists and men from the Riviera's sizeable gay community.*

Barry Dierks had received a thorough education in architecture at Pittsburgh, and finished his training in Paris. He was a modernist, an early practitioner of what would become the art deco movement, and his style – which typified the late Twenties and early Thirties, with its structured clean lines – was described by Noël Coward as 'impossibly beautiful'. In 1925 Dierks designed and built a villa on an isolated rocky peninsula with a small private beach at Theoule-sur-Mer, about six miles west of Cannes. It would be his studio, and also his home with his partner Colonel Eric Sawyer. This extremely elegant and charming couple were regarded as the darlings of the Riviera, and Dierks was well placed to attract commissions from rich incomers who were beginning to want residences in the region. His own house proved his ability. Built into the steep hillside, entry was via some thirty steps

---

* Although homosexual, in 1915 Maugham had an adulterous relationship with Syrie Wellcome, wife of Henry Wellcome the pharmaceutical tycoon, and they had a daughter Mary (usually called Liza). After the Wellcomes divorced in 1917 Maugham and Syrie married, although he had already begun his long relationship with the real love of his life, Frederick Haxton. Syrie eventually felt unable to tolerate the *ménage à trois* and divorced Maugham in 1929. Maugham was recommended to put the villa in his daughter's name to avoid death duties; he replied, 'Thank you, I have read *King Lear*.' Haxton died in 1944, and Maugham in 1965. The villa was inherited by Maugham's last partner, Allan Searle.

down from street level, which gave on to the top floor with seven bedrooms and five bathrooms. More stairs led downwards to the reception floor where the generous open-plan living and entertainment areas provided stunning sea views from every window and the large terraces. With its kidney-shaped pool set into the rocks and a stairway down to the tiny beach, the gleaming white Villa le Trident was as up to date as it was possible to get.

Maugham's commission in 1927 gave Dierks all the cachet he needed and spread his name far and wide. Soon he had embarked upon a series of art deco houses which have easily withstood time and changing fashions.

In 1930, after seeing the villa Dierks had built for himself on an inhospitable site, Maxine gave him the commission to build her a house. It was to be called the Château de l'Horizon, she said. And she knew precisely what she wanted.

PART TWO

5

Courtesans and Assignations

The Château de l'Horizon was in a sense Maxine Elliott's last love affair. She moved into the small workman's cottage on the site in order to monitor every detail of the construction.

A bridge, wide enough to take her Daimler, was built from the main road across the railway tracks, giving access onto the building site behind a six-metre-high wall built to provide the property with total privacy. To this day no one in Cannes can explain how Maxine persuaded the municipal authorities to grant permission for the bridge, and there must have been difficulties, too, during the building of the structure because of the frequent train services between Nice and Cannes.* It is said locally that there were internecine difficulties resembling those of a civil war when trains were

---

* This line is also the main line between Marseilles and the Italian border.

sometimes stopped by builders.* The jewel of a house which emerged was the result of Barry Dierks's genius, Maxine's passionate interest and many heated exchanges. Maxine was a woman used to getting her own way and she thought nothing of ordering a whole day's work to be ripped out if it failed to meet her expectations. In the main, though, she deferred to the thoroughbred-looking Dierks because she recognised him as something special.

The gleaming low white villa was set into the rocks behind it, as though it belonged there, and guests who glanced out of the windows or stepped onto the private balcony of their bedroom would get the impression that it was almost hanging over the blue sea. The swimming pool, considered the best on the Riviera, was housed in a basin blasted out of the rocks and featured a water-chute so that bathers could slide down into the sea below and swim to a raft tethered just offshore. The huge terrace between the house and pool was the centre for most of the entertainment, and at each end a curved stone staircase descended to the pool. Retractable sun awnings were installed, and card tables beneath provided shaded places for guests to drink and play card games – bridge, six-pack bezique – or backgammon. Any guest willing to play cards with Maxine for the whole day was one to be treasured and was sure to be re-invited.

She had gained weight since she gave up the stage almost a decade earlier, having decided that enjoying life was more important than her body shape. There is a story of how, during the build, Dierks one day persuaded Maxine to bend over to look at some detail of the swimming pool while

---

* It remains today the only road bridge across this stretch of railway line.

behind them his partner Eric Sawyer surreptitiously stretched out a tape measure in a tactful attempt to ensure that the water-chute was built wide enough to accommodate her.

Maxine began entertaining at the villa before it was even half-finished, with a fancy-dress drinks party (but most of the women wore the newly popular flowing beach pyjamas). Several hundred guests attended; familiar names from the London and Paris crowd, who swarmed to parties wherever they happened to settle – Cecil Beaton, Doris Castlerosse, Sylvia Ashley, Beatrice Guinness and her daughters Theresa 'Baby' Jungman and Zita Jungman* among them, as well as Cimmie Mosley and her sister Irene Curzon. There was no formal meal, just hors d'oeuvres and endless servings of champagne and cocktails.

Cimmie, who had just conceived her third child, crashed her car on a hairpin of the Corniche, after falling asleep at the wheel on the drive back to Monte Carlo at 5 a.m. Tom Mosley had returned to the UK the previous day having heard news of a change of government, but before he left the couple had quarrelled noisily and publicly in the bar at Eden Roc† over his latest extra-marital affair, with Diana Mitford. Maxine was always convinced that Cimmie had drunk too much deliberately, to forget her marital miseries, but maybe she had simply attended too many parties which ended at dawn. Fortunately, although the car was wrecked Cimmie was only bruised and she continued on a sort of frantic round of the cocktail parties, lunches, casinos, beach club parties and nightclubs – a never-ending hedonism that would

---

* Two of the leading 'Bright Young Things' in the Twenties.
† The iconic restaurant and bar, with a swimming pool and terrace, situated on a rocky outcrop adjoining the famous Hôtel du Cap at Antibes.

provide her with a road to self-destruction. Maxine went to many of these parties, without – now she was middle-aged – involving herself in the wilder excesses. She still had her own close group of friends from the old days; the younger set provided the fireworks and buzz, which she was content to watch.

By the late summer of 1932, although the villa was still incomplete (works would go on for another year), it was ready for limited occupation. As soon as the kitchen was in working order Maxine could wait no longer and threw her first luncheon party on the pool terrace. Fifty people sat down to eat while workmen sat on the scaffolding, watching and cheerfully serenading the guests with Provençal songs. From that day, there was a never-ending stream of visitors to the villa, from England, from America, from the length of the Côte d'Azur and beyond, while Maxine happily pulled her white mini-palace together. The villa was seldom empty as she hosted swimming parties, luncheon parties, dinner parties, bridge parties, cocktail parties; any kind of event that would give pleasure. She loved the Château de l'Horizon and never tired of showing it off to those who lived or holidayed on the Riviera.

Sunlight reflecting off the sea flooded the spacious white rooms, rippling on the ceilings and walls. The classic furnishings for an English country house, originally chosen for Hartsbourne and stored for years, were finally shipped in: huge squashy sofas, chairs, tables, side tables, sofa tables, sideboards, a grand piano, photographs of the King (Edward VII) and Maxine's closest friends – many now dead – in silver frames, crystal vases and lamps, gilded-frame pictures. Barry Dierks burst into tears when he saw it all, for he had visualised an uncluttered minimalist interior for his beautiful *pièce de résistance*. After the initial shock he came to accept that it was Maxine's world, her house, not his, and in later years he would give her much credit for the things he learned about providing elegant comfort as well as beauty.

Guests were driven across the narrow bridge and down the short, steep hill to arrive at the entrance door. They were invariably received by Maxine in the central hall, and several visitors wrote about the striking imagery which was possibly deliberate: she had allowed her hair to go naturally white now, and she usually dressed in white and waited for them at the foot of the sweeping pale marble staircase. To one side of the stairway was an immense salon, large enough to garage a hundred cars.[1] It had a vast marble fireplace and glass doors which opened onto the tree-shaded terrace looking over the pool. Beyond the salon was a small dining room, used only in the winter, and then two small rooms – a morning room used for card games and a library overlooking the sea. The kitchens and usual offices such as the flower room and housekeeper's room faced a small side garden, as did some ground-floor rooms for the staff of guests such as secretaries and maids or valets. Fresh flowers were everywhere; mostly great arrangements of white lilies, sometimes with their throats sprayed pink, or gold, or blue with food colouring to match the colour scheme of the table setting. Minutes before a guest arrived Maxine's maid would whisk through the hall and salon wafting an incense burner – Maxine knew a thing or two about staging and settings.

The first floor housed the bedrooms and Maxine's own suite. There were a dozen or so guest suites and bedrooms (even regular guests weren't sure of the number), all overlooking the sea and each with its own wedge-shaped bathroom. This was Maxine's clever idea: the thin end contained a high window for light and formed a wall to provide the balcony with privacy. As soon as the main guest suite was completed she invited her beloved sister Gertrude and Forbie, who was by now almost eighty, and recovering from pneumonia, a much-feared illness in those pre-antibiotic days. Maxine provided everything for his comfort and visualised him relaxing on the terraces, convalescing in the gentle warmth of the winter sunshine. Unfortunately, it was one of those occasional winters on the Riviera when the sun did not shine. Instead, residents suffered one of the biggest storms ever known, which bent iron girders on building sites, removed entire roofs and flooded villages. The storm was followed by weeks of cold winds and driving rain, with a grey and heaving sea as an outlook. In a house designed for a warm climate Forbie was thoroughly miserable. A local doctor, Dr Brès – who would become a lifelong and sympathetic friend of Maxine's – came to visit Forbie daily to cheer him up and generally look after him.

That winter Maxine built a small staff of devoted retainers, some of whom had been with her through the war and afterwards, and these 'permanents' were augmented by local people. At last, her stage was set. From May to October the Château de l'Horizon was to be a second Hartsbourne, and since the smart set had by now 'discovered' the Riviera for summer holidays there was a steady influx of visitors from New York, London, and Paris all year, roaming the Riviera in a relentless search for pleasure. Maxine rarely had more than ten house-guests at a time, but many travelled with staff – maids, chauffeurs, valets or secretaries – so there was often a large household to cater for and some favoured guests stayed for a week or more.

Breakfast was served to guests in their rooms, invariably eaten on the balconies in privacy, at whatever time they wished. Afterwards they would drift downstairs, often wearing pyjamas and dressing gowns, but usually dressed in swimsuits – 'The scantier the better,' observed one guest as a fellow visitor paraded her beautiful legs about while wearing a few small patches of yellow material many years before bikinis hit the fashion scene.[2] Older women wore more decorous costumes and loose silken cover-ups, while Maxine employed an arrangement where with the addition of a matching skirt her swimsuits were turned into sundresses for coffee or drinks by the pool, or for games of backgammon that lasted most of the day.

By 1 p.m. non-resident guests began arriving for lunch, and five days out of seven were likely to number up to thirty or forty. One visitor recalled that 'the whole of the Riviera wandered onto that terrace at some time or other during the season. Often Maxine had rather dim ideas of who these people were, but at least she always knew who brought them.'[3] She always knew a good deal about those she invited to stay at the Château de l'Horizon and could reel off their antecedents for a generation or two, but it was not unusual for luncheon visitors to be completely unknown to her. Sometimes they would be ferried in off a yacht; on one occasion the entire ward room of the Training Ship *Arethusa* came ashore. Sometimes friends with villas further along the coast or up in the hills of Provence would call, bringing their entire house party along. Old friends such as Elsa Maxwell and Elsie de Wolfe were always *personae gratae*, and could arrive almost without invitation, trailing friends. Most guests, having partaken of Maxine's lavish hospitality, would have been surprised to know that after a very full luncheon, while they were taking a siesta or maybe out touring the area, at 5 p.m. each day their hostess sat down to an English tea with cucumber sandwiches and little fancy cakes in the library. Maxine's nieces blamed her weight problem on this secret tradition.

With a very few exceptions, such as an occasional evening party, dinner was at 9 p.m., for house-guests only, always in evening dress, and always taken beneath the great umbrella pines which Barry Dierks had carefully preserved on the terrace. Citrus plants in pots provided a piquant top-note to the fragrance of the pines. The dark hump of Cap d'Antibes lay silhouetted against the sky at the eastern end of the huge bay delineated by a curve of twinkling lights that eventually blended into the illuminations of the resort of Juan-les-Pins some three miles away. On nights when the moon was full and the tranquil dark sea was bathed in silver light, with only the rhythmic rasp of cicadas and the odd wave slapping onto the rocks as a background, a soft breeze off the sea to stir the balmy air, rustle the pines and caress bare shoulders, diners were often struck dumb by the sheer beauty of it. Having witnessed the effect on her guests of dining by moonlight, Maxine conceived a solution for those evenings when the real moon refused to oblige for her: she designed and installed a large electric 'false moon', set in the top of the highest tree, which could be switched on whenever she wished, to provide the full romance of a thyme-scented Mediterranean night.

*

Just as at Hartsbourne, Winston and Clementine Churchill were among the earliest visitors to the Château de l'Horizon, first appearing in mid-August 1933, accompanied by their teenage daughter Sarah, for a two-week visit. Winston was much in need of a holiday.

Maxine was well aware through gossip and the newspapers that he was now regarded as a spent force. Although re-elected to Parliament as MP for Epping in 1924, he had served a surprisingly lacklustre term as Chancellor of the Exchequer in the Baldwin administration until the collapse of the Conservative Government in 1929. In the elections the Conservatives were trounced, but though Winston managed to hold on to his own Parliamentary seat, he was already past his middle fifties and by the time of the next election in five years' time (even assuming his party won it) he would be over sixty – retirement age.

Winston might sometimes console himself with the fact that his ancestor, the 1st Duke of Marlborough, was fifty-two before he began his successful campaigns against French ambition to dominate Europe and thus became a national hero, but not surprisingly, like most other political observers even Winston now suspected that he was facing the end of his career. His own party leaders did not entirely trust him, having never forgotten nor forgiven him for deserting the Tory party in 1904 to join the Liberals and bait them mercilessly on the subjects of Irish Home Rule, Free Trade and India Reform. But most of his enemies looked no further than the Dardanelles fiasco, for which – as most historians now accept – he was unfairly made to shoulder the blame. In the main, though, he was simply too clever for most of them; a troublemaker whether he was on the front or back benches, who was too famous, too eccentric, too attention-seeking. His supreme self-confidence in his own abilities was often a further irritant, and yet he knew only too well that Stanley Baldwin and Neville Chamberlain were unlikely to select him for further high office if and when they were returned to power.

Relegated to the periphery of politics, and faced with the urgent necessity to earn enough to support his family, Winston had turned his attention to writing; his major relaxation was painting. Being out of administrative power did not, however, mean he ceased to think and function as an MP; that was his *raison d'être*. Unlike most of his colleagues in Parliament he had front-line battle experience in three wars, and he now found he was a party of one, observing what was happening in Italy and Germany – especially Germany – and applying his substantial grasp of world history to assess and predict a likely outcome. During his first visit to the Château de l'Horizon in August 1933 Winston wrote a long article for the *Daily Mail* in which he wondered how it was possible to watch the events unfolding in Germany without feeling increasing anxiety over what the result might be. He had received credible information that Germany was quietly rearming in contravention of the Treaty of Versailles, and he warned that Germany's neighbours in Switzerland, Austria, Belgium and Denmark were seriously alarmed about this.

The early Thirties were a dark period for Winston in almost all areas of his life, not only his career. Unlike Maxine, he had lost a good deal of his wealth in the financial crash of 1929. The money had not been inherited but earned by him as a young man and invested after taking advice from well-placed friends. It could not be replaced easily or quickly.

Furthermore, he had 'plunged' in the Twenties, purchasing a virtually ruined country house, which now he could really not afford. He was constantly in danger of losing his beloved Chartwell, and as a result Clementine tolerated rather than enjoyed the house. Less than a year after the crash, his best friend, the brilliant F.E. Smith,* died suddenly, at the age of fifty-eight. Winston had wept openly and told Clementine that F.E.'s death had left him feeling 'so lonely'. And then, some months later, while in New York trying to earn money on a speaking tour he was hit by an automobile while crossing Fifth Avenue, which left him badly injured. The accident, and his recovery from it, was followed by a serious illness – paratyphoid – and subsequently a paratyphoid ulcer which haemorrhaged and nearly killed him.

Winston's children were much loved by him but were also a frequent source of worry. Randolph, twenty-one, tanned, fair, and as handsome as a matinee idol, looked as though any parent would be proud of him. But he had grown into an arrogant young man who, having discovered that he shared a birthday with Pitt the Younger, was convinced that he would emulate Pitt and be Prime Minister by the time he was twenty-five. He certainly had the pedigree, and everyone of importance in Great Britain in the first half of the twentieth century had probably at one time or another sat at the dining table at Chartwell while Randolph was growing up. To him, his future was a matter of predestination and he merely had to step into the role assigned for him, but he failed to take into account an Englishman's natural distaste of bumptiousness. He was heartily disliked, and although it is fair

---

* By now the 1st Earl of Birkenhead.

to say that Randolph inherited some of his father's ability (he thought he had it all, and more), he lacked his father's humanity and, even more damaging, he lacked common sense. He alienated the very people from whom he needed support to begin his career in politics. When he was turned down as a candidate by the Tories he was so determined to get into Parliament, which he regarded as his birthright, that – against his father's wishes and advice – he stood as an independent candidate and on three occasions split the Conservative vote, which enabled Labour to reap the benefit in two constituencies which should have been easily won by the Conservatives.

Some of the resulting odium felt for his son was transferred to Winston, and for a while each time he rose to his feet in Parliament he was shouted down by men who might otherwise have been his backers. Winston did not support Randolph's ambition to enter politics – at least not then – and he actually made a public statement to that effect. In those years, whenever Randolph visited his parents Chartwell rang with loud argument until eventually he was banned. The estrangement from Randolph went on for several years and besides harming him politically it hurt Churchill emotionally.

Diana, the eldest of the Churchill daughters, had married the son of Winston's old South African friend Abe Bailey, but the marriage failed after eighteen months, and she had since suffered from depression. Sarah, meanwhile, had decided she wanted to go on the stage as a dancer. Esmond Romilly was another source of concern. The rebellious son of Clementine's beloved sister, Nellie, who lived with them a good deal of the time, had run away from his boarding school after espousing communism, a doctrine loathed by Churchill and much feared by the upper classes.

Beset by problems in both his professional and personal life, powerless and unable to make any headway politically, Maxine's generous invitations to Winston to come and stay for as long as he wished at the Château de l'Horizon were welcome in what were grim times. He knew he would be in the lap of luxury there, spoilt by her, and that he would be surrounded by agreeable company because Maxine would make certain of it.

Winston was described by his secretary at the time as a dynamo, but Maxine found that the middle-aged Winston who visited the Château de l'Horizon in 1933 was more subdued and softer than the self-confident and successful young man she had first known when he was First Lord of the Admiralty, before the war. As a consequence she was very protective of him, behaving like a fond aunt, and without overt fussing ensured that everything at the villa revolved around him. Although he was going through a bad time, she still considered him superior to everyone else who visited the villa and she happily changed the timetable (normally absolutely fixed for Maxine's convenience) to suit Winston's peculiar hours. This set the pattern for all of Winston's future visits. Other guests, both house-guests and those invited for meals or card parties, were limited to those she knew would entertain and amuse him. He must be given everything of the very best. He must never be bored. Only rarely did Maxine invite the Antibes crowd when Winston stayed, but among the few who bridged the gap were Elsa Maxwell, who could be relied upon to enliven any party, and the ageing Aga Khan with his old-world courtesy bringing a waft of foreign royalty. Winston loved to hear a piano played well after dinner for it reminded him of his mother's playing, and though it is not what she was known for, Elsa Maxwell could play classical music.

Winston enjoyed serious conversation with those who were politically informed, but he also enjoyed the company of pretty women who knew how to enliven a dinner party with clever repartee. When he saw a beautiful woman, his face lit up with pleasure and admiration.[4] Maxine evidently noticed this, and among the most frequent guests when Winston was visiting were the 'Three Ds': Daisy Fellowes, Doris Castlerosse and Diana Cooper – the first two of whom might best be described as courtesans. They were old acquaintances (friends would be too strong a word); both were titled, and despite scandalous histories they managed to remain socially acceptable, although not to Clementine Churchill.

Of the two, Clementine most disliked Doris (Lady Castlerosse, née Doris Delevingne), and perhaps not without justification, for some years later a persistent rumour about Winston and Doris circulated in society. This is running ahead of the story, but in 1933 they clearly spent a fair amount of time together for although Winston worked each morning on the three-volume book he was writing about his ancestor the Duke of Marlborough, a telegram he sent to Lloyd George records that he had also spent a good deal of his time painting. He specifically mentions several landscapes: 'Yachts in Cannes Harbour', and one of the church of Notre Dame de la Vie. But he also produced – unusually for Winston – a portrait. It was of Doris Castlerosse and painted in the style of Lavery's portrait of Doris that had been exhibited in the Summer Exhibition, which had startled her husband Valentine into the comment 'It may be art, but it's not Doris.' Randolph had also pronounced that it was 'not at all like her'. Word of this portrait leaked out and it was reported in the *Daily Express* that 'Mr Winston Churchill is challenging the achievement of Sir John Lavery ... one of the few noteworthy features of this year's Academy.'[5]

Doris had grown up in Beckenham, a typical respectable middle-class suburb. She was the daughter of a tradesman but had the good fortune to look as though she must have 'good breeding'. There was only one way in which she could enjoy the things she wanted from life, which went well beyond the middle-class aspirations of her parents, and that was to marry well. Her looks were her passport. Along with thoroughbred streamlining she possessed what were often described as the best legs in the world; as famous as, but arguably even shapelier than, those of Marlene Dietrich or Betty Grable. Doris was fortunate that post-war styles meant she was able to make the most of these first-class assets. Had she been obliged to hide her legs beneath the ankle-length fashions of previous decades, history might have been different. With her fair looks, a little pointed face, cool, appraising blue eyes and porcelain skin, her small hands tipped with shiny red-lacquered nails, she was, as her favourite couturier of the time, Victor Steibel, called her, 'an enchantress with a jester's cap of pure gold hair'.[6]

Aged nineteen, having obtained a job modelling for a London fashion house, Doris went to London to seek her fortune and was introduced to the twenty-one-year-old up-and-coming actress Gertrude Lawrence, whose background, ambitions and flexible morals were not too dissimilar from those of Doris. The two women got on well, and when Gertrude announced that she intended to become the most famous actress in London Doris responded, 'And I am going to marry a lord.' Both achieved their goals. Doris's personal axiom undoubtedly helped her: 'There is no such thing as an impotent man,' she opined, 'only an incompetent woman.'

Following a failed early marriage, Gertrude was in a relationship with a cavalry officer, Captain Philip Astley. Part of their arrangement was a Mayfair flat to which he contributed most of the upkeep, and it was a long-running affair, though both had other lovers at the same time. Gertrude was hopelessly extravagant despite Astley's generous allowance and when she met Doris she was looking for someone to share some of the additional costs of her flat. Doris moved in and for a short time the two women shared one evening gown – the only one they had between them until Doris discovered that one of the perks of her job was the discreet acquisition at bargain prices of garments that she had modelled for potential clients and were consequently regarded as second-hand. Not only were she and Gertrude happy beneficiaries of this policy, but Doris also found an eager clientele, initially among Gertrude's actress friends and soon thereafter from society women on a budget.

By today's ideal, neither Gertrude nor Doris were conventionally beautiful, but they had perfect figures, were good-looking in an unusual and arresting way, and each had an ability to make men believe they were beautiful. Noël Coward first met Gertrude when they were both about fourteen and knew her all her professional life. He described her as 'not pretty but striking', but he also said that when she was about to go on stage in *Private Lives* she somehow lit up from within and in those moments, when he looked at her she took his breath away. Astley bought her the right clothes, taught her how to behave, took her to the right places and introduced her to the right people; the consummate actress absorbed all the tips her handsome escort offered.[*] Doris presumably benefited from this educational process too, and she evidently learned quickly for no matter where she moved in society she seemed to slot in seamlessly. There was another characteristic the two women shared: both were sexual foragers and sleeping with men who could further their ambitions was an accepted element of their strategy.[†] 'An Englishwoman's castle is her bed,' Doris declared. One friend wrote that she 'delicately exploited ... sex' and never hesitated to attack the standards of the age 'which forced women to accept the social, sexual and economic dominance of men'. She felt that the male should pay some tribute for being allowed to maintain the fiction of his superiority.'[7]

By 1923 Gertrude was already beginning to stretch towards her goal of stardom, playing the lead in a musical revue written for her by Noël Coward. As for Doris, in line with her ambition to marry a lord one of her first lovers was Tom Mitford, brother to the famous Mitford sisters and heir to Lord Redesdale. This was moving in the right direction, but it was soon clear that although there was a title, young

---

[*] Years later, when asked by Margaret, Duchess of Argyll, why he had never married Gertrude, Astley replied that it was because she was 'pure Clapham'.

[†] Early biographers hinted that Gertrude Lawrence was lesbian, and it is possible that she was bisexual for Daphne du Maurier claimed she slept with Gertrude, but there is no evidence of any other homosexual affairs. Conversely, Gertrude's daughter lists numerous male lovers from the Prince of Wales (later Edward VIII) to Gerald du Maurier (father of Daphne) and Yul Brynner, and she is on record as stating that Gertrude's appetite for men 'verged on nymphomania'.

Mitford had no money. The next important man in her life was Stephen 'Laddie' Sanford, an American professional polo player who had no title but was rich. So Doris fell madly in love with him.

Laddie set Doris up in her own smart little Park Lane apartment and 'looked after her'. Doris always claimed that he had been the love of her life, but within a year Laddie had begun an affair with a Park Lane neighbour, Lady Edwina Mountbatten. Doris was distraught, but then she sensibly remembered her goal and made the best of the split with a good settlement. Before long she was the mistress of a Canadian financier who bought her a Mayfair house, 6 Deanery Street off Park Lane – and this time she made sure her name was on the deeds. By the time she was twenty-five, Doris had made the most of well-placed investments and gifts from a series of rich lovers and she had indeed acquired not only the glittering lifestyle she wanted, along with a host of society contacts, but she also had an income from her own clothing business, which she expanded by opening a hairdressing salon on the Champs-Élysées. Her house in Deanery Street was staffed by a housekeeper, a lady's maid called Swayne and a chauffeur to drive Doris's Rolls-Royce. A hairdresser called every evening to style her hair. The title, however, still eluded her.

By now Doris could afford shopping trips to Italy, where she would purchase hundreds of pairs of expensive leather shoes at a time. She never wore any shoes more than two or three times, but probably she disposed of them along with the gowns in which she now traded. Similarly, she never wore her guinea-a-pair silk stockings more than once because (like her kid gloves) they never looked the same once 'stretched', and she happily wore several pairs a day. Her hosiery bill alone was more than three times the average weekly wage for a working man, but her cast-off stockings were swooped upon as welcome gifts at the great houses she visited, such as Madresfield, by daughters of aristocratic families whose dress allowance did not run to such luxury items. Her face was as recognisable then, from pictures in society pages, as is that of her great-niece Cara Delevingne in the twenty-first century. Always beautifully dressed, she was warm-hearted, impulsive, clever and witty; conversation stopped when she entered a restaurant. She was in great demand for her ability to make a party go with a swing, knew everyone worth knowing, always surrounded by an admiring crowd, and was blessed with unlimited energy. She cherished what might have been considered a flaw by other women – a gap between her front teeth – claiming with a laugh that it showed she was 'lucky and sexy'. Arriving at a party she would perform a little talisman sign-of-the-cross routine, touching her forehead, breast and shoulders, while reciting *'tiara, brooch, clip, clip'*. In her beautiful couture dresses, she was, as the French say, a *poule de luxe*,* but just occasionally she let her guard slip enough to admit to a dark underside of her gilded existence. When lunching in Quaglino's with a friend† one day, in the midst of a lively conversation Doris suddenly bowed her head and became silent – then she looked up and said vehemently, 'You may think it's fun to make love, but if you had to make love to dirty old men as I do, you would think again.'

---

* Literally 'luxury hen'; colloquially, a rich man's toy.
† The English socialite Vicomtesse Phyllis de Janzé (née Boyd).

Mainly, though, Doris enjoyed the life she had made for herself where she could choose from invitations to four great balls in one night, each trying to outdo the others in glamour and luxury. She was even invited to the summer Court balls and there was no great country house from Cliveden to Chatsworth, Belvoir to Blenheim, Hatfield to Holkham to which she was not invited. Driven by her chauffeur along with numerous trunks of glamorous gowns and country clothes, she would be accompanied by Swayne, who carried the jewellery box and was responsible for checking the twenty pieces of luggage, unpacking, pressing and laying out the various changes of clothes and accessories, including immaculately cut tennis shorts. Doris had only to bathe and change, and allow Swayne to dress her hair. Although she played an indifferent game of tennis, lounging around a court in the sun in tennis shorts was a perfect excuse for Doris to show off those wonderful legs.

It was in 1926 that she met Valentine Castlerosse, the vastly overweight, boisterous and eccentric playboy viscount who was heir to the Earl of Kenmare. Castlerosse was the leading society gossip columnist of the day and worked for Lord Beaverbrook's newspapers. 'There is nothing that enthrals me quite so much as the written word,' he once remarked, 'particularly at the bottom of a cheque,'[8] and his readers loved the way he lampooned pomposity in society. When he and Doris met Valentine was about to depart on an extended tour of the Mediterranean and Middle East with Beaverbrook, who acted as a sort of godfather and often bankrolled him because the younger man amused him. His chatty columns had the unique appeal of being written by an insider on intimate terms with those he wrote about, and he had become so well known that a few lines' caricature of a large man with a huge cigar would, in those days, suggest Lord Castlerosse.

Castlerosse was considerably struck by Doris: her slender figure, her exquisite clothes and the way she wore them, her trademark elbow-length white gloves. She was good-natured, quick-witted, with a confident personality, and her overt sex appeal and absolute elegance in everything she did – the way she rose from a chair, shrugged off a fur, or crossed her exquisitely long shapely legs while leaning towards him to listen as though everything he said was a pearl of wisdom beyond price – intrigued him. One special feature of Doris, unlike many of her contemporaries, was that unless she was involved in a face-to-face argument with someone she never made a throwaway comment at anybody else's expense; she was at heart a kind person and very much a woman of the moment.

The era belonged to smart young women who wore shingled hairstyles under close-fitting cloche hats and knee-length tubular silky dresses with dropped waists over bust bodices which flattened the breasts – an androgynous look was the ideal and indeed women like Doris who could get away with it sometimes wore no underclothes at all, apart from a silk slip as a liner. High-heeled strappy shoes and silk stockings were *de rigueur*. These women scorned chaperones, drank cocktails and smoked cigarettes in holders.

While Valentine was about to depart for the east, Doris was leaving for America and he arranged for them to meet again after playfully warning her that skirts were even shorter in New York, and drinks longer (despite Prohibition).

That Sunday his society column, 'The Londoner's Log',* which provided its avid readers with a diet of amusing personal philosophy and entertaining gossip about the mainly impenetrable, glittering and glamorous world whose population eddied between London, Cannes, Deauville, Monte Carlo and various stately homes, led with a photograph of Doris. In short, Valentine Castlerosse fell headlong under Doris's spell.

When they returned to London in the spring of 1928 from their respective trips, Valentine was a frequent visitor to 6 Deanery Street and their affair blazed across the backdrop of London society like a comet. One night at the Embassy Club the Prince of Wales, who was at another table, looked up and saw them together, the vast bulk of Castlerosse's three hundred pounds making Doris appear even daintier than she was. The Prince's companion recalled how the Prince whistled in admiration and sent a note over to Valentine which read 'Congratulations, my Lord.' In May, Valentine and Doris were married, to the consternation of Valentine's friends, who forecast his annihilation by Doris – chiefly because although he spent like a rich man he was not one. Beaverbrook vainly attempted to prevent the marriage and Valentine's mother refused ever to acknowledge Doris or receive her, clinging to the belief that since Doris was Protestant and because the ceremony was performed in Hammersmith Register Office it was not a real marriage in the eyes of the Catholic Church. Nevertheless, Doris

---

* 'The Londoner's Log' did not only appeal to those who wished to read gossip about the upper classes, it was so popular with those likely to appear in the column that the wise hostess of a house party would ensure a copy of the *Sunday Express* was delivered for each lady guest so that no one had to wait to read 'the Log'.

had finally obtained her title, albeit a courtesy one. Now Viscountess Castlerosse, her writing paper bore the appropriate coronet over the interlinked initials DC. In time, barring accidents, she could hardly avoid becoming Countess of Kenmare.

Doris was undoubtedly romantically attracted to Valentine Castlerosse but neither of these larger-than-life characters was cut out for a conventional marriage. All the evidence suggests that while Valentine loved Doris obsessively (albeit not exclusively) to the end of his life, she often drove him to the edge of madness. Their marriage was a disaster; their extravagance eye-watering. Valentine once told a friend that Doris's idea of economising on a short visit to Paris was to restrict her purchase of new couture gowns to just a dozen. Her jewellery collection was legendary (though to be fair many of the pieces had been gifts showered upon her by admirers), and she often referred to herself as 'Miss Goldsmiths and Silversmiths'. Unexpectedly invited to swim in a new pool when at a house party, she thought nothing of despatching her chauffeur on a four-hundred-mile round-trip in her Rolls-Royce to fetch her swimsuit from London.

Valentine was as bad; he drank only the best champagnes – in magnums, never bottles – smoked the largest, most expensive Havana cigars, employed the best tailors to make his colourful bespoke suits and distinctive beaver-collared cashmere overcoats (mink-lined in the winter months), ordered dozens of pairs of handmade shoes at a time in the belief that he got a discount for quantity, and gambled away small fortunes in the firm conviction that his luck was about to change. His annual salary from Beaverbrook of three thousand pounds,* which together with his allowance of about half that sum would have been perfectly adequate for most men in his situation, hardly paid his drinks bill. His idea of economising was to charge everything, and never spend any cash. Not surprisingly, he was always in debt, but when his creditors became a nuisance he sent his excess bills to Beaverbrook as expenses and 'the Beaver', after a little bluster at seeing delivery notes for multiple sets of expensive golf clubs, bouquets of red roses and dozens of cases of champagne, invariably paid them. On one occasion when Valentine had a sudden attack of guilt after opening his post which contained only overdue bills he asked Doris to cut down on her expenditure, but she retorted scornfully, 'All right, don't give me any money then ... I'll pay for everything myself in future.'

The couple fought constantly, each occasionally managing to inflict actual physical damage. Their house in Culross Street shuddered nightly as they fought and made up, and on one occasion Doris visited a friend of her husband's displaying an arm full of bruises. She asked the friend to warn Castlerosse that if it happened again she would involve the police. When the friend delivered the message Castlerosse rolled up his trouser leg and showed him a bandaged leg. '*She* did that,' he complained. 'With her *teeth* too.'⁹ Their public rows in restaurants – oblivious of other diners – became celebrated. An enraged Valentine would inflate his Billy Bunter figure, turn puce and produce a torrent of invective, but he was no match for his wife who knew all the chinks in his armour and could always produce a volley of witty jibes

---

* Worth about £180,000 today.

about the things that most concerned him; his obesity, his virility, his massive debts. Having delivered her poisonous darts she would depart with a triumphant laugh. However, Doris's devastating ripostes were often self-defence against Valentine's fearsome temper, and there is plenty of evidence from her closest friends to whom she ran for shelter to indicate that Doris smarted quite as much from these encounters as her husband.

Noël Coward based his character Amanda, the insouciant and sophisticated leading character of *Private Lives*, on Doris. To those in the know, certain of Amanda's lines made famous by Gertrude Lawrence – the first actress to play the part – seemed especially poignant. 'I think very few people are completely normal, really, deep down in their private lives,' she mused, and 'I believe in being kind to everyone ... and being as gay as possible'. Another line is, 'Heaven preserve me from "nice" women.'[10] The 1930 play was a huge success, playing to packed houses for years. It is still one of the Coward plays most frequently reprised. When after the first night a friend told him it was enjoyable but that certain parts of it – all the quarrels and rolling around on the floor – seemed quite unreal, the playwright snorted, 'You obviously don't know the Castlerosses.'

By the summer of 1933, when Doris was invited to stay at the Château de l'Horizon, Valentine had petitioned for divorce on the grounds of Doris's adultery, citing Sir Alfred Beit.* He had a list of men to choose from, includ-

---

* Sir Alfred Beit, Bt (1903–94) inherited a large fortune and was a well-known art collector and philanthropist. In 1931 he became a Conservative politician, and later married Clementine Mitford, a first cousin of the Mitford sisters and Clementine Churchill.

ing Randolph Churchill, who on one occasion telephoned Valentine from Doris's bed to taunt him. When Valentine bluntly asked him 'Are you living with my wife?' Randolph retorted that he was, since Valentine didn't have the courtesy to do so. A few nights later they met at a club to which they both belonged and Valentine angrily confronted his young and handsome rival, saying that for two pins he would hit him. 'I shouldn't do that, Castlerosse,' said Randolph evenly. 'I'm not your wife.'

Gossip that year said that Doris was Cecil Beaton's first heterosexual experience. Their intimate escapade occurred at a house party when Beaton wished to make his lover Peter Watson jealous by 'turning heterosexual', and was – probably unwittingly – overheard by fellow guests as Beaton's squeals of 'Oh goody, goody!' rang through the house. When the story reached Valentine's ears he merely remarked, 'I never knew Doris was a lesbian!' But despite his own infidelities, he was heartbreakingly jealous of Doris's lovers. He hired a detective agency to follow her for evidence and one evening at the Ritz in Paris he received a telephone call from the agency to tell him that his wife was staying at the hotel and a man had been seen entering her room. 'You blithering idiot!' he yelled. 'It's me. I am here with my wife.' His mother persuaded him to withdraw his divorce petition because of the disgrace it would cause the family name, and the couple agreed to a formal deed of separation with no financial clauses. Calling herself Lady Castlerosse, Doris was now free to roam through society like a vixen in a hen house.

The personality of Daisy, the second of the Three Ds, was no less distinctive, albeit she was less likeable than Doris.

She had first met Winston in Paris in 1919 when he was there for the signing of the Treaty of Versailles and immediately set out to seduce him. He was forty-four and staying at the Ritz when he was introduced to the twenty-nine-year-old Princess Daisy,* widow of Prince de Broglie, who had just become engaged to Winston's first cousin, the banker Reggie Fellowes (a former lover of Consuelo Marlborough).† Daisy invited Winston to come to her room after dinner in order to see her 'little child'. It was perhaps because of his own small daughter Sarah, who was four at the time, that Winston went along as requested, only to find that the 'little child' was Daisy, lying stark naked on a tiger skin. Winston declined the obvious invitation with amusement and left, but he told his wife about it: years later Clementine told a friend that she had 'quite forgiven Daisy' because her seduction attempt had been unsuccessful.

Doris Castlerosse slept with men because she needed them to provide the good things in life and she used what she regarded as her God-given assets as tools to achieve her aim. But Daisy, who was an heiress to the Singer sewing machine fortune and a princess by her first marriage, was as rich as Croesus; her lovers numbered in the hundreds and she appeared to regard the serial purloining of other women's husbands as normal behaviour. It is hard to come up with a reason for her obsessive sexual need other than straightforward nymphomania. She was Duff Cooper's mistress for a while, and in letters between Duff and his beautiful wife

* Born Marguerite Séverine Philippine Decazes de Glücksberg. Her husband died in the great influenza pandemic of 1918, though it was rumoured he committed suicide when he was exposed as a homosexual.
† Daisy married Reggie Fellowes later the same year.

Diana they referred to her as 'Daisy "Wanton" Fellowes' because Daisy smoked opium or sniffed cocaine before sex to render extinct any inhibitions that might have hindered the full extent of the experience. She kept a stash of cocaine handy for any visitors who felt similarly inclined, and once dispensed a large dose as a headache cure to a Diaghilev ballerina.

Daisy was yet another of those women with striking looks that seemed to typify the art deco period; in fact, she was almost ugly despite a nose job which she underwent without anaesthetic in order to be able to direct the proceedings. Stick thin through rigorous dieting, she lived on minute helpings of grouse, iced carrot juice and lashings of vodka in order to maintain the angular shape so beloved of Cecil Beaton's camera lens. She thought nothing of spending thousands of pounds – the price of a good family house in London – on a single gown to be worn once. Indeed, she is still remembered as one of the most daring trend-setters of the twentieth century, and arguably the most important client of the surrealist couturier Elsa Schiaparelli and the jewellers Cartier and Belperron.*

At the Ritz, fellow diners rose to their feet and some even climbed onto chairs to get a glimpse of her monkey-fur coat with gold embroidery. She mostly espoused a chic, stream-lined look – what Beaton called 'studied simplicity' – which made other women seem overdressed. She was never afraid to be stylishly outrageous; the colour Schiaparelli pink, so hot it was called shocking pink, was invented for her and she wore a surrealist hat shaped like a red high-heeled shoe with

---

* Today she would be described as a *fashionista*.

a haughty aplomb that stifled any ridicule. She entertained lavishly from her villa, Les Zoraides, at Cap Martin near Menton, and from two massive yachts, the more famous of these being the *Sister Anne*. Unlike Doris Castlerosse, who at heart was a kind person, conversation about mutual acquaintances with Daisy was likely to be maliciously droll, and at least one friend reported that she was always afraid to leave the room for fear of what might be said about her in her absence. Despite this, Daisy's witty conversation was much appreciated, and there is no doubt that she knew everyone worth knowing.

Diana Cooper, the third D, was a regular visitor to the Château de l'Horizon during the Thirties. Born Lady Diana Manners, the daughter of the Duchess of Rutland by her lover the dashing Harry Cust (but the Duke magnanimously accepted the child for the sake of good form), she had married Duff Cooper, one of the few young men of her acquaintance to survive the trenches of the First World War, in 1919. Although they were leaders of a group of young intellectuals, they were also very much part of the 'bright young people' set in the early Twenties, until Duff was elected to Parliament in 1924. Diana was a society celebrity – her classic beauty photographed wherever she went, her fashions copied, her sayings quoted, even her personality borrowed by Evelyn Waugh for his novels. Her parents were initially against the marriage because for a while it had seemed possible that Diana might marry the Prince of Wales, but despite Duff's serial philandering it was a happy union, and by 1933 they had a three-year-old son, John Julius.

Diana apparently tolerated Duff's on-off affair with Daisy,

was even reasonably friendly with her, and was amused by Daisy's 'secret' for getting a cocktail party off to a good start: 'Just pour some of this into the punch, darling' – 'this' was Benzedrine. Somehow Diana moved with the fast crowd without herself ever becoming sullied by it; maybe her exceptional beauty acted as a shield.

It was the Churchills' silver wedding anniversary in September 1933, and with arrangements made for a suitable family celebration at home, they had accepted Maxine's invitations to spend a few weeks with her in August, together with nineteen-year-old Sarah. Winston's letters from the Château de l'Horizon, including one to his cousin Lord Ivor Spencer Churchill recorded that he and Clementine were having a delightful time, bathing three or four times a day, and that he was painting hard. Clementine was not very delighted, in fact; she played a lot of tennis with Sarah but was necessarily thrown into the company of Doris and other women whose company she could not bring herself to enjoy. She worried quietly about Winston's reputation being affected by these fast women and she disliked sitting around listening to the social chatter that Maxine enjoyed. Furthermore, she especially did not wish to hear the stories (which she already knew) on people's lips concerning her son, nor did she wish Sarah to hear them.

One scandalous event still being discussed ad nauseam in 1933 had taken place in Venice the previous summer, and most people in this cliquey little world who mattered had been involved: among them Randolph Churchill; Diana Mitford and her husband Bryan Guinness; Tom and Cimmie Mosley; Tom Mitford; Bob Boothby; Emerald Cunard's lover Sir

Thomas Beecham; Edward James and his wife Tilly Losch (with whom Tom Mitford was in love); Doris Castlerosse; Winston's great favourite Brendan Bracken;* Chips Channon; Cecil Beaton; Evelyn Waugh; Oliver Messel; Sir Richard Sykes; and the Lucky Strike heiress Doris Duke, who the papers usually called the richest girl in the world.

The *on dit*, as they had all assembled in the various palazzos and hotels along the Grand Canal, was that Diana Guinness and Tom Mosley were together. Everyone knew about it; not that the lovers tried hard to hide it from the others, including their respective spouses. They gazed into each other's eyes at table, vanished for hours between luncheon and dinner, and Mosley once loudly commandeered Bob Boothby's room between midnight and 4 a.m., insisting that Boothby could sleep on the beach at the Lido. The cuckolded spouses, Bryan Guinness and Cimmie Mosley, could only pretend not to notice the scandalous behaviour and hope that by the end of the holiday the affair would have run its course. Cimmie cried a great deal.

There were so many romantic entanglements within this small group that it was hardly surprising that the atmosphere became overheated, and as Diana Mitford wrote in her autobiography, 'Our countrymen were not on their best behaviour'.[11] The Rubicon was crossed during a group outing when Sir Philip Sykes – angry at Doris Duke for ordering her chauffeur to turn him out of her car on a lonely road in the hills after he made a pass at her – began an argument with Miss Duke and burned the back of her hand with his

---

* There was a persistent rumour that Bracken was Winston's illegitimate son, which to Randolph's fury Bracken 'refused to dignify with a denial'.

cigarette. Randolph Churchill sprang to Miss Duke's defence and hurled himself at Sykes. Suddenly most of the men, who had been drinking like fish for several hours, were up and brawling with each other. Cecil Beaton and Bob Boothby – two most unlikely brawlers – were 'fighting like bears', while wives vainly attempted to hold on to their husbands to prevent them joining in the melee. Michael Parsons, the Earl of Rosse, was flung into the canal by a group of gondoliers. Diana recalled that the following morning she and many of the women received bouquets of tuberoses by way of apology.*

Various versions of this outrageous behaviour were retold in England, appeared in gossip columns and were recounted over coffee tables. It was considered very shocking; reprehensible for Englishmen abroad to let the side down when the country was still in grave recession and unemployment was at its highest-ever level. It set such a bad example, and it is hardly surprising that Clementine did not wish to be associated with this raffish crowd, even though a number of them were kinsmen or close friends who were *personae gratae* at Chartwell. Her fastidiousness made her disapprove of the way Maxine and her guests sat around and gossiped about their peers. There were a few diversions for her when Maxine's great friend the Duchess of Sutherland came for a few days with her husband, who had served in the Cabinet with Winston during the last Conservative administration, as well as Viscount Ratendone, former Governor-General of Canada. Clementine could see that both appreciated

---

* Sixty years later, when I interviewed Diana for a biography of the Mitford sisters, she chuckled when she told me that she could never smell tuberoses without recalling the fight on the beach.

Winston's after-dinner talk, which earned her approval. But usually the others returned to the same gossipy subjects – and there was plenty to discuss.

Although withheld from British newspapers, it was already common knowledge by the summer of 1933 that the Prince of Wales was involved with an American divorcee, Wallis Simpson, and also that Diana Guinness, having run away from her 'nice' husband that spring, was now living in a flat off Eaton Square with her small sons as the mistress of Tom Mosley. Valentine Castlerosse and Randolph Churchill had attacked each other in print, Castlerosse witheringly dismissing Randolph as 'a little London peacock' living on his father's reputation, while Randolph accused his persecutor of 'ridiculous jealousy of any success his juniors might gain'. Most people in their circle knew the real reason for this extraordinary public quarrel.

Another matter still on everyone's lips that summer followed the sensational King and Country debate at the Oxford Union some months earlier when the motion, that 'this House will in no circumstances fight for its King and Country', was carried by 275 votes to 153. It is one of the most famous and notorious debates conducted at the Union, and was described by newspapers of the day as 'a tour de force of pacifist rhetoric'. Winston described the result as 'abject, squalid and shameless'. However, even he could not excuse his son's subsequent behaviour when, having tried and failed to reverse the decision by debate, Randolph marched into the Union and tore out the page which recorded the transaction. Such behaviour by her son was unfailingly agonising to Clementine.

So there was plenty to gossip about, and the other guests

were somewhat wary when Valentine Castlerosse showed up without an invitation to see what Doris was getting up to. For a change the Castlerosses behaved beautifully, no quarrels were reported and Valentine spent most of his time playing bezique with Winston under a shady awning. The strain of behaving well was probably too much for him; after three days he left for Paris, but was taken ill on the train with violent stomach pains. After a few days in hospital he had himself removed by stretcher and taken to his usual room at the Ritz to recover. Beaverbrook was very anxious about him for these few days and he cabled Doris who, although they were legally separated, was still fond of Valentine. She was just leaving for Biarritz, so she wired Valentine to join her there to convalesce – which he did.

As soon as he was up and about he was taken over the border to a bullfight, which he loathed. That evening he went to a party at a casino where their Spanish host placed a fond arm around Doris. Valentine took a glass of sticky sherry and threw the contents in the man's face, saying that Spain was a barbarous country and should be reported to the RSPCA for the manner in which they treated their horses. Doris was reported to have hooted with laughter as Valentine was physically thrown out of the casino – possibly she was the only one present who had noticed Valentine's extreme horror and anger at the bullfight. Next day, Valentine departed for London. One friend said, 'These two understood each other – and forgave each other, so long as they were not together . . . the trouble was that, fond as they were, they just could not live with each other.'[12]

Perhaps one of Maxine's most welcome local guests in 1933, and one who was approved of by Clementine, was the Aga

Khan, who owned a house in Antibes. His full title was His Highness Sir Sultan Mohammed Shar, Aga Khan III, but to most people in British society he was always simply known as the Aga. Not only were he and Winston old acquaintances, but they knew many of the people from the old days at Hartsbourne, such as Lloyd George and Lord Curzon. Maxine knew that this courteous man could be relied upon to engage Winston in the sort of conversation Winston relished, for India had been in the news for the past three years.

Few men knew as much about Indian politics as the Aga Khan and Winston may have gained a good deal from their conversations for, some months later, when he gave evidence at the India Joint Select Committee, Winston was congratulated by sympathisers on both sides of the question under debate* for the scope of his information.

---

* The method of bringing Indian princes into a federation.

6

Winston

Maxine was delighted when Winston returned to the villa in August 1934. Clementine had chosen to holiday in Scotland with their daughters Sarah and Mary, so, he wrote, he would be coming alone. Alone, that is, but for a secretary, Miss Violet Pearman, who was needed to take several hours of dictation each day; his butler Inches; a large collection of boxes and suitcases; his painting kit; and his son. Winston arrived fresh for his holiday thrilled at the ease in which he had travelled: he had stayed with Sir Philip Sassoon at his luxurious house in Lympne, Kent, following which Sassoon had flown him to Paris in his private De Havilland Leopard Moth, which took only an hour and forty-five minutes. He was then met at the Ritz by Randolph (they were now on speaking terms) and after lunch the party caught the

Blue Train* overnight to Antibes and from there were ferried to the Château de l'Horizon by Maxine's driver.

Winston's good spirits flowered in the hot sun, and Maxine ensured that the house revolved around him. He was soon ensconced in the best guest suite, where he was visited each morning by Maxine's latest pet – a lemur called Kiki, which guests referred to as 'the monkey'. This little primate, the latest in a long chain of beloved pets of Maxine's, had the run of the house in the way a cat would have, and while it was charming to see it hanging by its tail from the trees on the terrace, or the glass door leading from the salon, it was a cause of great consternation to some guests, especially when it leapt from the trees to land on the dining table. Female guests were especially nervous of it, and if it nipped anyone with its sharp needle-like teeth Maxine would brush off complaints and call for iodine. Elsie de Wolfe was nipped in a vulnerable spot one day while standing on her head beside the swimming pool. She complained loudly to Maxine and said it was her or the monkey. Maxine (whose own hands were often covered in small red bites) responded that it would have to be the monkey, although she did eventually agree to have the vet rasp the animal's teeth to make them less sharp. Winston, who loved all animals, mentioned that the monkey came into his bed sometimes in the mornings while he was working, and would caress him gently, but one day it misbehaved and left behind its 'calling card ... *on the bed!*'[1] he wrote with semi-amused irritation.

During this visit Winston's fellow house-guest was Kitty de

---

* An all first-class sleeper train which ran between Calais, Paris and Nice, dubbed 'the train to Paradise'. It made its first trip in 1922; later it added second and third classes and during the Thirties it ran daily.

Rothschild,* who was, Winston thought, 'very sprightly' (she was forty-nine) and made herself most agreeable. Usually this meant someone who was prepared to play cards with Winston whenever he wished, but in Kitty's case her knowledge of Germany made her an especially interesting person to chat to. A year earlier Hitler had become Chancellor of Germany and – knowing from his own visit there and his further investigations – that the country was secretly re-arming, Winston was increasingly anxious about the adequacy of Britain's defence policy, having concluded that if Germany was allowed to obtain military parity with France or Poland it would mean another war in Europe. His insight and his warning message went unheard, chiefly because he was at odds with leaders of his own party, but also because the man on the street in Britain was far more concerned that unemployment had reached three million in the depression following the world crash of 1929.†

Winston was above tittle-tattle over drinks around the pool, so this generally took place while he was off painting; Maxine always made sure that whenever Winston was around the conversation was more appropriate. She had noticed how he came alive and delivered his most memorable lines when matters of politics, history and literature were discussed, but if the conversation sank to trivialities he lapsed into a bored silence. When irritated, his wit could be pitiless, such as when a fellow guest asked if Winston had read his latest book. 'No,' Churchill replied, 'I only read for pleasure or profit.'²

---

* Born 1885 in Philadelphia to an Austrian father and orphaned as a small child, she was raised in Munich by an aunt and so spoke fluent German. Two early marriages ended in divorce before she married Baron Eugene de Rothschild, one of the richest men in the world, in 1925 though she retained her Roman Catholic faith. She was a friend of the Prince of Wales from the days before he met Wallis Simpson, and it was to Schloss Enzesfeld, Kitty's eleventh-century Austrian castle, that he fled after the abdication in December 1936.
† The population of UK in 1933 was forty-six million. Now sixty-four million.

Although he never appeared before noon, unlike other guests at the villa Winston was not having a holiday lie-in for he woke at eight o'clock each morning and immediately sent for his secretary. He sat propped up with pillows in a bed littered with letters, papers and books, while he dictated at a furious pace. No single secretary could have coped with Winston's daily output at home, where he had a number of shorthand typists who worked in shifts from 8 a.m. until 10 p.m. But when on holiday he usually managed with one over-worked female secretary, often Miss Pearman, who worked harder at the Mediterranean villa than at Chartwell (when Winston had finished three or four hours' dictation he rose, showered and dressed for lunch, and her work had only just begun). Everything had to be typed, letter perfect, for signature before dinner. Any corrections meant a total retype.

Another of Winston's secretaries, Phyllis Moir, recalled how he dictated pages of his book without hesitation until his mind was emptied and he could move on to the next section of his research, while he reeled his letters off 'to men and women in English political and social life ... more formal letters to members of government ... letters to statesmen in India, Africa and Australia, letters to his secretary [at home] with whom he corresponded almost daily; orders and instructions to his estate manager, his lawyers, his political secretary in London ...' To Winston, she wrote, 'a secretary is a completely impersonal adjunct, a machine that must have no personal needs ... somebody who must be on call whenever he wants them ... perfectly efficient and completely dedicated to the needs of Winston Churchill.' 'Yet it was difficult,' she added, 'not to fall under his spell, despite his terrifying impatience and unpredictable fits of irritability.' He was not a fearsome person, she recalled. 'When something amuses him – and he found life in general very entertaining – the corners of his mouth pucker up roguishly ... and his round pink face lights up with an impish grin.'[3]

Nor was his book and his correspondence Winston's only activity that holiday, for by the end of it he was able to write to Clementine that he had painted four pictures, including another of the church of Notre Dame de Vie, which he thought was very luminous and would look good in her bedroom – in fact, he thought it was the best painting he had ever done. There was also a painting of a quiet bay at the Cap d'Antibes, and another portrait of Doris Castlerosse, who was also staying. A small black-and-white photograph exists of Doris lying on a garden chaise wearing her signature short shorts while Winston stands in a dressing gown chatting to her. He used this photograph to paint his second portrait of her.

Among others at the villa were David Herbert, son of the Earl of Pembroke, and Ralph Milbanke – always called Toby – who worked for a Cuban cigar company. Elsie de Wolfe's husband, the British diplomat Sir Charles Mendl,*

---

* Elsie de Wolfe was sixty when she accepted a proposal of marriage from Mendl, a handsome and well-connected attaché at the British Embassy in Paris. He apparently liked the kudos of being married to a rich woman who could act as his hostess without any strings; she just wanted a title. On 9 March 1926 the *New York Times* ran a banner headline, 'Elsie de Wolfe to Wed Sir Charles Mendl'. The piece was full of innuendo since Elsie had lived openly and happily for over thirty years with the masculine-looking Bessy Marbury. 'The marriage comes as a great surprise to her friends,' it read. 'When in New York she makes her home with Miss Elisabeth Marbury at 13 Sutton Place.' Gossips had long referred to them as 'the bachelors'. The Mendls agreed in advance on a *mariage blanc*. They each maintained their own apartment in Paris and lived separate lives, though sharing the Villa Trianon whenever they wished. This arrangement was completely accepted in their circles; the couple liked each other and were a wonderful foil at parties, so the unusual partnership worked well. Elsie, who now styled herself Lady Mendl, continued to live with Bessy Marbury until Bessy's death in 1933, and in her 1935 autobiography *After All*, Elsie entirely forgot to mention her husband.'

came in most days from a neighbour's house to use the swimming pool, and there was a constant stream of luncheon guests, including friends whose yacht had broken down so they had all been found accommodation in nearby villas. Violet Cripps was another guest – in her previous marriage she had been a duchess, wife of Bendor, the fabulously rich Duke of Westminster whom Winston had met in Paris on his journey south. It was a congenial party constructed to guarantee interesting conversation for Winston. Ten days after Winston's arrival his eldest daughter, Diana, arrived. She had recently parted from her husband after only eighteen months of marriage and was depressed and sad. Winston had mentioned to Maxine that a visit to the Château de l'Horizon might cheer her up and she was immediately invited to join the party.

Last to arrive was Professor Frederick Lindemann ('the Prof'), a near-genius scientist who had become a good friend. He drove down just so that he could drive them both home, stopping en route to enable Winston to paint. Specifically, Winston wished to drive along part of the route taken by Napoleon when he escaped from Elba, landed near Antibes in March 1815 and made his way to Paris by way of the Alps to avoid recapture. By coincidence, the *Route Napoléon* began about a mile from the villa and had recently been opened as a section of Route National 85. Winston's interest was piqued when Stanley Baldwin teasingly wrote to him a few weeks earlier to say that he was staying in an *auberge* near Aix-les-Bains used by Napoleon on his march to Paris – which, he said, made him one up on Winston. As a result Winston read Henry Houssay's biography of Napoleon, published in 1904, which gave him a desire to write a book about the emperor. Despite the fact that he was contemplating enforced retirement from politics, he wrote to Clementine that he had so many literary projects in mind that he might not have enough time left to do them all.

Maxine hated her guests to go out in the evenings and encouraged them to make their own entertainment at the villa. She would have been quite content if this was card games every night, but usually there was someone among them who could play the piano and sing or recite. Elsa Maxwell was always happy to oblige, as was Noël Coward (though he was not present when Winston was there in 1934). Winston had an encyclopaedic memory for songs from musicals and he would sing them, word perfect, in his booming baritone. He also enjoyed acting the part of various animals in the game charades, and reciting long poems that he had committed to memory as a young man.

However, they did venture out sometimes. Winston took them all into Cannes one night and they somehow found their way to a seamy dance hall frequented by sailors, where a woman in a fit of jealousy kicked another woman in the backside. On another evening – much to Maxine's annoyance – Randolph tempted his father to stray as far as the Cannes Casino, and this was noted and appeared in the papers in England. Clementine wrote to tell Winston that he was reported to have lost heavily at the roulette table but he corrected this, saying that he had only played chemin de fer and that although he had lost 'uniformly' the amounts had been small; Randolph, however, lost heavily enough to stop him playing.[4] On the night before his departure Winston threw a dinner party in the best hotel in Cannes, partly to repay Maxine's hospitality and partly to entertain some friends who were staying in the area. Maxine pressed Winston to stay on but he felt that though it had been a welcome change, and he had achieved a good deal in the relaxed atmosphere, it was time to go. He had the bit between his teeth on a new project and was anxious to begin the drive on the *Route Napoléon*, making five stops along the way to paint, and also to visit Stanley Baldwin, fortuitously still on holiday in Aix-les-Bains. He planned to talk to Baldwin about Britain's ability to develop an effective air defence against Germany, and his own opposition to Indian reform.

Just before he left Winston reported to Clementine that he thought Maxine was not very well. She had been fine at the start of his holiday, he wrote, but had gradually become morose and low-spirited, playing endless games of bezique for small points. He discovered the likely reason for this when Maxine confided that she was feeling the effects of the recession that year because prices on the Dow Jones were still low, and the conversion rate for the dollar was unfavourable. The result was that whereas for some years she had received an income from her investments of $150,000 a year, it was presently only $48,000. She said it was painful after having worked so hard, when finally she had built herself the house she had always wanted, to suffer this drop in income for, with the exception of Hartsbourne, she had never loved a house more than the Château de l'Horizon. Her theatre was now closed down and the site was on the market, but no one was buying property in New York at present and it was costing her $22,000 (almost half her income) a year in taxes and ground rates. She had therefore decided to close the villa in September to travel and stay with friends around Europe during the winter as an economy, and maybe rent out the villa until things improved. In Clementine's reply she sent her love to Maxine but remarked to Winston that although she felt sorry for Maxine for losing two-thirds of her income, £10,000 a year still wasn't too bad for a single woman.

The Churchill party broke up, Winston and the Prof to head for Grenoble in the footsteps of Napoleon, Randolph to drive Diana to Paris in a hired car. The butler and secretary took most of the luggage and made their way home by train.

One of the most remarkable things about this two-week holiday taken by Winston was how much he managed to cram into it besides his card playing, his painting, his long conversations and the regular swimming sessions of which he wrote. The multi-volume authorised biography of Churchill by Sir Martin Gilbert is accompanied by hefty companion volumes containing transcripts of Winston's daily correspondence (and despite their size even these are not fully inclusive), so his output during that short period is clear to see and one cannot help but be impressed, not only by the sheer number of letters and articles he produced but by the breadth of subjects, from world issues such as India and Germany to correspondence concerning his books, and personal letters to friends. What is more, each letter is a marvel of composition yet his secretary states that he rarely hesitated when dictating, even more rarely did he edit the typed documents and only paused when he was savouring a humorous or apposite phrase – saying it out loud, repeating it to himself and rolling it round in his head to gauge the effect – and then he would nod to himself with humour or with satisfaction and carry on dictating. As if this was not enough for holiday productivity, he also worked at proof-reading the second volume of his Marlborough biography, which he admitted had been 'laborious', wrote an introduction to a book by the artist Paul Maze, and an article on Viscount Snowden's life for the *Daily Mail*. He also arranged to take part in a set of talks for BBC radio on India, and agreed a thirty-thousand-word series on the subject 'My Life to Date' for the *News of the World*.

No wonder he was satisfied as he left, promising Maxine that he would return the following year.

On 1 September 1935 Maxine's youngest niece Diana and her new husband Vincent Sheean, an Irish-American journalist, arrived at the villa for a week's stay. The couple had met a few weeks earlier, fallen in love and decided to get married immediately. They flew to Vienna in a friend's airplane for the ceremony, and only afterwards thought to tell Diana's parents. It was not a secret marriage per se, but it was done so hastily that Diana knew that, unlike her forgiving parents, her aunt would be disapproving and she was nervous. The pair arrived at the Château de l'Horizon late that night, to find all of Maxine's other house-guests out at the Casino and Maxine complaining about how rude it was for guests to go elsewhere for entertainment when she had gone to so much trouble to make things perfect for them at the villa. However, she welcomed the young couple and told them that they had a treat in store, for Winston was arriving the following morning on the Blue Train.

Vincent Sheean was a drinking friend of Ernest Hemingway and – like Churchill's nephew Esmond Romilly – was a radical left-winger. He had produced incisive articles on international incidents, from the Palestinian-Jewish riots in Jerusalem 1929 to Mussolini's growing powerbase. During a recent assignment for the *New York Herald Tribune* covering

1. Rockland, Maine, a sleepy little port during Maxine's childhood

2. & 3. Maxine in her early twenties. Her beauty helped propel her to fame as an actress

4. Maxine begins the transformation into an English 'lady' – with Gertrude at Jackwood

5. Maxine and Nat in the drawing room at Jackwood

6. Gertrude (left) and Maxine in the study at Jackwood

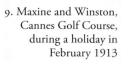
7. Maxine with Lady Diana
Manners at Belvoir Castle

8. Even in this photograph with the
Hon George Keppel (right) Maxine
appears to cold-shoulder Nat

9. Maxine and Winston,
Cannes Golf Course,
during a holiday in
February 1913

10. Walking on the
Croisette at Cannes;
Maxine and Lady
Portarlington (left)

11. Hartsbourne Manor, Hertfordshire. By now Maxine's transformation was complete

12. Maxine's famous 'Saturday to Monday' house parties at Hartsbourne included
a host of celebrity visitors

13. Regular visitors to Hartsbourne were best friends F.E. Smith (Lord Birkenhead) and Winston Churchill

14. Maxine as the cool 'Duchess of Harts' . . .

15. . . . . and the smouldering stage presence.

16. Maxine with the King at Marienbad in 1909

17. (inset) Tony, the love of Maxine's
life: tennis ace Anthony Wilding

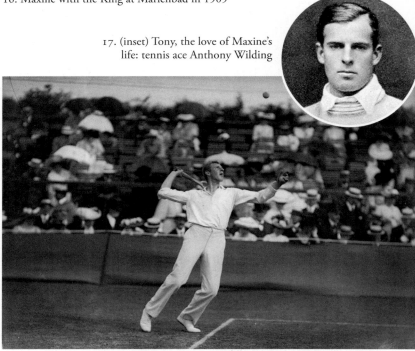

18. Anthony Wilding, Wimbledon champion for four consecutive years

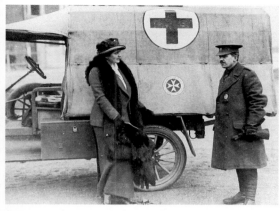

19. Maxine with her chauffeur turned ambulance driver with one of the ambulances she provided

20. Maxine's barge *Julia*, which brought food and medical supplies to 350,000 displaced people in Belgium

21. Winston and Archibald Sinclair visited Maxine on the *Julia* in February 1916

22. Above this photo in her album Maxine wrote 'some of my poor refugees'

23. Maxine's theatre on Broadway

24. Post-war friends, Cole Porter and Elsa Maxwell

25. The Murphys at Antibes gathered an eclectic set around them

26. & 27. Eccentric genius: Elsie de Wolfe (Lady Mendl) credited her robust health to standing on her head for long periods every day

the open violence in Spain (which would soon lead to civil war) he was firmly in the anti-Franco camp. To Maxine and her other two guests – Peggy, the Marchioness of Crewe* and Napier, Lord Alington – he was almost a Bolshevik, but Maxine knew that good manners would ease the way for him, and she felt that Vincent and Winston would find plenty of subjects for lively conversation even though they might not agree.

Taking his cue from his bride, Sheean also admitted to a little nervousness at meeting the famous Aunt Dettie because of everything he had heard about her and her odyssey from the clapperboard cottage in Maine to what he called her 'white palace on the water'. His politics made it impossible for him to be wholly admiring of Maxine and her lifestyle, yet he found he could not help but be impressed by her manner. He noted that she had adopted the mannerisms of an aristocrat from a bygone era, peering through her lorgnette which she kept clipped onto a string of pearls, and she spoke, he wrote, with an Edwardian absolute certainty of her superiority, almost as a dowager duchess might absently address a groom.

Sheean's first sight of Maxine's favourite guest came the following day as Winston descended to the pool terrace just before noon, wearing a red silk bathrobe over his swimsuit, a large floppy hat and slippers. A cherubic grin completed the ensemble. His financial situation had caused him to make a few economies and Sheean recorded in his memoirs the first words he heard Winston speak: 'My dear Maxine, you have

---

* Born in 1887, Margaret 'Peggy' Primrose was the daughter of the 5th Earl of Rosebery. It was while attending a ball at her house in 1904 that Winston first met Clementine.

no idea how easy it is to travel without a servant, I came here all the way from London alone and it was quite simple.' And Maxine's contralto voice answering in an amused tone, 'Winston! How *brave* of you.'[5] Sheean knew that Maxine had once travelled all over America by train on her own, yet somehow her manner was that of someone who had never known that such inconveniences existed. If nothing else, Sheean decided, it would be an interesting visit.

He listened to Maxine and Winston chatting about the old days at Hartsbourne. Both said they felt sorry for anybody who had not known London before the war. Sheean recognised that these two had known a vanished world, the passing of which would be a lifelong bereavement. He also saw how completely Maxine had become integrated into the aristocracy. She thought like them, spoke like them, shared the same memories, was steeped in the complicated family trees, and shared their interests and prejudices. And yet Sheean also recognised that Maxine had a strong intelligence which never allowed any worldly or business matter to be influenced by sentiment. He came prepared to dislike her and ended admiring the way she pulled together around her an international fashionable set into which these *ancien régime* aristocrats somehow fitted, and in which she had taken the role of *grande dame*.

When Winston wrote to Clementine on 15 September, towards the end of this holiday, it was to apologise for not writing previously (which was extremely unusual for him). His letter now, he said, was prompted by four reasons. One, to let her know he was staying on an extra day, which would give him time to advise his return date, and he hoped not to be rebuked for having not written earlier. Two, to say he had been 'rather successful' at baccarat the previous night; three, the euphoria of completing a painting that he thought was beautiful; and four, a general contentment due to some excellent old brandy after lunch and the fact that he was now alone with Maxine, all other visitors having left.

He had enjoyed his holiday immensely, he wrote, and had done nothing but paint 'ferociously' from morning to night – often having to stand to avoid indigestion, so his legs ached. He said he had not dictated a word of Marlborough and instead had painted 'careless of time' both outdoors and in his bedroom, which had made him late for everything. He was giving a dinner that night at the Casino, he reported, and he hoped his winnings would pay for it. The dinner was principally for Maxine, but he also invited some guests who were holidaying in the vicinity, including the Liberal politician Leslie Hore-Belisha (appointed Minister for Transport that year), 'a Spanish Duchess-something-or-other' whom Hore-Belisha appeared to have in tow, and Arthur Evans.* Hore-Belisha gambled at the tables for high stakes that Winston knew he could not afford, but it was his political ability that came in for most criticism; how irritating it must be, Winston wrote witheringly, to be in government and yet know nothing whatever about government policy.

Winston certainly painted a lot in those weeks; his fellow guests have noted how he went off into the thyme- and rosemary-scented hills at Saint-Paul-de-Vence. There is a record of Winston setting off for a day's painting and the upheaval caused to the domestic arrangements of his hostess:

---

* Henry Arthur Evans, Conservative MP for Cardiff South at this time.

The painting paraphernalia with its easel, parasol and stool had to be assembled; the brushes, freshly cleaned, to be found; the canvases chosen, the right hat sorted out, the cigar box replenished. At last, driven by our chauffeur ... he would depart with the genial wave and rubicund smile we have learned to associate with his robust optimism. On his return he would amuse us by repeating the comments of those self-sufficient critics who congregate round easels. An old Frenchman one day told him, 'With a few more lessons you will become quite good!'[6]

Sheean wrote about this holiday with Winston in his memoirs and he recorded how, 'in spite of the fact that [Winston] was on holiday, painting and taking the sun, [he] could not keep his mind off these ominous foreshadows of the day of reckoning. He spoke constantly of the Ethiopian crisis, of the League [of Nations], of Mussolini, of relations between England and Italy, of Italy's relations with Germany and of German rearmament.'[7] The latter subject was his chief worry, for he had just come across incontrovertible evidence that Britain was under threat, and yet his warnings had fallen on deaf ears, with the exception of Anthony Eden, an ardent anti-Fascist whose name was spat on in Italy. Even as Winston spoke Mussolini was preparing for his attack on Ethiopia which would ally him with the Germans – somehow, Winston could see clearly what few others recognised, the sinister series of moves being made on the European chessboard that would ultimately lead to a world war.

Curiously, there was no mention in Winston's sole letter to Clementine during that holiday of a meeting with the Prince of Wales and Mrs Simpson, who were staying at a villa five hundred yards away (though it was not visible due to the rocky outcrops between them) with the Marquess and Marchioness of Cholmondeley. The Villa le Roc was originally a nineteenth-century art nouveau castle that had been unoccupied for years and fallen into ruin. When Maxine heard from her old friend Rock Cholmondeley* and his wife Sybil, that they had bought it and were to be her neighbours, she immediately advised them to call in Barry Dierks. Like Château de l'Horizon the tiny building was perched on a ledge of rock and Dierks expanded it and turned it into an art deco cube with a covered swimming pool held in the rocks.

Lady Cholmondeley, the fabulously rich sister of Churchill's friend Sir Philip Sassoon, had organised the royal visit. 'We got here,' Wallis Simpson wrote to her aunt, 'to find a lovely villa *in the water* – our own rocks and all the privacy in the world.'[8] Maxine always called it 'Rock's place' and she slightly disparaged it, claiming that the noise from passing trains was so much louder there than in her own villa; her guests found they could not tell the difference. It is from Wallis Simpson's surviving correspondence that we know Winston and Maxine were invited there for drinks with the couple in September 1935, for a brief handwritten note to the Prince survives: 'I think it would be nice to have the Churchill drinks on the porch outside the drawing room,' she wrote.[9]

Winston had an almost feudal loyalty to his sovereign, and when he saw them together and realised that the pair were in love he gave them his support. Maybe he felt disinclined

---

* George Horatio, 5th Marquess of Cholmondeley (1883–1968), was styled Earl of Rocksavage until 1923, when he inherited his father's title. He was a direct descendant of Sir Robert Walpole, the first Prime Minister of Great Britain, and was a well-known tennis and polo player who had been a visitor to Hartsbourne.

to write about this to Clementine, who was not impressed by Wallis, but felt he needed to tell her about it in person after he got home. He only briefly mentioned Doris Castlerosse who, he told Clementine, had now left for Baden Baden to go to Dr Dengler's spa, which Doris and Maxine frequented. Yet it seems there may have been something more between Winston and Doris during that holiday, when he painted a third portrait of her. Three separate, trusted sources reported that while Winston was at the Château de l'Horizon Doris had climbed into his bed one night, the inevitable happened, and that afterwards Winston said to her, 'Doris, you could make a saint come!'[10]

The biographer John Pearson also mentioned the incident in his Churchill biography *Citadel of the Heart*, but placed it at the red, white and gilt palace that is the Ritz Hotel in Paris, which suggests it may have become confused with the Daisy Fellowes incident in 1919.* Yet another source stated that while Winston was staying at the Château de l'Horizon, Doris Castlerosse was 'popped' into his bed.[11] While it is hard to imagine who might have popped Doris into Winston's bed, other than Doris herself, this story is well known by members of a set of people who were likely to have heard about it from those in the know at the time.

We will never know the truth, of course, but it is certainly true that if ever the Churchills' long and happy marriage hit a rough patch it was in that period. Earlier in 1935, Clementine had joined Lord Moyne's yacht, the *Rosaura*, for a cruise in the South Seas with friends, during which she enjoyed what can be best described as a shipboard romance with another man, which she later admitted to her daughter Mary.

---

* See page 117.

This is the only extra-marital sexual incident ever mentioned about Churchill, apart from an alleged remark by Thomas Thynne, 5th Marquess of Bath, that Churchill had only ever been unfaithful once, and that was with Maxine Elliott. It would be hard to know when *that* might have been supposed to have occurred, and reading the loving letters Winston wrote to Clementine throughout their marriage it seems extremely unlikely. It has been suggested that it occurred when Winston and Maxine were in Cannes in February 1913, and a photograph certainly survives of them together there, walking on a golf course. But that occasion can easily be discounted for Clementine was with Winston on that trip to the South of France; indeed they were part of a large group which included Winston's cousin Sunny (the Duke of Marlborough), Maxine and one of her closest friends at the time, Millicent, the Duchess of Sutherland – not to mention Tony Wilding, the love of Maxine's life.

Although Maxine had initially come to know Winston through her friendship with his mother, she was only six years older than he and admitted to being only two years older. It is possible that Lord Bath knew of their wartime encounters in Picardy, when Winston visited her on the barge a number of times. We do not know if he ever called on her unaccompanied, and it is certain that both were extremely vulnerable at that point, and lonely. Maxine was recovering from the death, eighteen months earlier, of her fiancé, and Winston, still raw from the Gallipoli tragedy,[*] had been away from Clementine for many months.

There is, too, a letter from Winston to Clementine in which

---

[*] The ill-fated Dardanelles campaign some six months earlier.

he wrote that he was upset that she should harbour what he called 'such absolutely wild suspicions' about him.* He felt this dishonoured the love he felt for her – and would always feel for her. It was unworthy of her, he wrote, and of him and filled him with an embarrassment he had not known since he was a teenager. She must trust him, for he would never love any other woman.[12] That was in the early years of their marriage, but still, a relationship between Winston and Maxine seems highly unlikely. Doris is a different case.

Apart from the fact that he painted four portraits of Doris while staying at the Château de l'Horizon – as many as he painted of Clementine – there is the evidence of other guests that Winston and Doris got on well. This was inexplicable to Vincent Sheean, who recognised Winston's genius but described Doris as an 'unrivalled nitwit' who was only interested in her appearance. He recorded that one afternoon when Winston was speaking she idly looked up from scratching her shapely thigh with a red-tipped fingernail and asked, in what Sheean described as a piercing nasal voice, why politicians always chose Geneva for their meetings. It seemed to her they could choose a nicer place. Winston looked at her benevolently from under his floppy straw hat and said genially, 'Because, my dear, Geneva happens to be the seat of the League of Nations. You have heard of it, no doubt?'[13]

There is also the fact that after the first holiday at the villa in 1933, when Doris was there, he had not been able to persuade Clementine to accompany him there again. Her

---

* I asked Mary (Lady Soames) about this in 2010. She replied that she had questioned her mother about it when she published the letter in *Speaking for Themselves* (pp. 37–8) and that Lady Churchill could not recall what it had been about. Lady Soames said she could only assume her mother had heard some gossip about her father.

daughter said that her mother was not fond of the people that she met on the Riviera who amused Winston. Then, too, Winston must have at least suspected that Doris had had an affair with Randolph, for gossip columns had not only hinted about their friendship in unmistakable terms, but had divulged her favourite name for Randolph – 'Fuzzy-Wuzzy'.

All the same, one might be inclined to dismiss this story as mere gossip were it not for one small item buried in the Churchill archives. It is a letter from Doris to Winston in 1936, in which she regrets having heard that he will not be at Maxine's that September, as she will be there as usual from 1st to 15th. She writes that she has heard he is going to America that month, and as she intends to travel to New York after she leaves Maxine she hopes she might see him there. She ends her letter, intriguingly, 'I am not at all dangerous any more ... do ring me sometime, Mayfair 3731. My love, Doris.'[14]

Set against these anecdotes and suggestions of a possible dalliance between Winston and Doris, it is important to remember that when, in old age, Winston was asked what he considered his greatest achievement, he replied that it had been his ability to persuade Clementine to be his wife. One only has to watch newsreels of the Churchills together in their later years to see that this was a couple who remained in love despite the many tribulations thrown at them.

However, on balance, given the slight differences in the Churchills' marriage at the time, and Doris's casual attitude towards sleeping with men, it is entirely possible that she jumped into bed with him on this one occasion and was not rejected.

7

A New King

In the spring of 1936 the Château de l'Horizon was in the national news as it had been rented by the new King for a month's holiday. After lunching there with Maxine, the British Ambassador spent some time arranging all the details with the authorities at Nice. As a result, newspaper reports announced that during the royal visit 'no car will be allowed to stop on the sun-drenched road which runs behind the villa', no speedboats could approach the little harbour without coming under the strictest scrutiny, fishermen had been warned that they must avoid the waters near the château, and enterprising long-distance swimmers would be severely discouraged. 'Invisible eyes will keep a constant watch on the King from sea, land and air during his holiday,' and 'an army of gardeners' had been engaged to put the final touches to the lawns, flower beds, and 'the little winding pathways under the pine trees, where the King used to walk last year with his favourite Cairn terrier'.[1] Gigantic parasols had been placed on the pool terrace for meals to be taken by the swimming pool, and a powerful wireless receiver had been installed at the villa to ensure good reception despite the Alps.

This was all in great contrast to the informal royal holiday at 'Rock's place' the previous year, when the King had still been Prince of Wales.* Furthermore, although British newspapers were not publicising it, most foreign newspapers were fascinated by the story of the King's romance with Wallis Simpson.

In the event the holiday was called off when the King was advised that it was unwise to holiday in such a public place as the Riviera. The French had recently elected a left-wing administration under Léon Blum, and the Foreign Office claimed there were intelligence reports from Paris of a communist plot to assassinate the King. It was therefore announced that the King believed it inconsiderate to give the French extra responsibility in the light of the Spanish problems,† and he was cancelling the holiday. Maxine returned the King's cheque for one hundred pounds happily, for she had not really wanted to move out at the best time of the year, and he sent her an eighteenth-century silver snuff box as a thank-you gift. Her niece Diana recalled how Maxine opened the gift, looked at it and gave a *humph* sound, possibly because she recalled 'more kingly gifts' in her past, such as the gold dinner service rumoured to have been given her by Edward VII.

With the villa empty of guests for the period when the King and his party had intended to stay, Maxine entertained

---

* He succeeded to the throne on 20 January 1936 as Edward VIII.
† The Spanish Civil War began in July 1936.

her niece Diana and Vincent Sheean, and his publisher Hamish Hamilton, who was in fact a former nephew-in-law of Maxine's, for he had once been married to Diana's sister Jean. Some American celebrities also came and stayed for a few days: among them Douglas Fairbanks, whom Maxine liked and admired; and Johnny Weissmuller, who dived from the top terrace, over the lower dining terrace into the pool.

Winston had written that he would not visit in the late summer of 1936, but evidently changed his plans for on 1 September he arrived at the Château de l'Horizon after all. Again it was a painting holiday, but he found time to lunch with his old girlfriend, the former Muriel Wilson. She was now a widow, and staying in a nearby villa. Muriel and Maxine were old friends and so Winston invited her back to lunch at l'Horizon. His fellow house-guests were Loelia, the Duchess of Westminster; a young French film actress whose name Winston forgot when he wrote home, but about whom he remarked that she was 'very pretty but not very successful'; and the Marquess of Queensberry's younger brother Lord Cecil Douglas. 'But many [others] come as usual to bathe and lunch,' he wrote to Clementine, and he had not been able to avoid being taken out to lunch with Laura Corrigan.*

He would rather have been painting for he had found a spot on the River Loup about twenty miles away, which was remote and quiet, and also he hoped to paint the small port at Saint-Jean-Cap-Ferrat. He was writing a series of articles

---

* Wife of a billionaire American steel magnate who bought her way into English society in the Twenties by renting the Keppels' London house at a huge rent, and giving away costly 'prizes' such as gold cigarette cases at her fabled parties. She was uneducated and notorious for her malapropisms, but she was a kind person and never nasty to anyone.

for the *News of the World*, had arranged to go and see some French army manoeuvres on the 9th and 10th and was to visit the much-vaunted Maginot Line on the 14th and 15th so, as usual, time was his enemy.

Doris Castlerosse was there too, finally in the throes of divorce from Valentine. In a letter containing a tip to him to 'buy U.S. Steel' written prior to this holiday, she told Winston that she needed to give Valentine better evidence and so she had 'let Rootes* out. It seems ridiculous when I have sworn statements of Valentine's indiscretions with three different women, but it would have meant a beastly fought case.'[2] Eventually Valentine divorced her on the uncontested grounds of adultery with Robert Heber Percy, which caused a few raised eyebrows if not outright titters since Heber Percy – the 'mad boy' of the Brideshead set – was the live-in boyfriend of the eccentric Lord Berners.† Valentine claimed that the alleged misconduct had taken place 'in a hotel in Paris and on the liner *Strathair* last year', and also mentioned that his wife's extravagance had caused much unpleasantness during their married life.

But Valentine's and Doris's divorce was not the hottest topic of discussion that September. Having cancelled his holiday at the Château de l'Horizon, the King and Wallis Simpson were cruising in the Adriatic with a party including Duff and Diana Cooper aboard a chartered yacht, the *Nahlin*. Unlike the UK,

---

* William Rootes (later 1st Baron Rootes), founder of the Coventry Rootes manufacturing group which produced Hillman, Humber, Singer, Sunbeam and Talbot cars.
† Lord Berners was renowned for his waspish humour and exotic way of life: guests were summoned to dinner by a music box; the doves in his dovecote were dyed many and various colours so that in flight they looked like a handful of confetti. Nancy Mitford parodied him as her fictional Lord Merlin. In 1942 Heber Percy married a woman he had impregnated and all three lived at Berners's Faringdon House. It was an unusual ménage, but Berners was kind to Heber Percy's wife and treated her as a daughter-in-law until the divorce in 1947. Berners left his estate to Heber Percy.

where reporting about the King's affair was self-censored by loyal press barons such as Lords Rothermere (*Daily Mail*) and Beaverbrook (*Daily Express*),* it was open season in the European newspapers and magazines. Each day a new report appeared of the King and his mistress pretending to be ordinary tourists, mobbed by well-wishers waving and chanting 'Long live love!' Against Clementine's inclinations, Winston had thrown his lot in with the couple and supported them on the grounds that, despite the fact that Wallis was a divorced woman, the King should be free to choose his own wife. Whether he would have done so had he known that the Foreign Office had stopped sending the King any confidential reports because they had evidence of leaks through Wallis to her friend Joachim von Ribbentrop in the German Embassy in London is doubtful.

In mid-September Winston left to drive north, reporting that the days he spent with Maxine had been very pleasant with beautiful weather and 'every comfort'. He had painted six pictures at l'Horizon as well as three at Consuelo's château at Dreux.† In this mood of content he heard the first hints of an unfolding horror, something still virtually unknown about in Britain. While in Toulon he had dined with Madame Marie-Anne Goldsmith Rothschild, who had formerly been married to Clementine's cousin Jack Mitford. He wrote to tell Clementine that Madame Rothschild was a remarkable woman and she had told him 'terrible' tales of the treatment of Jews in Germany.[3]

On 10 December, unable to force his ministers to agree to marriage with Wallis, and despite Winston's unwavering support throughout the crisis, the King abdicated in a storm of

---

* Before the diluting influence of television, daily newspapers were hugely powerful. The *Express* was the first paper to reach a circulation of two million.
† Château de St Georges Motel.

national ferment. It was, one American newspaper said, 'the greatest news story since the Resurrection'. A week earlier, on 3 December, Wallis had fled from England accompanied by the King's Lord-in-Waiting, Lord Brownlow, to avoid press attention. After a nightmarish journey she arrived in Cannes to stay with Herman and Katherine Rogers* at their ancient (and reputedly haunted) Villa Lou Viei, on the sunny south-facing hills of Californie. It had been partly renovated by Barry Dierks in 1928, but to his chagrin the owners had insisted on keeping the perfumed flowering creepers which festooned the house, except where the wonderful view of the Mediterranean was affected. Wallis had stayed there previously and enjoyed the hot sunshine and outdoor life. But now it was winter, and cold and wet most days, so she hardly even went into the garden. It was from Lou Viei that she urgently telephoned to the King telling him he should not abdicate, but should put several alternatives to Prime Minister Baldwin, including that of a morganatic marriage which would make her a duchess but not queen. In any event, she urged him, he should not make any decisions until autumn of the following year. But it was at Lou Viei on 11 December, sitting with Herman and Katherine, that she heard on the radio the King's abdication broadcast. Winston heard it at Chartwell and wept.

When she heard afterwards that the King – now to be known as the Duke of Windsor – was planning to go to Zurich and stay at a favourite hotel there while they waited out the requisite time for her divorce to become final, Wallis was horrified,

---

* Katherine had known Wallis since 1918, when they were young navy wives in San Diego. Widowed, she married millionaire Herman Rogers who worked for the State Department and while on transfer in China she met Wallis again. Herman retired to the South of France aged thirty-five to write 'the great American novel' (he never did).

realising how he would be besieged by the press if he stayed in such a public place. She consulted Elsie de Wolfe and the result was the Duke went instead to stay with Kitty de Rothschild at her Schloss Enzesfeld near Vienna. Winston wrote to the Duke as soon as he heard, to say he was pleased that he had found such an agreeable temporary 'shelter' for he knew Kitty well from having once been 'a guest with her at Maxine's'.[4] The Duke agreed, and initially found his hostess kind and hospitable, but as the weeks went on he upset her by running up international phone bills of over eight hundred pounds, calling Wallis several times a day, as well as contacts in England, and treating Kitty's staff as though they were his own servants. 'We are not the rich Rothschilds,' she complained to a friend.* Her husband Eugene de Rothschild left for Paris in mid-January 1937 to transfer all their liquid assets out of Austria after stories began to circulate about confiscation of Jewish property by the Nazis. Kitty stayed on till the end of January out of consideration for her guest, but when she felt obliged to leave the Schloss and join her husband, the Duke did not even rise for breakfast to say goodbye to her.

Wallis was more considerate of her hosts, for she knew they had sacrificed their normal life to shelter her. 'Nobody asks them [out] because of me,' she wrote to the Duke, but in a subsequent letter she described her disgust on wandering about Lou Viei and finding that the kitchen, run by an elderly Provençal couple, was dirty and smelly. Their cooking was not up to her standards either, and it was instantly clear to her that they could not be married from Villa Lou Viei. The

---

* In fact they were very rich, although all of their properties in Austria were subsequently confiscated by the Nazis.

couple had hoped that the wedding would be held soon after the coronation in London, but it was all very much in the hands of the King's Proctor who was investigating a charge of collusion, and so the couple was unable to set a specific date with any degree of certainty.

Wallis made enquiries and through Daisy Fellowes located a secluded house on the tip of Cap d'Antibes which was empty and available to rent. It was a large seaside villa called Château de la Croë, built only ten years earlier for Sir William Pomeroy Burton, president of Associated Newspapers Limited, but on Victorian lines. Since then, Sir William had bought another place on Cap Martin, which he preferred, so he wanted to sell or lease La Croë. Daisy was 'longing' to see the Duke again, Wallis wrote from Villa Lou Viei, but although recognising that Daisy had been a stalwart friend in their crisis she advised the Duke against becoming too friendly with her, 'not from jealous reasons but you know what the press is and [what] the gossip would say – as we know her reputation is not too steady'.[5] Wallis has been accused of being uncaring of the Duke in contrast with his obsession with her, but her letters show she was jealous of any attentions he paid other women, and at one point she even ludicrously accused the Duke of having an affair with his hostess Kitty.

After a shopping trip to buy a number of new gowns and a fur jacket, Wallis paid a short visit to Willie Maugham's villa La Mauresque, where she was joined by Sybil Colefax* and they discussed decor. Along with Syrie Maugham, who had pioneered the 'all-white room', and Elsie de Wolfe, Sybil

---

* Sybil, Lady Colefax, was a socialite and in the Thirties became an acclaimed interior decorator with her business partner John Fowler. The firm remains a favourite for redecorating English country houses.

Colefax was the *dernier cri* in interior decoration. All four of them then went to visit Daisy at Les Zoraides in search of ideas for La Croë.

In the event, the idea to lease La Croë for the wedding was temporarily shelved when the new King advised the Duke that a wedding in a villa on the French Riviera might appear too frivolous.[6] Wallis had anyway realised that it would be impossible to recruit the necessary staff in the time available to them, as well as adequately furnish and make the château ready. Instead, she accepted an invitation to stay at and be married from a palatial château a few miles south-west of Tours in central France.

La Candé was owned by Charles Bedaux,* a wealthy French-American industrialist who was a friend of Herman Rogers. Bedaux and his wife Fern offered to move out of their château while Wallis and the Duke needed it for their wedding. He stipulated one condition: it should be announced that the Duke and Mrs Simpson were there as his guests; Bedaux did not wish it to be assumed he had rented out his house in case it reflected adversely on his financial standing. Wallis decided that it was no bad thing to marry in the French countryside; it was somehow more dignified than the Riviera with its playground-of-the-rich reputation, she thought, and even her enemies in the Royal Family agreed that it was more suitable for the former king to marry in a Renaissance castle than in a

---

* Charles Bedaux invented a time and motion study called the Bedaux system. His promotion of it to international big businesses earned him a substantial fortune (he was the fifth richest man in America at one point), but also the hatred of trade unions. During the Second World War he collaborated with the Germans and made a fortune. In 1944 he was arrested in Algeria by the US Army while constructing a pipeline for the Germans. He was charged with treason and committed suicide while awaiting trial.

seaside villa. Wallis had been very upset by rumours and news-paper stories that she had been delivered of a child at Lou Viei, just one of dozens of nasty tales about her, so she attempted to show herself by taking a walk along the Croisette wearing an ermine coat and white hat. She was mobbed and had to be rescued and returned to Lou Viei which she was by now begin-ning to regard as a prison. She was also anxious to get away from what she called 'the smallness of Cannes'.

By contrast, at La Candé she was totally protected, waited on by a flock of almost thirty liveried servants, as well as her own maid and a top Paris chef. The ancient château had been expensively renovated, with American plumbing, and among its more outstanding features were a swan-shaped bath with gilded plumbing, a pipe organ rumoured to have cost forty thousand dollars, and its own telephone exchange. Eventually Wallis asked Fern Bedaux to return to help her prepare La Candé for the Duke's arrival prior to the wedding, which had finally been agreed for 3 June 1937.

Right up to the last minute the Duke hoped that at least one member of his family would attend the wedding, despite the new King having told him explicitly in April that it was not possible because of the risk to the image of the throne. In the event, nobody from the Royal Family attended, and – in place of a wedding present – the Duke received word that Wallis was not to be allowed to use the title HRH. Wallis had only her favourite aunt, Bessie, to represent her own family.

The couple invited three hundred people to their wedding but only sixteen guests showed up; they included Herman and Katherine Rogers and the owners of La Candé. The Duke's friend – said to be his only male friend – and aide Edward Dudley 'Fruity' Metcalfe was his chief supporter (best man), and Metcalfe's wife Baba (Alexandra, daughter of Lord Curzon)* was the most senior of the guests. In London the Palace had let it be known that to attend the wedding would mean the end of royal approval, and in some cases the end of plum careers. In May Daisy Fellowes had written to Winston: 'Will you let me know if you come over for *the* wedding as we could arrange to go together? I have a daughter who has a house near Candi [*sic*.] – it might facilitate things to spend the night there.'[7] However, neither Daisy nor Winston attended. Daisy was not invited, and Winston – the couple's greatest supporter – declined, saying he was otherwise engaged, but he sent Randolph as his representative.

The fascinating wedding portraits taken by Cecil Beaton show the Duke and Duchess exhibiting the strain of the past months, and they look many years older than the pictures taken of them on their holidays less than a year earlier. Wallis looks almost ugly with stress, and her square-shouldered, floor-length Mainbocher gown of 'Duchess of Windsor blue' did her slim figure absolutely no favours. It made her look gaunt – a disappointment to the millions of women who had breathlessly followed the royal romance.

That September Winston wrote to Maxine that he was still tied up trying to finish volume four of his epic biography of Marlborough, but admitted that he was 'thinking much of you all and the pool'.[8] Doris was at l'Horizon as usual, though, and she had brought along her new best friend, Margot Flick Hoffman.† She had met the Hoffmans in China

---

* Sister of Cimmie Mosley.
† Margot Flick, a noted polo player and pilot, had married Richard Sanford Hoffman, a writer, in February 1936.

the previous winter, while they were on honeymoon, and Doris and Margot immediately became close friends. When the Hoffmans' marriage failed after a remarkably short time, Margot joined Doris in Europe and offered to buy her a palazzo in Venice in return for introductions to the right people. Doris had brought along her personable brother Dudley as well, and there was the extremely handsome, golden-haired young Duke of Sutherland,* who had come directly from a garden party at Holyrood and was able to tell them first-hand about the new Royal Family.

Having missed his usual holiday at l'Horizon, Winston asked Maxine if he could visit her instead during January, a period when she normally had the villa closed up while she went to a spa or to St Moritz. Maxine immediately changed her plans and invited him and Clementine, but he explained that 'Clemmie . . . has made all her plans' and was taking Mary skiing. He would stay in Paris for some important discussions and arrive in Cannes on 5 January, he wrote. However, he then had to go and see the Duke of Windsor for luncheon, because the Windsors were leaving the Riviera the following day. He had not seen them since the 'dark day' of the abdication, he wrote, and 'as you know I am a devoted servant'.[9]

A few weeks earlier the Windsors had arrived at Cannes to spend their first Christmas together at Lou Viei, which had been loaned to them while Herman and Katherine Rogers went to America for a few months. Following their wedding the Duke and Duchess had been living at the discreet though luxurious Hôtel Meurice in Paris while they searched for a

---

* 'Geordie', the 5th Duke of Sutherland, son of Maxine's beloved friend Millicent from the Hartsbourne days.

permanent home. They found Lou Viei 'a welcome change', the Duke wrote to Wallis's aunt Bessie on 28 December. They had spent a quiet and peaceful Christmas and had only once been out to dinner as it was so much nicer on their own at the château. 'I expect you will find us ensconced in some French château when you next visit us here,' he ended.[10]

As usual, Winston lapped up being spoilt by Maxine for a few weeks at the start of 1938. Although not guaranteed in January, the sun shone and it was mild, so that apart from lunch with the Windsors on the day of his arrival he hardly stirred from the villa for the first week, working every morning in bed at his proofs. He had had to cut almost a hundred pages of text which, he complained to Clementine, was like cutting off his own fingers and toes, but Maxine had arranged an extra comfort for him with the services of a masseur. It was too cold for swimming and he could not paint as the winter afternoon light was no good (as Clementine had warned him) – it was dark by 6 p.m. at that time of year – and so he had fallen into the habit of playing Mah Jong all afternoon with Maxine, who was an expert, but, he wrote to Clementine, he had only lost two pounds after many hours of amusement. The only other house-guests that week were Maxine's niece Diana and her husband Vincent. The big event of his holiday had been a dinner with the Windsors a few evenings earlier.

On learning while lunching with the Duke and Duchess that they had put off their departure from the Riviera for a week, Winston asked Maxine to invite them 'and no other outside guests' to dine one evening at l'Horizon. Although she was not opposed to the couple Maxine had made it clear she disapproved of the abdication, sniffing (and no doubt recalling King Edward VII's arrangements with Mrs Keppel) that 'we did things better in my day', but she could never refuse 'dear Winston' anything. Lloyd George was also staying locally, at the Hôtel du Cap d'Antibes, and at the very last minute Winston asked that Lloyd George be invited to the dinner, since many years earlier it had been Lloyd George who had officiated at the Duke's investiture as Prince of Wales at Caernarvon Castle. It being winter and too chilly on the terrace, they dined in the pretty dining room.

Over luncheon that day the matter was raised by those attending the dinner of how they were to address and treat the Duchess. Much ink had been spilled at Whitehall and Buckingham Palace over the matter of Wallis's title, and she had been famously deprived of the prefix HRH. It was without precedent for a married woman not to take her husband's title on marriage, and seems a remarkably petty act by the Palace to withhold it in the case of Wallis, especially when the Duke made clear his deep hurt over the matter. There were those in society who did call the Duchess Her Royal Highness, and those who used 'Her Grace'; those who curtsied to her and those who refused to do so. In the case of the dinner party at the Château de l'Horizon it was agreed that since it was a purely private dinner no harm would derive from their addressing Wallis as Your Royal Highness and then ma'am, and Diana and Maxine (Margaret Lloyd George did not attend) would curtsey to her when she arrived.

There was a certain amount of nervousness before the dinner as it was the first time the former King had set foot in l'Horizon, although while staying at 'Rock's place' he had several times strayed along the narrow footpath when out walking his dog, and once got as far as the terrace before he vanished, to the consternation of bathers in Maxine's pool. When Winston came downstairs to meet Maxine prior to the Windsors' arrival he found her in front of a looking glass. He joined her in a last-minute preen and as always had a *bon mot* for the occasion: 'You have a strange party tonight, my dear. It consists entirely of the *ci-devant*; ex-Kings, ex-Prime Ministers and ex-politicians. It is like Voltaire.'[11]

Winston reported to Clementine that 'the poor Duke' was bright and charming although now that he was no longer King 'he had had to fight for his place in the conversation like other people'.[12] However, Sheean's memory of the event was in sharp contrast. 'From the beginning,' he wrote, 'the Duke of Windsor dominated the conversation. He sat at the head of the table, like a King, with Maxine at his right, Mr Lloyd George at her right; the Duchess sat between Lloyd George and me; Winston and Diana completed the circle.'[13] At some point the conversation turned to Welsh coal mines and the Duke compared them with the more favourable conditions that existed for miners in Hitler's Germany. He and the Duchess had toured the German mines, he stated, and been impressed by the facilities including compulsory installation of hot showers at the pithead. This led to a discussion on the manner in which the poor, and specifically mining families, lived in England and Wales – a matter on which the Duke held himself to be something of an expert.

Sheean, an intellectual socialist, sat back in amazement as he listened to the other three men debating the matter. 'The seriousness in the question could not be doubted,' he wrote, 'and yet it was confounded with an incurable frivolity owing to their astronomical remoteness from the conditions of life of which they spoke.' The Duke undoubtedly wished to see the people who worked in the mines clean, healthy and contented – just as he might wish his horses or dogs to be, Sheean thought. As for the Duchess,

> so slim, so elegant, so suggestive of innumerable fashionable shops, dressmakers, manicurists and hairdressers, [she] seemed at the uttermost remove from the pithead of a mine . . . in the exquisite little room, gleaming with glass and silver over the flowers and champagne, all so enclosed and private and secure . . . what did they have to talk about but the dirt on a miner's neck?[14]

Winston, though, considered the dinner a great success, and Maxine told him she had not enjoyed a dinner more since the great days at Hartsbourne. He thought the Windsors looked somewhat pathetic but also very happy, and Wallis had made a very good impression on him, so that he believed their marriage, so dearly bought, would be a most happy one.

Maxine was as popular as ever and had not lost her knack of attracting top politicians as well as celebrities. During the time that Winston was at l'Horizon in early 1938 she entertained Anthony Eden as well as Lloyd George and his daughter Megan several times. Winston, too, accepted invitations to other villas, such as that of Lord Rothermere, who had a place at Cap Martin close to Daisy Fellowes. Maxine only dined out occasionally and almost always with friends; she was treated with huge respect having come to be accepted as the *grande dame* of the Riviera. At a dinner at a neighbour's villa, also attended by the Duke and Duchess of Windsor, Diana Sheean recorded how, at the end of the evening, 'the entire roomful of guests rose to their feet, including the Duke of Windsor and

Mr Churchill, when [Maxine] came to the door to indicate that it was time she took her house-party home. She was dressed all in white, all diamonds flashing, hair white. That was when I fully recognised the stories of her beauty.'[15]

Before he departed Winston gave a dinner at the Casino for some Dutch friends of Maxine's, at which he was captivated by a parrot: 'The most lovely parrot I ever saw ... He is a millionaire and keeps a sailor to look after him,' he wrote.[16] The parrot knew a number of French swear words and party pieces, and kept whispering in his keeper's ear and then roaring with laughter. He could also miaow like a cat and imitate the sound of drums of a military band, and generally showed off to loud applause. In fact, Winston reported, he brought the house down.

After twelve pleasant days at the Château de l'Horizon, Maxine reluctantly waved Winston off in her chauffeur-driven car to Cap Martin to spend a week or so at Les Zoraides with Daisy and his cousin Reggie. He liked to paint there – there was a different quality of light from that at Cannes and Antibes, and Daisy's garden had some beautiful settings. During Winston's visits Daisy thoughtfully declined to have her swimming pool covered each morning with fresh pink rose petals. Maxine had been so genuinely upset at his departure that Winston promised to return soon and said he would try to bring Clementine next time. This could be as early as the end of the month, and he wrote to his wife asking if she would consent to join him in France. Knowing her feelings about the company one met at Maxine's, he assured her that this time they would be quite alone. The golf course at Mougins, near where he liked to paint, was within an easy drive, and he was sure they could find a good golfing partner for her, he cajoled, or there was tennis.

There was no one else at Les Zoraides as Daisy was recovering from a facial injury sustained when the train on which she was travelling threw her from her seat, and apart from a few lunches out Winston worked at his editing until lunch and in the afternoons and evenings joined his hosts – he did not tell Clementine when he wrote to her that he spent several evenings at the Casino with Reggie, for he knew how it would worry her. However, to his enormous pleasure, Clementine agreed to his suggestion that she join him for the last week of January, so she was able to attend the celebratory luncheon party at the Hôtel du Cap which Winston organised for the Lloyd Georges' golden wedding anniversary. Also present were Daisy and Reggie, and Maxine. Lord Derby had sent his apologies and a gigantic basket of orchids; the King and Queen had sent a telegram, as had the Windsors, who had by now departed for Paris. The wives of fishermen from Nice came bearing flowers, an old Riviera custom for golden wedding days, organised by Daisy on this occasion. The 'bride and groom' ceremonially cut a three-foot-high wedding cake (Lloyd George earned local approval by distributing most of this to the children of the town of Antibes).

Despite his promise the Churchills were not entirely alone at l'Horizon as there was one fellow visitor: the sculptor Clare Sheridan, Winston's bohemian first cousin. She was highly intelligent and outspoken, and despite the fact that she was a strident communist sympathiser, and Winston was the leading spokesman in England against the Bolsheviks, he enjoyed their lively debates. Perhaps he also recalled that when they were both young at the beginning of the century she had written to him to say she wished to become a writer in order to be independent of her father. Winston (it should not be forgotten that he was born and raised in the Victorian era) told her that a better occupation for women was to 'please and inspire the male sex'.

She had since sculpted Winston,* and among her other sitters were such prominent men and women as Guglielmo Marconi, Lord Asquith, Gladys Cooper, H.G. Wells, Mahatma Gandhi, Lord Birkenhead (Winston's best friend, F.E. Smith) and Marie of Romania. Clare had been widowed in 1915, just days after the birth of her son,† and set to work as a war widow to support her children. After the war she became a tireless traveller on her motorcycle and wrote books about these travels in Russia, Poland, Germany, Czechoslovakia and Turkey, and her adventurous and unusual life, during which she spent several months living with American Indian tribes. She had a much-publicised love affair with Charlie Chaplin and the two notoriously camped out together in California with her small son, Dickie, until they were discovered by Chaplin's fans. When asked by the press if it was usual in England for married women to take lovers, she replied frivolously that it was. 'As many as they can get,' she added, which caused outrage. Winston's great friend the financier Bernard Baruch took her aside and explained that she couldn't behave so flippantly in America and keep her reputation intact. Dickie was sent to England with a nanny to stay with the Churchills, and Clare went to Mexico.

During the summer of 1920 a Russian trade delegation on a visit to London invited Clare to travel to Russia to make busts of their senior revolutionaries. Subsequently she sculpted Lenin

---

* And would do so again in 1942–3 in a famous wartime 'bulldog' pose.
† Richard Sheridan; he died aged twenty of peritonitis, in 1936 in Algeria. Clare's daughter Elizabeth died in 1914, also of peritonitis.

(exhibited at the Royal Academy in 1924), Trotsky, Dzerzhinsky and Kamenev. It seems she took Winston's early advice somewhat literally, for reputedly she slept with all of these sitters and was cited by Kamenev's wife in their divorce. Among her best friends she numbered the Mountbattens and Lady Diana Cooper, Princess Margaret of Sweden and Vivien Leigh, none of whom apparently took her left-wing credentials too seriously. Certainly she was happy to enjoy Maxine's capitalist luxury.

When the Churchills returned home Winston felt a renewed vigour and wrote to Maxine telling her it was the first 'really good rest' he had enjoyed for a long time. 'I do not know when I have had such a pleasant month.'[17] He had noted, however, that Maxine was not her usual bouncy self, she had gained a great deal of weight now and had lost much of her old sparkle. He only hoped, he wrote, she had not tired herself out by entertaining them. Clare wrote to say that after their departure l'Horizon had filled up with its usual quota of guests, who were – she wrote – an odd mixture, and as well as good friends of Maxine from the old days included an Italian duchess who was very anti-British. Maxine could not bring herself to be rude to a guest, but took a little revenge by playing 'Land of Hope and Glory' constantly on the gramophone. Eventually the duchess asked, 'What is the name of this pretty tune?' and Clare took huge pleasure in telling her. However, she reported fairly, the duchess was agreeable and funny as long as they kept off politics.

Clare continued her gossip to amuse Winston: Mary Herbert* had lost three thousand pounds, a huge amount

---

* Mary Herbert, Baroness von Hügel (1849–1935), wife of the theologian and Austrian ambassador Friedrich von Hügel; daughter of the 1st Baron Herbert of Lea.

of money, at the Casino and the *caisse* was asked not to extend her any further credit so she had been obliged to leave early. But as for Maxine, she 'was very sad after you left ... seeming comatose and uninterested in daily life, but Winnie Portarlington forced her to live on 2 bananas a day and a glass of milk for a week, which did much good'.[18] Lady Portarlington* had seen Maxine through depressions in the past. Now she tried to keep her old friend buoyed up with the latest gossip, and the news that, having leased a house in Versailles next door to Lady Mendl's Villa Trianon, the Duke and Duchess of Windsor had also finally signed a two-year lease on Château de la Croë on Cap d'Antibes, to begin in May.

The narrow winding road that led from Cap d'Antibes to La Croë ended in a cul-de-sac. On the promontory itself there were only three other houses: the Aga Khan's Villa Jean-Andrée, formerly the Villa Taormina, which he had rebuilt and renamed in 1929 for his third wife; Sir Henry† and Lady Norman's Château La Garoupe; and the Château Eilenroc, which was then unoccupied. All were grand, and like La Croë protected from sightseers by huge park-like grounds. La Croë was a typically Mediterranean mansion, white with green shutters and a red-tiled roof. Set in twelve acres of cool woodland and lawns, and facing the sea over some rocks, no other house could be seen from its windows. Apart from yachts which sailed past the Cap between the town of Antibes and Juan-les-Pins, the Duke and Duchess hoped they would be untroubled there by outsiders.

---

* Winnifreda Yuill, the Countess of Portarlington. A lady-in-waiting to Princess Marina, the wife of George, Duke of Kent (youngest son of King George V).
† Sir Henry Norman, Bt (1858–1939) was a retired journalist and Liberal politician.

Wallis immediately threw herself into an orgy of decoration and furnishings. They had planned to be in Paris during the spring months to begin setting up a permanent residence there, but they received orders from the Palace – through the British Embassy – that they *must not* be in Paris when the King and Queen made their state visit to the French capital;* it was strongly recommended to them that they should return to the Riviera.

Before his marriage, as the Prince of Wales and later as King, the Duke had devoted a great deal of his energy to creating a beloved private home, Fort Belvedere. The romantic small fortress, which dated from 1703, was set in woodland at Virginia Water, near Windsor, and had been given to him by his father. He had spent tens of thousands of pounds of his own money on 'the Fort', and one of the few favours the Duke asked of his brother, the new King, was that it remain his own property after the abdication. This favour was, he thought, granted. However, the Fort was soon emptied of the Duke's personal belongings, which were sent into store at Frogmore House in Windsor Great Park. Many of these furnishings, paintings, silver, porcelain and crystal were now transported to La Croë, where the Duchess was spending huge sums to recreate the conditions to which her husband was accustomed in royal palaces. Wallis had known the Fort intimately for some years while she was the King's mistress, because it was the place he did most of his private entertaining, so she knew exactly how she wanted the house to look.

La Croë was built around a huge central hall leading off

---

* Winston and Clementine were part of the royal entourage for this state visit. Although Winston's image at home was tarnished he was well-regarded in France.

to wide lofty rooms, all richly furnished, 'a dream-like place, cool, serene and aloof', the Duke's secretary recalled. 'As you entered the front door,' she wrote,

> you found yourself looking straight across the whole length of the house and through the tall French windows at the back onto the woods and lawns beyond the terrace. On the right of the hall, suspended from the lower gallery, its rich red and gold colours softly floodlit, was the Duke's banner from the Chapel of Knights of the Garter in St George's Chapel at Windsor ... antique chairs had red leather seats and black and gold backs ... The broad terrace, facing the sea, ran the whole length of the house ... The great rooms were French in character. The high ceilings and walls were elaborately moulded in white and gold. Tall mirrored doors, standing always open, led from one room to another and looking-glass covered some of the panelling.[19]

There were huge mirrors above the great fireplaces and Wallis used mirrors with skill, reflecting objects back and forth, creating effects of light and space. 'Mirrors delighted her,' the description continued. 'As she walked about La Croë she would glance in the glass-covered panels ... and if she stood talking to you her eyes would often wander away to the nearest mirror, so noticeably that some of her friends called her "Wallis through the Looking Glass" ... It had the charming appearance of an English country house in a French setting ... It was all done in a remarkably short time causing Rebecca West to comment admiringly, "There are not many women ... who can pick up the keys to a rented house, raddled by long submission to temporary inmates, and make it look as if a family of good taste had been living there for two or three centuries.'"[20] Wallis had the assistance of two 'interior' experts, Lady Sybil Colefax and Lady Mendl, but she also had innate good taste.

When it was completed the Duchess held sumptuous receptions at La Croë, with the help of thirty-three uniformed employees – peculiarly, they were all blond-haired – all trained to treat the Duke as if he were still King.[21] Those who visited recall how the Duke adopted full Highland dress at dinner: kilt, jabot, sporran, and a *sgian dubh* tucked into his stocking. His kilt, or as a member of his French staff called it, 'his little skirt', was in Balmoral tartan. One guest – Debo, the Duchess of Devonshire – wondered how he could stand it in the climate. Pipers after dinner were a regular feature, and she recalled that it was a goosebump-provoking experience to be sitting over drinks on the terrace on a balmy night, looking over the sea, to hear the faint skirl of pipes as the pipers marched up from the woods towards the house – all the same, she thought, 'it was all probably more suited to the misty glens of Scotland than Antibes in high summer'.[22]

By the swimming pool there were wicker chairs with black cushions and a large white and red tent which flew the Prince of Wales standard and acted as a changing room. This pennant mirrored the Garter standard which hung in the entrance hall. The Duke told Harold Nicolson, who was a guest in August 1938, that when he became King there was no Prince of Wales, so the standard was taken down. He therefore saw no reason why he shouldn't use it at La Croë. 'I saw why,' wrote Nicolson. 'But he didn't. It is his insensitiveness to such things which brought on all the trouble.'[23]

*

One regular Château de l'Horizon guest was missing from the Riviera that autumn: Doris Castlerosse. Margot Flick Hoffman had kept her promise to buy Doris a Venetian palazzo in return for introductions and presented her with the delightful single-storey Palazzo Venier dei Leoni which had formerly belonged to the Marchesa Casati and would in turn become Peggy Guggenheim's European home. Margot and Doris spent a year there, during which time Doris's brother* and his bride visited them, only to find the palazzo deserted when they arrived, but with all the doors open. They discovered a bedroom with the bed made up and retired. At 4 a.m. they were woken by a full orchestra playing music in their room – Doris had been at a party and had suddenly recalled they were due to arrive, so she gathered up the orchestra and brought them home to welcome the newlyweds.

Looking back from the twenty-first century we can see that the enticing frivolity and sheer glamour of life on the Riviera in those sunlit, apparently carefree days of the late Thirties – when Elsa Maxwell, Mrs Laura Corrigan, Lady Mendl, Daisy Fellowes and others (including Maxine) vied for the informal title 'Hostess with the Mostest'† and beauties drifted around in silk pyjama suits – seems even more alluring when viewed against the shadow of the approaching war. But the recipients of the lavish entertainment, who danced and sunbathed and swam and gambled in the sun, were unable to see this. It was all, to quote one of the most enthusiastic participants, Cole Porter, 'delightful . . . delicious . . . de-lovely'.

---

* Edward 'Dudley' Delevigne. His second wife was Angela Greenwood, daughter of the Tory MP Hamar Greenwood (created Viscount Greenwood, 1937).
† Maxine would not have agreed that she vied for this she thought it was hers by right.

Another song that owes its inspiration to the Riviera is Noël Coward's 'I Went to a Marvellous Party', which describes five parties he attended in 1938. The first was a beach party given by Elsa Maxwell, and another a 'come-as-you-are-party' to which he and the actress Beatrice Lillie went casually dressed, only to find that everyone else was wearing full evening fig. When he performed the song Noël always spoke 'Elsie's' line with an American accent: it is safe to assume he meant Elsie de Wolfe.

> We talked about growing old gracefully
> And Elsie who's seventy-four
> Said, 'A, it's a question of being sincere,
> And B, if you're supple you've nothing to fear.'
> Then she swung upside down from a glass chandelier,
> I *couldn't* have liked it more.

Most members of the Riviera set read the same daily news as Winston, but they assumed Germany was no significant immediate threat to their lifestyle, while Winston, though fully enjoying the dinners, lunches, parties, casinos and performing parrots, could plainly see the growing danger. On his journey to Maxine's he had stopped in Paris to dine with the former Prime Minister of France, Pierre Flandin.* It was not a pleasant evening, he reported to Clementine: Flandin had been most depressing and pessimistic, and he (Winston) had come away seriously concerned about what he had heard. It appeared that the French right-wing

---

* Pierre Étienne Flandin, French conservative politician and Prime Minister of France November 1934–May 1935.

administration assumed Germany would become undisputed ruler of Europe in the near future, and it all stemmed, Winston wrote, from the fact that Ramsay MacDonald, Stanley Baldwin and John Simon 'would neither make friends with Germany nor prevent her re-arming'.[24] He thought that a thousand years in the future historians would look askance at the fact that the victorious allies of the First World War had so meekly delivered themselves up to a vengeful enemy whom they had once overcome.

8

Final Fling

Politically, relationships in Europe grew steadily worse during 1938. Within weeks of Winston's return from Cannes in early February Anthony Eden, the Foreign Secretary, resigned his office in protest against Neville Chamberlain's wish to try to renegotiate with Mussolini. Soon afterwards, in mid-March, following his triumphal state visit to Italy which served to demonstrate the strength of the German-Italian Axis, Hitler marched into Vienna and annexed Austria in the Anschluss.

In June Germany imposed anti-Jewish laws requiring Austrian Jews to register all property, at home and abroad, within a few weeks. The following month, in order to emphasise Anglo-French unity, and as a belated response to Hitler's visit to Rome, King George VI and Queen Elizabeth made a second state visit to Paris. Then in August, while negotiations continued in Prague between Czechoslovakia and Sudeten Germans, Germany called up three-quarters of a million troops for an unprecedented series of military manoeuvres. In response, the British government announced the mobilisation of the Royal Navy by September, and warned that the British would not back down over Czechoslovakian interests as they had done over Poland.

That summer some of Maxine's family came to stay, among them her niece Blossom with her husband, the British aircraft designer and manufacturer F.G. Miles. The talk on the terrace turned to investment, and Fred Miles suggested to Maxine that as Rolls-Royce was seriously expanding into aircraft engine production they would probably make a good investment. Maxine shook her head shrewdly. When the war came, she said, any assets in England would be frozen. She intended to keep her assets in America, although she made it clear she was not to be persuaded to leave the Château de l'Horizon.

In August 1938 the Windsors, who had already decided to purchase Château de la Croë, dined at La Mauresque with Somerset Maugham and his daughter Liza Paravicini. Although things looked decidedly grim in Europe, Maugham wrote in his memoir *Strictly Personal*, at this time that he still believed, as most people did, that the British and French had great armies and if the time came for them to fight they would acquit themselves 'valiantly'. So on the Riviera life went on as before. Harold Nicolson was staying at La Mauresque when the Windsors visited. 'I am glad I came here,' he wrote in a letter to Vita Sackville-West. 'It really is the perfect holiday. I mean, the heat is intense, the garden lovely, the chair long and cool, the lime-juice at hand, a bathing-pool there if one wishes to splash, scenery, books, gramophones, pretty people – and above all, the sense that it is not going on too long.'[1]

He described how in the soft warm evening he had sat alone by the swimming pool among the banks of red and white oleander in the pink dusk and watched the sun set over Cap d'Antibes until the lighthouses began to wink across the purple water. Then he had to go and bathe and change to greet the Windsors, having been warned by Maugham that the Duke became cross if the Duchess was not treated with respect, and there was the usual discussion about how to address her.

In they came ... she has done her hair in a different way ... it gives her a placid less strained look ... He entered with his swinging naval gait, plucking at his bow tie. He had on a tussore dinner-jacket. He was in very high spirits. Cocktails were brought and we stood around the fireplace. There was a pause. 'I am sorry we were a little late,' said the Duke, 'but Her Royal Highness couldn't drag herself away.' He had said it. The three words fell into the circle like three stones into a pool. Her (gasp) Royal (shudder) Highness (and not one eye dared to meet another) ... They called each other 'Darling' a great deal. I called him 'Your Royal Highness' ... and 'Sir' the whole time. I called her 'Duchess'. One cannot get away from his glamour and his charm and his sadness, though.[2]

Meanwhile, at Eden Roc twelve-year-old Bobby Kennedy, son of the American ambassador to Britain, danced and swam with Beatrice Lillie. The Kennedys had found Antibes, liked it and would make several visits during Joseph's term as ambassador.

In mid-September, during a speech at Nuremberg, Hitler demanded the right of self-determination for Sudeten Germans, causing widespread panic in Czechoslovakia. Martial law was declared in an attempt to restore order and several leading Sudeten German leaders escaped to Germany. To try to defuse the situation, Neville Chamberlain, with French support, called for a meeting with Hitler, hoping to find a compromise and negotiate an end to German expansionism. The seventy-year-old Prime Minister overcame his fear of flying to attend a conference in Munich whose chief delegates were Hitler and his Foreign Minister Joachim von Ribbentrop; Benito Mussolini and his Foreign Minister Galeazzo Ciano; Chamberlain; and the French Premier Édouard Daladier. Czechoslovakia was not represented. Hitler did not concede; instead he issued a new set of demands to include the immediate surrender of predominantly German areas by 25 November.

After a second trip to Germany, this time to the Berghof, Hitler's mountain retreat near Berchtesgaden, Chamberlain returned from Munich on 29 September declaring that there would be no war. He assured the electorate that he had Herr Hitler's personal signed assurance of this. The agreement reached in Munich, he claimed to great public ovation, celebrations and huge relief, meant 'peace in our time'. But history would show that the Munich Agreement had simply met all of Hitler's immediate demands. Germany emerged as the strongest power in Europe, and it was a clear step towards war. Winston and his supporters saw it as 'peace with dishonour' and Duff Cooper immediately resigned his post as First Lord of the Admiralty in protest.

Winston was first stunned by the outcome of Munich and then enraged. He had already cancelled a very lucrative speaking tour in the United States during the coming winter in order to be available to speak in Parliament when the new session opened on 2 November. He had also replied to a query from the Duke of Windsor that he would probably not stay with Maxine that September as usual; anyone could see the reasons behind his decision, he wrote. In a speech in Parliament he bluntly told Chamberlain that he had been given a choice between war and dishonour; 'You chose dishonour, and you will have war.'[3]

Despite the fact that, for most people, Munich had taken the heat out of the situation, Winston was working in overdrive. Maxine, who had been looking forward to his visit, suggested he might still like to spend a few weeks resting at the villa. 'Can't you possibly turn up?' she wrote. 'Bring a man with you if you like?' Kitty Rothschild would be there, she cajoled, and the Windsors never stopped asking after him. 'I am beginning to feel desolate in fearing you might not come.'[4] He replied that it was not possible at present, but he would try to fit in a short break later.

In November the Duke of Windsor met his brother the Duke of Gloucester in Paris. It was his first meeting with a member of his family since the abdication. The British Embassy found they were unable to oblige the Dukes with a room for the meeting, so they met informally at the Hôtel Meurice with their wives. The brothers embraced – they had been good friends in the past having travelled together in the old days a good deal, including several safaris in Kenya (where Gloucester had met his wife).

The two duchesses kissed on the steps and a street musician played the National Anthem, causing wide smiles.

On the Riviera the *on dit* was Tom Mosley's surprise announcement that he and Diana Guinness had married in secret two years earlier, at the home of Joseph Goebbels. It was rumoured incorrectly that Hitler had been Mosley's best man, though the Führer had attended the wedding as guest of honour.

At the time Winston was trying to finish a book, *History of the English-Speaking Peoples*, before war began: he was convinced this was imminent, despite the Munich Agreement, and in a letter to Clementine dated 22 December 1938 he told her he expected Hitler to move against Poland in February or March. Clementine was cruising in the Caribbean aboard Lord Moyne's yacht *Rosaura* for the winter months so Winston spent the Christmas holidays at Blenheim with Randolph and Mary, after which, helpless to change the political situation, he became bored and dispirited with the 'unbroken routine'. He loathed the cold and snowy weather, which when it gave way to wet thaw was no better. In London parks the newly dug air raid trenches filled with water and were pronounced a danger to children. Feeling that there was nothing he could usefully do at Chartwell Winston felt he could be more productive working on the proofs 'in bed, in the sunshine,' he wrote to Clementine, 'of that room you know at Maxine's'.[5] So he wrote to Maxine proposing himself as her guest.

Maxine had spent Christmas 1938 at Roquebrune, in a villa next to Coco Chanel's La Pausa, but when Winston wrote to take up her standing invitation she made plans to return home at once and cabled him that he was welcome. On 7 January he flew with Prof Lindemann in thick fog to Paris and late that morning they met his secretary Mary Penman at the Ritz. Leaving her with enough dictation to keep her occupied all day, Winston disappeared off to Versailles for a series of meetings with various French leaders, as well as Sir Eric Phipps and Sir Charles Mendl at the British Embassy. He roared back into the hotel at 7.30 p.m. looking pleased with himself, to find his secretary and the Prof, who was not travelling south with them, waiting anxiously with the luggage packed and ready to be loaded into two taxis. They raced to the Gare de Lyon, arriving with only minutes to spare for the overnight Blue Train to Antibes. The description of Winston's day – little more than a half-day, really – in Paris, recorded by his secretary, reads breathlessly; a typical day for Winston, probably. He merely noted that after a good dinner he 'slept blissfully'.

For Winston it was a thrill to leave Paris on a dark mid-winter evening and wake next morning to radiant sunshine on the Riviera, even if there was a slight winter nip in the air. All his life he loved sunshine; it energised him and enabled him to work at an even higher rate. Maxine's chauffeur Jules was waiting, as always, to whisk them to the Château de l'Horizon.

Maxine had been overjoyed to see him, Winston wrote to Clementine, and there was hardly anyone visiting the Riviera out of season, just local residents. The Windsors were expected to dine at l'Horizon on the following evening, and as usual there was much discussion about curtseying to 'the lady', he wrote. 'Feelings run high on the point. But all accounts show them entirely happy and as much in love with each other as ever.'[6] A few weeks earlier there had been a small furore in the press over a reception in Paris when Lady Diana Cooper and

Mrs Euan Wallace* had curtsied to the Duchess of Windsor. Diana Cooper declined to comment, but Mrs Wallace said it was a very informal occasion and she had done it purely to please the Duke. It had become common practice in the South of France: certainly the newspapers reported that women had curtsied when the couple, with the Duchess glittering in diamonds and emeralds, saw in the new year at the Sporting Club Monte Carlo with Lord and Lady Brownlow and a small party of guests. The Windsors' circle there were pragmatic about the matter. It gave much pleasure to the former King, and most people considered it a small thing to do.

At Maxine's dinner, the HRH courtesies were again extended to Wallis. And Maxine and her house-guests (including Diana and Vincent Sheean, who had become regular visitors) were invited to dine at La Croë the following week. The Windsors' dinner was 'very grand', Sheean wrote, the guests consisting of

assorted notables from up and down the coast, mostly English people of high rank. My Lords Rothermere and Beaverbrook had been prevented from attending by colds. (Lord Beaverbrook recovered sufficiently to attend the Casino, where we saw him afterwards.) When some of the more overpowering guests had departed after the long and stately meal in the white and gold dining-room, the Duke and Mr Churchill settled down to a prolonged argument with the rest of the party listening in silence. The Duke had read Mr Churchill's recent articles on Spain and the newest one (out that day, I believe) in which he appealed

---

* Wife of the Financial Secretary to the Treasury.

for an alliance with Russia. We sat by the fireplace, Mr Churchill frowning with intentness at the floor in front of him, mincing no words ... declaring that the nation stood in the gravest danger in its long history. The kilted Duke in his Stuart tartan sat on the edge of the sofa eagerly interrupting whenever he could, contesting every point but receiving – in terms of utmost politeness ... an object lesson in political wisdom ... The rest of us sat in silence; there was something dramatically final, irrevocable about this dispute.[7]

Winston also commented on this dinner at La Croë, to tell Clementine how 'extremely well done' it all was with the staff in red livery behaving as though they were in royal service. He marvelled at the Duke's formal Highland evening dress, recalling how, at the Fort when he was Prince of Wales, it had been difficult to get him to wear a dinner jacket and bow tie.

Even though the weather had turned grey, damp and cold, the cossetting that Maxine ensured Winston received at l'Horizon allowed him to remain contented and focused, enabling him to exceed his daily target of a thousand words.* Dressed in the brightly coloured silk dressing gown that Clementine had given him for Christmas, and looking like an extravagant peacock,[8] he sat up in bed every morning, his papers and books strewn around him while he dictated to Miss Penman until it was time for lunch. In the evenings, when not playing cards with Maxine, he admitted he had been gambling – it was unusual to confess this to his wife

---

* He wrote that since his arrival he had averaged 1500 words a day and had reached a word count of 221,000, which put him sixty-three days ahead of his self-imposed schedule and should give him seven months to revise and polish his manuscript.

for, having lost her brother to suicide because of his gambling debts,* Clementine strongly disapproved. But as he was unusually successful on this occasion he felt able to tell her that he had been several times to the Casino at Cannes, where he had played hard and had built up a substantial advantage. He had even, during evening sessions, attempted to learn a new dance from a couple who performed there. The dance required the dancer to take three steps and give a hop. He tried his best but he kept hopping in the wrong place, which, he grumbled, provoked 'small-minded people to laugh'.[9]

Maxine invited enough people to amuse Winston, and more to his taste the once-glamorous chit-chat of former years was now interlaced with stories of the situation in Germany and how German Jews were being treated under Hitler. When they were alone Winston discussed investments with Maxine, for he lived habitually beyond his income while she was known to be an astute manager of money. After two weeks at l'Horizon, Winston left by train for Monte Carlo, where he was to stay overnight with Lord Rothermere at his villa La Dragonnière – so called because local legend had it that a dragon had once lived on the site before being slain by a brave local lad.

Rothermere, originally Harold Harmsworth, was the immensely rich proprietor of the *Daily Mail*, which he began publishing in 1896 under the slogan 'a penny newspaper for half a penny'. It was the first daily newspaper aimed at the working classes, and rapidly became the most popular newspaper in the country when its circulation reached over a million during the Boer War. In 1903 he and his brother Alfred (later 1st Viscount Northcliffe) launched the *Daily Mirror*, which

---

* Her brother Bill shot himself in 1921 because of his debts.

was aimed at women readers and filled with pictures – a brilliant innovative move. The brothers gradually took over less successful publications such as the *Sunday Pictorial* and the *London Evening News*, and eventually the business became the newspaper empire Associated Newspapers Ltd. After the death of his brother in the early Twenties Rothermere became sole proprietor – the 'other bookend' to Lord Beaverbrook of the *Daily Express* – and between them these two press barons more or less controlled popular public opinion in the United Kingdom between the wars.

Harold Harmsworth's elevation to the peerage had not brought him much happiness.* Two of his sons were killed in the First World War and he never recovered from their loss, although he had another son, Esmond, who eventually succeeded him. After his marriage failed he spent increasingly long periods in the South of France, where he was a passionate and successful gambler at the Monte Carlo Sporting Club. The amounts of Rothermere's wagers became as legendary as the name of his villa, and he had a series of mistresses, the most notable of whom was an Austrian princess (Stephanie von Hohenlohe) who introduced him to Hitler and was eventually unmasked as a German spy.

For years Rothermere paid Princess Stephanie an annual retainer of five thousand pounds. In 1938, however, he dropped her when MI5 made known to him that she was regarded as a very dangerous person; shamelessly she took him to court for alleged breach of contract, but did not win her case. Fiercely anti-communist following the Bolshevik

---

* Harmsworth was created Baron Rothermere in 1914, and Viscount Rothermere in 1919.

revolution, Rothermere adopted a right-wing stance that initially – due to the influence of his glamorous princess – had led him to support Hitler, and caught him up in a web of intrigue. He was not alone: many educated people looked to the right during the Thirties as an antidote to Bolshevism, without realising that with Hitler the pendulum had swung too far. Only with war pending had the scales dropped from Rothermere's eyes.

No politician of any era would turn down the opportunity of a personal relationship with a newspaper magnate such as Rothermere, and Churchill was no exception. Furthermore, the old myth of the slain dragon somehow lent an air of enchantment to Rothermere's villa, basking in its peaceful sunny acres of orange groves, scented flowering trees and shrubs on Cap Ferrat, overlooking Monte Carlo and the sea. Whenever he visited La Dragonnière Winston was inspired to get out his easel and start painting. Usually he also enjoyed the mix of guests his remarkable host gathered to his dinners, but on this overnight stay in January 1939 he dined with only Lord Rothermere and the Duke of Windsor, in order to discuss the ducal couple's return to England in the event of war. The establishment wouldn't like it, Winston confided to Clementine, but they had no power to stop it, and if anyone could help to ease the way for the Windsors it was Rothermere.

From La Dragonnière Winston went to stay with the Fellowes for two nights at nearby Les Zoraides, and lunched on their yacht in the bay below their villa. Winston and Daisy went on to the Casino at Monte Carlo on at least two occasions. He assured Clementine that he did not gamble large amounts; he could not afford to, but Daisy could and she played big (although on one occasion even she pulled out when the stake reached forty thousand francs).[10] Winston treated the casinos as though he was an errant schoolboy enjoying a treat of which he knew his parents would disapprove, corroborated by Miss Penman's account of how, as they were driven to the station at Monte Carlo to catch the Blue Train to Paris, they had to pass the Casino. To Miss Penman's dismay, for – as usual – they were already short of time to catch the train, Winston ordered the driver to stop. He leapt out and ran off into the Casino, his coat unbuttoned and flapping. A few minutes later he reappeared, still running. He jumped in beside her and told the driver to push on to the station. Then he told her that he had just won enough to cover their fares home. 'What do you think of that?' he asked her, grinning.

Winston found a letter from Maxine awaiting him at Chartwell: 'What a sweet little note you gave me at the station, Winston dearest,' Maxine wrote. 'I am so happy that you enjoyed your all-too-brief visit. Never have I seen you in such good form and our jaws ached with laughter continually – your *joie de vivre* is a wonderful gift and on a par with your other amazing gifts – in fact you are the most unusually gifted creature in the whole wide world.'[11] He had, she said, quite literally taken the sunshine with him for it had been dull and overcast ever since, but she was so glad that he had decided to return at Whitsuntide. Maxine was looking forward to it for she had been ill in bed almost since he left. L'Horizon was now filled with her women friends, such as Lady Portarlington; her 'Adamless Eden', she called it, and she complained that 'men are rare birds on the Riviera. Only pansies grow here, and they are not my favourite flowers'.[12] It was a curious, unkind remark when some of her most constant visitors and good friends were Barry Dierks, Willie Maugham and Noël Coward.

Before Winston departed he had chatted with Maxine about building a small house in a wooded hilltop site at Chartwell, overlooking the Weald of Kent. It was to be a small family home for a man and wife, and maybe two or three children – it would cost about three thousand pounds to build, he thought, if he did a lot of the work himself. If he could sell it for six thousand pounds it would provide him with a profitable occupation once the latest book was off his hands. He enjoyed bricklaying. He stressed that of course he would not begin it unless he was convinced that there was no danger of imminent war. Winston being Winston, he planned to ask the distinguished architect Sir Edwin Lutyens to pop down and have a look at the site. But the basic design of the house was Maxine's, and she turned to Barry Dierks, who was not used to designing houses for working men in England, to set down her ideas. There was a flurry of correspondence on the subject and the first plans showed a small mansion with en suite bathrooms in each bedroom and an integral garage (an unbelievable luxury in England at the time), but at Winston's request Maxine had them redrawn on a more practical scale. 'The Riviera is a dull place without you,' she wrote, 'and we miss you more than I can say.'[13] Still, she looked forward to Whitsuntide when she would see him again. Neither knew it yet, but his visit in January 1939 was to be Winston's last to the Riviera for some years, and he would never again see Maxine or the Château de l'Horizon.

Other members of his family visited the Riviera, though, for that February, while convalescing from a nose and throat operation, Sarah stayed at Saint-Jean-Cap-Ferrat and lunched with Maxine in order to discuss her ambition to become a serious actress. A worry to her parents, she had gone onto the stage as one of Mr Cochran's Young Ladies and she had shown a real aptitude for it. It was not what Winston and Clementine wanted for her, but they might have come to accept it had Sarah not then fallen in love with the Jewish-American comedian Vic Oliver, who was the star of the show in which Sarah was a member of the chorus. Winston forbade the marriage, so Sarah ran away and married Vic on Christmas Eve 1936. The Churchills managed a veneer of acceptance but the marriage did not work out. By February 1939 Sarah had begun to get some half-decent parts in stage productions but at the time she visited Maxine she knew her marriage was in deep trouble and she wanted advice about this and her career. She also visited Daisy, but in letters to her sister Sarah disparaged these 'elderly' women who were friends of her father.

In June Maxine suffered a mild stroke. Her weight – 230 pounds – had begun to take its toll, and a sudden spell of abnormally hot weather was an intolerable strain. Friends and neighbours rushed to l'Horizon to be told by a tearful Fanny that her mistress was barely conscious, but there seemed to be no paralysis. Dr Brès was still with her, but they could wait if they wished to see her later with his permission. Looked after by Maxine's staff they waited in the shade by the pool: Charlotte Boissevain,* to whom Maxine had introduced Dierks to build her a covered swimming pool for her Cannes mansion; Princess Julia Ottoboni; Madame Louise Edvina, the Canadian soprano – all

---

* Formerly Charlotte Ives, the actress. When her husband, Jan, died she moved to Cap d'Antibes, having agreed to rent the villa of a friend. When she saw another villa she preferred she signed for that instead and was sued for breach of contract. She ended up paying for two villas for a year.

anxiously waiting for news. After a while Elsie Mendl (now almost eighty) arrived, striding onto the terrace dressed in shorts and wearing her trademark conical hat. She lectured them, saying she had been telling Maxine for years that she must 'diet and exercise, diet and exercise. Like me,' she said, patting her flat stomach before she launched into her daily exercise routine, which ended with her standing on her head. At this point Charlotte Boissevain began praying fervently for two things. One, that she could contain her giggles, and two, that Maxine would live so that she could describe to her this bizarre scene.[14]

Winston wrote a concerned letter and as soon as she was sufficiently recovered to reply Maxine wrote that she was touched when he had so much else to think about. 'I am proud that you should worry ... I seem to have come back from an illimitable distance and find the world more beautiful than I remember it,' she wrote in reply, explaining that she was something of a limp rag at present and had to learn to walk again. Dr Brès got a famous Parisian specialist down to treat her, and with his own daily care he promised Maxine that if she did as she was told there was no reason why she should not be up and about and feeling almost normal by August. That would leave her two months of the best weather to enjoy, and she would still be able to entertain Winston since he had now suggested a visit in August or September. 'Promise you will come and stay as long as you can,' she begged him. 'And Clemmy too if you can persuade her.'[15] The Churchills planned to stay with Consuelo at the Château de St Georges Motel during the Parliamentary summer recess of 1939. Winston was to paint and also tour the Maginot Line at the invitation of the French, but he thought it might just be possible to pop down to l'Horizon and see Maxine during this time.

In early July Dr Brès moved Maxine to the Royal Palace Hotel at Royat, a town in Puy-de-Dôme surrounded by forests, that had been renowned since the Roman occupation for its hot springs providing a natural spa. The cooler, fresher air at over three thousand feet enabled her to sleep well and stopped the palpitations she had been suffering in the heat of the Riviera. She had been thrilled to receive a signed copy of Winston's latest publication, *Step by Step*, a book of essays on the present political situation, and she was looking forward to his visit 'if that fiend Hitler', as she put it, did not begin any more wars that summer. By now large sections of the public and the newspapers were agitating for Winston to play a larger part in government. 'Was there ever such a triumph for a public man?' Maxine wrote from Royat. 'Press and public alike, hotly demanding the one man who has told them the frightening truth all these years; and now they run to him to try and pull their burning chestnuts out of the fire.'[16]

The countdown to war had begun. Winston had told Daisy in a letter that spring that he believed they were approaching a showdown, but that now he felt more confidence and certainty in the country than previously. In March Hitler had marched into Czechoslovakia and Mussolini – wanting his share of the loot, as Winston put it – annexed Albania a few weeks later. Winston looked at all the pieces of the jigsaw and decided that if there was to be a crisis it was likely to be in September.

Meanwhile, life on the Riviera continued as normal. Soon after Winston's departure Cannes held its Fête du Mimosa and visitors breathed in the quiet perfumed air, gazed over the tranquil blue sea, sipped wine at beach cafés and strolled along the Croisette on balmy evenings under the necklace of lights stretching off to the Cap d'Antibes. It seemed inconceivable that war was imminent. The hotels had been full over Easter and all along the coast the traditional springtime 'battles of flowers' took place, including La Joute Fleuri at Nice. Cannes advertised its first film festival, which would be held in September. At the International Cinematographic Festival the top films would vie for the Grand Prix du Festival, among them *Union Pacific*, *The Wizard of Oz*, *Goodbye Mr Chips* and *The Four Feathers*.* Throughout the summer horse shows, golf matches and firework displays continued to convey confidence and an air of normality; and in anticipation of the forthcoming Film Festival, Hollywood stars began to arrive: Tyrone Power, Gary Cooper and Merle Oberon among them.

On 22 June the Duke and Duchess of Windsor, who had recently signed a lease on a twenty-bedroom house on Boulevard Suchet, near the Bois de Boulogne, had dined at the German embassy in Paris and were greeted with Nazi salutes. The Duke believed it was possible to negotiate with the Germans, little realising he would be branded a Nazi-supporter by many for the remainder of his life. Two months later the Duke presided with charm over the prestigious charity ball in Cannes, Le Bal des Petits Lits Blancs, where the rich, titled and famous flaunted jewels that normally lived in bank vaults. One of the worst electrical storms ever known on the Riviera occurred during the ball, delaying the spectacular fireworks. It was the final fling of the pre-war Riviera.

Maxine would certainly have attended some of these events had she been well enough, but she was still convalescing at Royat. During August, while painting with Paul Maze on holiday at the Château de St Georges Motel, Winston looked

---

* This festival never took place, but it was revived after the war.

up and remarked that these would be the last paintings that they would do in peacetime. A fellow guest, annoyed with Winston for speaking in this manner, rounded on him accusing him of being a warmonger, but the news became worse each day and on 22 August Winston flew home early. On the same day Germany and Russia signed a pact of mutual non-aggression. With Germany's eastern front protected Hitler could turn on Poland without fear of retribution and now, at last, everyone began to realise what this meant. Within a week German troops had invaded Poland, Britain and France declared war and Winston was offered a seat in the Cabinet, though initially 'without Ministry'. He did not have to wait long, however: a few days later he was offered the Admiralty, a post he had never dared hope would be his again.

The extensive grounds of Château de la Croë now housed a squad of Senegalese troops, and an anti-aircraft battery to protect the Cap d'Antibes from attack from the sea. All house-guests had departed. On 28 August the Duke, in the mistaken belief that he was still a man with power, cabled Adolf Hitler and King Victor Emmanuel of Italy, urging them to work for the preservation of peace. Hitler replied unequivocally that it was England, not Germany, who was responsible for the situation which now prevailed, and that whatever happened was England's fault. King Victor Emmanuel answered that he would do what he could to persuade Italy to remain neutral. Even on the day war was declared the Duke refused to believe war would actually happen.* His equerry, Fruity

---

* The Duchess had her cards read by a clairvoyant and as a result was convinced Italy would remain neutral. This may have affected the Duke's attitude.

Metcalfe, however, thought otherwise so he drove into Nice and somehow organised an entire compartment to be reserved on the train to Paris for the Duke's servants, Metcalfe's own valet, and a secretary; they left on the evening of 2 September. Apart from Metcalfe, the Duchess's French maid and a few local servants, the Duke and Duchess of Windsor were now totally alone. On the 3rd it was a very hot day and just before noon they decided to swim, but the Duke was called back indoors to take a telephone call from the British Ambassador. When he rejoined Wallis and Fruity he told them that Great Britain had just declared war on Germany. 'Then there came a splash,' Wallis wrote. 'He had dived into the pool.'[17]

During the last week of August Noël Coward, who had a new play due to open on 11 September in Manchester, had decided on a dash to the Riviera for one last irresponsible escape to the sun before, as he put it in his diary, 'the destruction of civilisation'. His two leading ladies were already staying in Antibes, at the Hôtel du Cap, learning their lines while picking up a tan. Other friends were on yachts along the coast, and although most English visitors were now on their way back home there were still, he decided, 'countless' expat friends such as Somerset Maugham, Barry Dierks and Charlotte Boissevain available to lunch, drink, dine and swim with. He looked forward to the well-remembered picnics on the Îles de Lérins* with

---

* Islands off Cannes. One contains the ancient fortress which became famous as a prison of which the Man in the Iron Mask (*L'Homme au Masque de Fer*) was an inmate. The name was given to a high-status prisoner arrested as Eustache Dauger in 1669 or 1670 and held in a number of jails, including the Bastille, for a period of thirty-four years during the reign of Louis XIV. He died on 19 November 1703, by which time he was known as prisoner Marchioly, but his true identity is unknown. No one ever saw his face, which was hidden by a mask covered in black velvet. The mystery of his identity has been the subject of many books and films. Another famous inmate was King Louis XVI.

hot *langouste* in butter and garlic, crisp French bread and the local rosé de Provence, day trips by car to Nice, Monte Carlo and St Tropez, and elegant evenings gambling in the casinos. He flew to Cannes and checked into the Carlton Hotel, arriving in time to watch the sunset and see the lights come on along the Croisette. He decided that he could still enjoy all his usual pastimes, but only with the aid of a very fast speedboat hired at a ridiculous price, an extravagance he considered – given the extreme situation – a justifiable expense.[18]

On the final evening of his holiday Noël recorded in a memoir how he took his boat over to Golfe-Juan to say goodbye to Maxine. While America remained out of the conflict she was not in any immediate danger, and despite the entreaties of her family in England she declined to leave her beloved villa. He had heard from her friends how unwell she was:

I landed at her little private jetty below the swimming pool and walked up the twisting path, shaded by oleanders, to the house. There was no house-party because Maxine was very ill, and the terrace and pool, in the past invariably thronged with people, wore an air of sadness . . .

I went upstairs into Maxine's bedroom. She was in bed, bitterly against her will, and looking more beautiful than I had ever seen her.* She joked about her illness and said that she was a cat with nine lives, eight of which had been lived to the full; the next attack, she said in her charming deep voice, would be the grand finale. She grumbled a good deal about being forced to stay in bed, and railed against the

---

* He had known her over twenty years, since the First World War.

doctor and Fanny, her beloved maid, for refusing to allow her to get up and walk about and play games and go for drives.

Noël stayed and gossiped with Maxine for an hour or so and then, seeing that she was very tired, he kissed her and left, making his way to the speedboat which made a loud roar as the engine caught. Maxine evidently heard it, for when he was a little way from the shore he turned and looked back at the villa:

... there was Maxine, leaning against one of the supports of her balcony and waving a white handkerchief. Her white hair, her white night-gown, and the handkerchief were tinged with pink from the setting sun. I waved back and the lovely picture became blurred, because I knew, in that moment, that I should never see her again, and my eyes were filled with tears.[19]

9

The Lights Go Out Over Europe

Maxine was still too unwell to go to London for the hastily arranged wedding of Randolph Churchill to Pamela Digby on 4 October 1939.* The bride was the daughter of Lord and Lady Digby, of Minterne House in Dorset, and Randolph had met her only a few weeks earlier. Meanwhile, Maxine's recovery was slow. She lost over forty pounds in weight and was pleased to have her figure back, she wrote to Winston: 'I can look forward to the time when we can all gather round the pool again and sit in the sun shine and lick our wounds. [But] I am afraid there will be many blows in store for us before those happy times arrive!'[1]

There were no more amusing luncheon parties with smart house-guests from London and the *gratin* from Paris bringing the latest gossip. Her visitors now were mostly her oldest

---

* He proposed to her after he had known her a few days and insisted on their marrying quickly before he was sent off to fight. By a curious twist of fate, although Maxine never met Pamela Digby she would one day become chatelaine of l'Horizon.

women friends, some of whom she had known since the horse-and-carriage era of Edward VII with its endless house parties, unlimited servants and discreet 'cinq et sept' trysts: Winnie Portarlington, Millicent Sutherland, Kathleen Drogheda – and they, Maxine could see to her dismay, were ageing before her eyes.

Not all her visitors were women. The Aga Khan called and spent several hours with her. And another old friend, George Cornwallis-West, called at l'Horizon to demonstrate to Maxine that it was possible to make a full recovery from the stroke he had suffered a few months earlier. As a young man he had been known as the most beautiful man in England. 'I must say he looked wonderfully well,' Maxine wrote.

And went gaily off for a round of golf only to be laid low with phlebitis the next day, so he could not have been fit enough to attempt golf so soon ... Millie Sutherland came to see me last week, I am not supposed to see visitors for more than 15 minutes, but she stayed 2½ hours and I cried continuously for three days afterwards. I have known Millie in her radiance and to see her now is too much for me. One sees just a placid old lady ... and with rather a silly smile. Muriel tells me she takes drugs and who can blame her – poor soul – if it makes life easier. God knows she has had more than her share of shock and grief. Geordie* is at Monte Carlo nursing a bad throat and more or less surrounded by his little bits of fluff ...

---

* Millicent's son, the 5th Duke of Sutherland. He was released from a deeply unhappy marriage by his wife's death in 1943. Meanwhile, he became a notorious womaniser, and the writer Barbara Cartland claimed that he was one of two possible fathers of her daughter Raine McCorquodale (later Countess Spencer and stepmother of Diana, Princess of Wales). Prince George, Duke of Kent, was the alternative candidate.

The Château de l'Horizon was apparently not in any immediate danger of being taken over by the military – Maxine was
a prominent American citizen after all, and she was living in
only part of the villa and using the rest to help the war effort.
Having immediately offered to assist the French army in any
way she could, she now had eighteen soldiers billeted with
her. 'They are nice and give no trouble,' she wrote. Indeed, she
adopted them as her own regiment; 'my chasseurs', she called
these sturdy young men of the Chasseurs Alpins, who were
trained to fight in mountainous areas, clad in their blue uniforms and distinctive huge floppy berets. And soon they did
indeed become 'hers', for they were termed the Poste Château
de l'Horizon and she was their happy *bienfaitrice*.

Part of the villa was also given over to a workshop, where
a team of local women, overseen by Fanny, Maxine's maid,
produced hundreds of children's garments for the local poor,
especially those children of men conscripted into the army
in the general mobilisation which threw many poor families
onto the breadline. When the women could not obtain any
further material to make clothes, Maxine threw open her
wardrobe and glamorous gowns and day dresses from Paris
fashion houses were pulled from their protective bags to
become numerous small pinafores and playsuits.

In November 1939 the Communist Party was banned in
France, and most declared communists were imprisoned as
possible subversives, and as there was a strong communist
element in Vallauris, the nearest small town to l'Horizon,
this meant another group of wives and children left destitute.
Maxine hated communism, but she refused to stand by and
watch the innocent starve. She began sending regular amounts
of money in cash to the mayor of Vallauris to provide aid for

the affected families. Her chauffeur Jules was conscripted and sent into the hills at Saint-Paul-de-Vence where, as winter began and the rains came, he complained to her, they were totally idle and sat about in the cold. Just waiting.

By November the Duchess of Windsor had joined the Red Cross and was photographed wearing the uniform of an officer, visiting the sick in hospitals and helping to pack boxes of comfort items such as soap, cigarettes, socks and magazines to be distributed to French troops.

Maxine looked closer to home and at Christmas organised a local children's party from her bed. In the cinema in Vallauris she had a large Christmas tree erected, and every one of the two hundred children who attended received a wrapped gift. For many of those children the party remained a bright memory throughout their childhood: it would be more than half a decade before they saw another. In the first six months of the war Maxine contributed thousands of dollars to help local people; 'The reserves of the Château de l'Horizon are often strained,' she wrote to Winston on 18 February – he was now her most frequent correspondent – 'but we are happy to help where we can.'[2] This was to be her last letter to him.

In London the declaration of war had immediately precipitated practice air raid alarms which sent terrified people scurrying for shelter. Within days a more *laissez faire* attitude was adopted and people took such alarms in their stride as they went about their business, wondering how long it would be before the alarms were for real. Things remained quiet on the Riviera, too, during this phoney-war period; the sun still shone, the sea was still blue, the raspy chirrup of cicadas still filled the air. Somerset Maugham recalled how everyone there talked a good deal about the possibility of war, but it still seemed remote to them:

We continued to bathe and play tennis; the weather remained fine; the new moon appeared one evening when it was hardly yet dark, a pale sickle of light in the evening sky, and we bowed to it three times and three times turned the money over in our pockets. The moon waxed. The peaceful days passed one after another. And then they were over.[3]

To coincide with their declaration of war the French had announced a general mobilisation, in which six million Frenchmen between the ages of nineteen and forty-five were conscripted, while an order was issued for the immediate requisition of all property, cars, aeroplanes, private vessels and animals (horses, cattle and other livestock). The effects of this were gradually felt on the Riviera. Cap Ferrat was only a handful of miles from the Italian border; indeed, the area from the border as far as Nice had been governed by Italy until 1860, and it was much feared that Mussolini wished to take it back, despite his promise that Italy would never attack France. Little by little it dawned on the expats who lived on the Riviera, especially in the area nearest to the border, that they were vulnerable and internment in a POW camp was the very least they might expect from the allies of Britain's now implacable enemy.

Foodstuffs began to disappear from the shops and markets within days of the declaration of war; mainly hoovered up by army victualling depots. Most adults were only too able to recall the hardships and shortages of the Great War just twenty years earlier, so there was inevitable hoarding. Fear and confusion began to grow. Within weeks banks refused to take cheques drawn on English banks. A friend of Maugham's who said goodbye and departed for Paris returned from the station reporting that it was impossible to get a place on the Blue Train, even with a reservation! In fact, the last Blue Train left Nice the same week. The roads were bumper-to-bumper with overloaded cars streaming away to the north and west. Before they had gone too far they would meet those who were hurrying south to evade the German armies invading in the north. Armed troops suddenly appeared on Cap Ferrat and were seen guarding a railway bridge, having been moved in by trucks overnight. Maugham's staff came to him one by one; some were being called up, and others – like the many Italians who had more or less settled in France to work in the service industries – now wished to return home. A staff of thirteen was instantly reduced to two. All owners of sailing vessels, including Maugham, were notified that privately owned craft must leave the harbour within twenty-four hours or be confiscated. Maugham's long-term partner, Gerald Haxton, was an American and therefore considered neutral, so it seemed safe for him to stay on to protect the house from possible looting. Maugham took the converted fishing boat they used as a yacht and sailed west, making for Cassis.

On 5 March 1940 Maxine died very suddenly. Fanny had helped her to the bathroom and left Maxine to wash while she remade the bed. On hearing a soft thump she went to investigate and found Maxine dead on the bathmat. There had been no call for help. Paul Brès had looked after her throughout her long illness, often spending several hours with her, so Fanny called him at once. Two hours later the doctor sat down and wrote to Winston. When he had seen her earlier in the day, he explained,

> she was as well as possible – blood pressure normal; heart regular, steady. She was cheerful and for the first time in many months making plans for the spring. We had a nice little chat and she spoke of you in her usually friendly and affectionate way she always had where it was a question of you ... at 7 p.m. she had a brutal seizure and in two seconds she was gone. When I arrived it was too late! I cannot write this without trembling (excuse my handwriting). We have lost a great friend and I know what a terrible shock the sad news will be to you ... There is in the ears her last words said this morning, about you, 'Winston knows how to take his responsibilities – nothing can frighten him – he should be Prime Minister!' ... I feel tonight so desperate and lonely. Her dear and beautiful face was so peaceful and radiant – only her splendid eyes were closed forever.[4]

Barry Dierks was the first of the friends who were left in the area to reach the villa and he broke down at the sight of one of her Chasseurs Alpins – standing guard at the door of l'Horizon, his head bowed over his rifle as an honour guard. Other visitors recalled how tiny Maxine appeared, lying in her bed, all white, with her unique vivacity stilled. Winston wrote to Dr Brès expressing his deep sadness at the loss of his old friend, and his gratitude for the tender skill with which Brès had always looked after Maxine. The lights in the world were being put out one by one, Winston wrote grimly, and as for the happy sunlit days at the Château de l'Horizon, they were 'gone forever'.[5]

They were not gone for ever, of course, but they were gone for a long time, and when it was possible for the survivors to return there would be a new set of people and life would never be quite the same.

Maxine's closest friends had already left the Riviera. Many had headed for London, while Millicent Sutherland had moved to Angers and would be forced to make her way to Spain as the Germans overran France, but among the few expats left in the Mediterranean, hanging on by fingernails and a measure of hope, were George and Alice Keppel. Once leaders of society, they had moved to Italy soon after the death of King Edward VII, when the new Queen made it clear they were no longer *personae gratae* at Court. Rather than be downgraded and shunned they went abroad. They had kept a home in England but had mostly lived in their villa near Florence (once owned by Galileo) since the Great War. In September 1939 they fled from Italy, and spent the winter and spring in a rented villa at Cap Martin. Winston cabled them to request that George represent him at Maxine's funeral. It was more fitting than Winston possibly realised, for in 1901 it had been George Keppel, with whom she almost certainly had a brief dalliance, who was chiefly responsible for Maxine's acceptance by the upper echelons of British society.

With all civilian travel restricted and overseas travel almost impossible, Maxine's niece Blossom was the sole family representative at the funeral. She and her husband had been able, with Winston's help, to get permission for a short trip to France. They flew a demonstrator model of their Miles

Mentor aircraft* to Cannes, where they had a permit to stay for three days.

Maxine was buried in the Cannes Protestant cemetery with a plain headstone which read simply 'Maxine Elliott 1873–1940' and the word 'Beloved'. Blossom believed this birthdate to be correct, but over the years Maxine had shaved five years off her age, and was actually seventy-three when she died.† The Chasseurs Alpins sounded the last post and fired a volley of shots over the grave. On the following day Blossom presented the regiment with a *fanion* which Maxine had commissioned some months earlier, and Blossom was made the *marraine* (patron) of the regiment in Maxine's place.

In the short time she had in France, and conscious of the weight restrictions of a small aircraft, Blossom could only clear the contents of Maxine's safe and jewellery boxes, and collect any papers that she thought looked important. Maxine had bequeathed virtually everything to her sister Gertrude and her four nieces, including the Château de l'Horizon and its contents, the London house she had bought for Diana and Vincent, her Paris flat, the theatre in New York and her investments. Eventually, the estate was valued at over a million dollars.‡

Maxine had left explicit instructions that all correspondence from Tony Wilding, Lord Curzon, Lord Rosebery,

---

* Blossom, together with her husband Miles (Frederick G. Miles), owned and ran a company building aircraft designed by the husband-and-wife team. It became the Miles Aircraft Company in 1941, and produced a large number of training aircraft during the war.

† Not only the date was incorrect: the mason misspelled Elliott as Elliot (see photo in plate section).

‡ Now worth about three times that much in cash, although the property values would be around twenty times that amount. Maxine's theatre was demolished in 1960 after Maxine's family had sold it; the Paris flat was somehow appropriated by the tenants, a family of White Russian semi-royalty. Despite a lengthy law suit Diana was never able to gain repossession after the war.

George Keppel, Churchill, King Edward and other important friends was to be destroyed unread, and this was done at
once.* Fanny and Jules (who seemed to have obtained leave
to return to the villa) were to stay on for a while to gather
together portable items such as the more valuable paintings and silver, and prepare them for transport out. When
it looked as though the villa would be occupied they were
to retreat into a village in the hills, taking with them what
they could. As Blossom left to fly home none of them knew
whether they would survive the coming fight.

---

* A few letters between Maxine and Winston that were not at l'Horizon survived.

PART THREE

10

War on the Riviera

In early April 1940 Germany invaded Denmark and Norway, and within four weeks German forces began an invasion of Belgium, Holland and Luxembourg. On 10 May Belgium declared a state of emergency. Germany looked unstoppable, and as the British Expeditionary Force (BEF) and the French army steadily retreated, there appeared to be very little to prevent an invasion of the United Kingdom. Neville Chamberlain, having lost the confidence of both the nation and of Parliament, was forced to resign and sixty-five-year-old Winston Churchill became Prime Minister. Immediately, he began to form a coalition government. Three days later he gave his famous 'blood, toil, tears and sweat' speech which gave the nation great heart; how proud Maxine Elliott would have been had she lived a few weeks longer.

Anthony Eden's first task as Secretary of State for War was to form a Home Guard from men exempted from serving in the forces. It may – thanks to TV sitcoms – be considered an amusing anachronism seventy years on, but invasion seemed almost inevitable, and in the desperation that prevailed even old men and boys armed with pitchforks felt like a better option than standing by to allow the enemy a walkover victory, as was happening in France. Anyone suspected of being a fifth columnist was arrested under hastily written new regulations and thrown into prison for the duration. Among them, on 23 May, was Oswald Mosley, followed a month later by his wife Diana. She had been denounced as the more dangerous of the couple by – among others – her sister Nancy, her former father-in-law Lord Moyne, and Baba Metcalfe, who was in love with Mosley herself and deadly jealous of Diana, despite herself being involved with Lord Halifax at the time. After Belgium capitulated, the British spent eight days evacuating the BEF from the beaches at Dunkirk.

Following the declaration of war the Duke and Duchess of Windsor, accompanied by Fruity Metcalfe, had left Antibes and made their way to Paris and then Cherbourg. They had been advised by Sir Walter Monckton,* who flew down to Antibes in a three-seat De Havilland Leopard Moth to discuss their return to England, that there would be no official welcome for them, and that contrary to the Duke's insistence they would not be offered any royal residence in England. The house he considered his own in England, Fort Belvedere, was unfit for them to live in as the building had been unheated and uncared for since the abdication. So, Monckton told them, they would have to make their own arrangements for accommodation. He further warned that the Duke would

---

* Monckton had served as legal adviser to Edward VIII at the time of the abdication.

be offered only two insignificant posts – face-saving roles in effect – to choose from, one in Wales and the other in Paris. The Windsors felt they had little option but to leave France, however, for there was concern that if they remained they might be captured and used as hostages. After much discussion they set off from La Croë by car, declining the use of the Leopard Moth, since Wallis was petrified of flying.[*] At Cherbourg, courtesy of Winston Churchill, who was at that time First Lord of the Admiralty, they were met by Randolph in the uniform of the 4th Hussars[†] and piped aboard the K-class destroyer HMS *Kelly*, commanded by a faintly hostile Lord Mountbatten, for the journey across the Channel to Portsmouth.

Only Winston's fondness, and sense of what was proper for his former King, ensured a dignified return to England for the Duke of Windsor. The ship was met by Baba Metcalfe and Walter Monckton, who went aboard briefly for a glass of champagne in the ward room. Although it was almost 10 p.m. and very dark on a cloudy, cool night in a blackout, Winston had arranged for a red carpet, a guard of honour of one hundred men and a military band to play the National Anthem as they disembarked. No official car was provided, but arrangements were made – again by Winston – for the Duke and Duchess to spend the night at Admiralty House in Portsmouth Dockyard, rather than the hotel the Metcalfes had been obliged to book for them. On the following day the party left for South Hartfield House, the Metcalfes' grey stone house at Coleman's Hatch in the Ashdown Forest, about

---

[*] During her first marriage, as a young bride on a naval air base, she had witnessed several fatal flying accidents.
[†] The Duke immediately noticed that Randolph's spurs were upside down.

forty miles south of London, which was to be the Windsors' base. The couple motored up from Sussex every day to the Metcalfes' London house at 16 Wilton Place; it had been closed up, was unstaffed, sparsely furnished and unheated, so they more or less camped out there with sandwiches and flasks of coffee brought in from a nearby hotel while the Duke attempted to arrange what he was to do for the war effort.

The King saw his brother on one occasion, in private, but neither Queen Elizabeth nor the Duke's mother, Queen Mary, would receive him. The Duke had fully expected to play a major role in the war but this was considered inappropriate given his abdication, and there was the disclosure by the Intelligence Service that Wallis was giving information (intentionally or otherwise) to friends in the German Embassy. This was later revealed as low-level material which might have easily been read in London gossip columns, or mentioned at any dinner table of those in government. However, no one at the time knew for sure *what* she might be passing on and Wallis was regarded as indiscreet, at the very least, and therefore a danger, since everyone knew the Duke confided utterly in her. After much discussion, traumatic to him, the Duke accepted a posting to the British Military Mission in Paris with the rank of major-general (he had previously held the honorary rank of field marshal) and he, Wallis and Fruity returned to Paris on 29 September 1940. The trip across the Channel was rough and Wallis reported that she spent most of her time on the floor of the captain's cabin not knowing whether to cry or be sick. Her relief that the voyage was over turned to horror when she saw that there was a crowd of British troops on the dock waiting to receive them. Every woman will feel sympathy for her immediate reaction:

'I regretted my sallow appearance,' she wrote, 'realising that several hundred men and a goodly smattering of nurses were wondering "How could he have done it?"'[1]

They did not go to their house on Boulevard Suchet, which had been closed, but to the Trianon Palace Hotel, so that Wallis could be within hailing distance of Elsie Mendl, one of her few close women friends. The Duke was away a great deal of the time, on duty at the Mission headquarters at Vincennes, where he came under the orders of Major-General Sir Richard Howard-Vyse. His position was deeply unsatisfactory to him, and to officers serving under him, and the Duke lost much sympathy when at a parade he unconsciously accepted the salute intended for his commanding officer. He also had a constant need to see Wallis, when of course he told her what he had been up to while they were apart. The perceived dangers of his passing on information about the dispersal of French troops which might (and did) end up in the hands of the enemy, and his total inability to accept that he was a relatively unimportant officer and could not simply operate as he wished, made the situation hopeless.

The Windsors were watched continuously by the British Secret Service for the months that this arrangement continued, but eventually on 10 May the Germans invaded the Low Countries, broke the French lines and swarmed into France. It was now obvious the Germans could not be held and that Paris was lost. The Windsors were ordered to leave at once. The Duke drove Wallis to Biarritz, returning to Paris alone twelve days later. He stayed only a short time: within a few days he left very early one morning, their two cars loaded to the roofs – the chauffeur Ladbrooke driving one and the Duke driving the other – in such secrecy that he did not even tell Fruity Metcalfe, who had worked loyally without pay as the Duke's aide-de-camp since the abdication. Fruity was left stranded in Paris with no transport, and when he eventually returned to England to join the war effort he was understandably nursing a massive grievance.

The Duke collected Wallis and they drove to Antibes, arriving there on 29 May. They remained at La Croë for some weeks, enjoying what Wallis described 'days of peaceful calm'.[2]

On 10 June Italy declared war on France and Britain and invaded France. Within hours Monaco emptied as more than half its population fled westwards. The Duke and Duchess of Windsor were entertaining Maurice Chevalier that day, in the hope of lightening the gloomy mood that prevailed. When the declaration was announced on the radio Chevalier left without finishing his lunch to join his lover, the cabaret singer Nita Raya, in his Cannes home.[*]

Four days later the German army entered Paris. All English who were still in France were ordered home, causing the Germans to issue the propaganda statement that the English would fight to the last Frenchman. Within days Marshal Pétain began collaboration negotiations, and a month later announced an armistice with Germany, establishing his puppet government at Vichy. At this point the Italian air force were flying daily sorties over the towns along the Riviera, and

---

[*] Later, although refusing to perform for the Nazis, Chevalier agreed to entertain French captives in exchange for the release of ten French POWs from the same camp where he was prisoner during the First World War. This story was misreported and he was accused of collaboration but cleared of all charges thanks to evidence given by Charles de Gaulle and Marlene Dietrich. He spent most of the war years in the unoccupied zone of France – anxious not to draw attention to himself because Nita was a Jew. He sheltered her family in his Paris apartment and after the war he and Nita married.

although no serious bombing occurred there was some straf-
ing, which alarmed the inhabitants. After France fell on 25
June, Italy and France signed a pact agreeing an Italian Zone
of Occupation, an area which was formally annexed to Italy
and under Italian economic control. Nice, however, lay within
the Demilitarised Zone, which was administered by Pétain.

Fanny and Jules, Maxine's servants, had talked with
Blossom after Maxine's death about what to do if France
fell, and now decided that this was the time to act. They
loaded up the car with most of the Churchill paintings, a few
Impressionist paintings and a portrait of Maxine, together
with the portable silver and items they knew Maxine had most
treasured, and retired to a cottage up in the hills where they
eked out the war years having hidden the items in their charge.

The Duke and Duchess of Windsor, meanwhile, were
advised not to remain in France, but the Duke wasted some
days by insisting on certain royal privileges, all of which were
refused. Eventually on 19 June – Wallis's birthday – they set
off for Spain with Ladbrooke driving their Buick limousine
and towing a small trailer containing their most prized pos-
sessions, in a convoy which included the American consul at
Nice and some other officials. It would be 1 August before
they were able to get berths on a ship crossing the Atlantic
from Lisbon.

As they drove through Cannes the Duchess saw in the
roadstead of the port two rusty old cargo ships that had been
sent to pick up the remaining British expats, among them
the Duke's Scots Guard piper and Somerset Maugham, who
had sold his converted fishing boat on which he had been
living. The two ships – old coalers out of Liverpool were all
that could be spared from the war effort – had been sent to

Cannes to evacuate any British subjects who wished to leave via Gibraltar. At the dock pandemonium reigned; cars were given away for packets of cigarettes and sundry food and supplies to take with them on the ill-equipped vessels. The passengers had a long and weary voyage in overcrowded ships not prepared for either the Bay of Biscay or the battles being waged in the Channel. It would be weeks before they arrived in England, and meanwhile Somerset Maugham had been reported 'missing, after the fall of France'. He arrived in good time to experience the effects of the Battle of Britain, when, after attacking RAF bases, the Luftwaffe began to concentrate its efforts on the major cities. From 7 September 1940 London alone was bombed on fifty-seven consecutive nights; more than forty thousand people were killed and a million homes destroyed.

Those who had been part of the pre-war Riviera set did not allow their partying to be interrupted by such inconveniences. Many headed for London, where those who could afford it – including Laura Corrigan, Duff and Diana Cooper, Emerald Cunard and many others who had graced the terrace at the Château de l'Horizon – had taken up residence at the great hotels on Park Lane. At the supposedly bomb-proof pre-stressed concrete Dorchester Hotel,* 'The Dorch', they met almost nightly, and the serious hostesses such as Emerald Cunard (who had made a circuitous journey from New York because she felt it her duty to be in England at this time) continued to entertain as before. Sybil Colefax remained in her Westminster home, but she held one of her 'ordinaries' – dinner – at the Dorchester every Thursday night for about thirty people. Guests knew that

---

* The hotel never received a direct hit so the claim was not put to the test.

they would receive a discreet bill for ten shillings and sixpence later in the week, but it was one way of continuing the old way of life: as Diana Cooper said, 'Living in this hotel, one need never wrestle with the blackout.'[3]

Among the regular guests was Randolph Churchill's young wife, Pam. With Randolph in the army, and baby Winston safely ensconced at Cherkley Court, Beaverbrook's country home, with his nanny, Pam found a job as a secretary in order to help pay off Randolph's gambling debts. This took rather a long time as she stayed at the Dorchester – actually not quite as lavish as it sounds since she occupied a room at roof level; because of the nightly bombings these rooms were unpopular and cost only six pounds a week. She lived fairly cheaply, eating at the nightly dinners and parties, and more often than not ended up sleeping in the basement 'dormitory' with nervous guests, until she started a romance with Averell Harriman* and moved into his suite.

On the Riviera there was no partying. Farmers had their crops annexed – a troop of soldiers would move in and harvest the crop for them, and cart it off to feed the army (although after 1942 it was mostly shipped to Germany). For the remainder of the war food was uppermost in most people's minds in Provence: queues outside shops began before daylight, winter and summer, but within minutes of opening everything was gone. Coffee was unobtainable, and an unpalatable, bitter-tasting alternative made from roasted acorns was introduced. Eggs, milk, butter and cheese were available only on the black market. A few staples got through from the north but nothing

---

* Averell Harriman was President Roosevelt's personal representative on shipping and supply questions. He inherited an immense fortune soon after graduating from Yale and was close friend of the Roosevelt family.

came in by sea to Vichy France because the British blockaded the coast with submarines. Everyone who could cultivated small handkerchief-sized plots for salad leaves, potatoes, a vine, a fruit tree, hidden away and too small to catch the eye of food inspectors, who would wait for apple and citrus trees to bear fruit before stripping them. Lucky were those who managed to keep a chicken or two in a secluded location.

The United States joined the war in December 1941, but throughout 1942 and 1943 all these existing problems worsened. Leather became unobtainable; worn-out shoes were replaced by clogs, or a wooden sole with a piece of fabric fastened across the top. Electricity and gas supplies were unreliable, more off than on, and running water was often a luxury. Frail and elderly people, or sick children, died of malnutrition. As the year dragged to an end the Allies invaded North Africa, in Operation Torch in November.

German and Italian troops then occupied Vichy France, but it was mainly the elite Italian mountain troops, the Bersaglieri, their black helmets decorated with knots of black cockerel feathers, who rode gaily into the Riviera resorts astride their motorcycles to occupy the coastal towns. Most big hotels housed troops, and luxury villas were allocated to senior officers. The Château de l'Horizon would, during the next two years, house officers from both the Italian and German armies, including some Gestapo chiefs. While Operation Torch was taking place the Italians began expanding their zone of occupation, with every intention of annexing the entire Alpes-Maritimes, plus Monaco and Corsica. This plan was never completed because in September 1943 Germany took over the Italian zones, and the four divisions of the Italian army of occupation surrendered to the Allies.

Unlike the experience of the occupying Germans in France, almost no resistance was offered to the Italians in Provence and they were accepted by residents as 'cheerful boys ... farm workers or fishermen'[4] who regarded their posting to the Riviera as *La dolce vita*. The worst part of the occupation was shortages of food, drink, transport and electricity, to which the occupying army had priority at the expense of local inhabitants, but there was another aspect to the Italian occupation. Mussolini was Fascist, but he was not anti-Semitic – indeed he had a Jewish mistress, Margherita Sarfatti – and Italian troops were ordered not to hand over Jews to the Germans, nor to assist with any deportation orders sending Jews to Germany. The Italian occupied zone thus became a refuge for Jews fleeing from Vichy France and elsewhere.

At the beginning of the war Prince Aly Khan, son of Maxine's friend the Aga, was serving as an officer in the French Foreign Legion in Syria. After France fell, the French in Syria felt that the British had betrayed them, having run away back to their island leaving them to face the Germans, and as a result they were in favour of surrendering to the Axis invaders in Syria. Aly duly resigned his commission, crossed into Lebanon and had to flee from his Beirut apartment across the rooftops, carrying his favourite saddle. He made his way to Egypt and at El Mansura, where he found an elite outfit of British yeomanry camped at an old Roman aqueduct, he simply walked in and asked to join them. Among the officers were some old friends including Lord Weymouth and the Earl of Cadogan (who had married Aly's sister-in-law), so he was welcomed and given a commission as second lieutenant. Shortly afterwards, because of his intimate knowledge of Mediterranean and Middle Eastern geography and his linguistic skills, he was posted to military intelligence in Cairo. Under the command of the eccentric Major Alfred D. Wintle,* he had an entertaining war, and was certainly useful to the Allied effort: he was engaged in special propaganda and intelligence, which included making broadcasts in many languages to Muslim audiences to rally them to the Allied cause, and setting up a network of Ismaili agents throughout the Middle East.

In August 1944, some weeks after D-Day, Allied forces landed in St Tropez and Aly, now a major attached as British liaison officer to the US Army, was in the vanguard of the liberation force. He regarded the Riviera as home and made sure he was among the first ashore on a landing craft in order to see how it had weathered the war years. As soon as he could get away he grabbed a jeep and made straight for Cannes – hardly recognisable despite the hot Riviera sunshine under its wartime adornment of tank traps, barbed wire and Nazi roadblocks. The Carlton Hotel was closed and the front entrance barred by an unoccupied German concrete lookout post, but Aly guessed (or possibly knew from intelligence received) that there was a skeleton staff in the hotel, probably hiding away until the fighting subsided, so he went to the side door and banged on it until someone answered. Once admitted, because he knew his way around, he made straight for the director's office, where he 'liberated' the Carlton. For the few staff crowding round Aly, he had personally liberated the Riviera. The director insisted

---

* Wintle lost an eye and a hand in the First World War, and spoke both French and German well enough to pass for a native of either country. He is now mostly known for a television biography, *The Last Englishman*, and a letter written by him to the Editor of *The Times* which read: 'Sir, I have just written you a long letter. On reading it over, I have thrown it into the waste paper basket. Hoping this will meet with your approval, I am, Sir, Your obedient Servant, AD Wintle'.

the Royal Suite should be got ready for him immediately, but Aly had some personal business to attend to. He wanted to see what had happened to his father's Villa Jean-Andrée on the Cap d'Antibes. Among those who had stayed behind in Cannes was Tommy Burke, the professional tennis player and an old friend of Aly's, and he was sent for and roped in to accompany Aly on his mission. Nobody knew whether they would encounter opposition for Aly was ahead of the Americans. They met no gunfire, and within five minutes were motoring along the empty coast road to Juan-les-Pins when they saw the bridge across the railway line which was the entrance to the Château de l'Horizon. Burke knew the villa as well as Aly, having often coached Maxine's guests there, so they decided to drive in and take a look.

It was deserted, the grounds neglected and overgrown, the house in need of painting, the bottom of the pool covered with dirty stagnant water and rubbish. Everywhere was full of weeds and huge coils of barbed wire lay about. They trod warily, suspecting (correctly) that it might have been mined. Peering through the locked windows, they could see that although the house needed attention it was undamaged. Next they drove on to Villa Jean-Andrée, which for many years had been the home of Aly's stepmother. In full battle-dress Aly was not at first recognised by Kitty, a friend of the Princess Andrée's, who came to the door at the top of the steps and shouted at them from a distance to go away. She had protected the villa from the Germans and Italians, she told them, and she wasn't going to hand it over to the Americans now. When she saw who it was she fell weeping into Aly's arms. He also checked out the villa that had once been his mother's, where she had had her sculpting studio and produced notable works exhibited under the name Yla (her son's name reversed). A quick tour of Antibes followed and he savoured the views from the hill and the unique peppery, dusty, herby scent of the air under the hot sun before he returned to his unit. His commanding officer in those first months in Provence as the Americans took over was Henry Cabot Lodge, Jr, who stated that Aly proved to be invaluable, winning over the suspicious locals with his native French and charming manner. Aly once said that he had never been happier than during the years 1941 to 1945.

Return of Peace

Prince Aly Khan was not the only old friend of Maxine's to visit Château de l'Horizon as the war came to an end. Air Chief Marshal Sir Arthur 'Bomber' Harris, who had twice visited the villa with Winston prior to 1939, looked in during March 1945 and found it intact except for a badly leaking roof which had damaged the decoration in most of the bedrooms.

He wrote to tell Winston that the villa had been occupied by 'the Boche', but according to Fanny they had taken little apart from a painting of the swimming pool by Winston, and some autographed volumes of *Marlborough* dedicated to Maxine. It was believed that these items had been sent direct to Hitler. In fact, several pictures were later found to be missing, including some full-length portraits of Maxine, too large to be moved by Fanny and Jules, that were never traced. As a parting gift the Germans had seeded the garden with landmines: Jules narrowly missed being blown up when he put his foot down just a few inches from one. The US Army, who were about to take over the area, cleared them and set a work party to empty the pool of rubble. Even so, 'It all looked somewhat sad,' Bomber Harris reported, adding news about the general situation in Antibes where the local people were 'terribly hungry'.[1]

Apart from the German occupation, the Château de l'Horizon had another wartime record. Barry Dierks worked with the French Resistance, and whenever he learned that the villa was unoccupied he used his own set of keys to gain entrance. It made a safe rendezvous and base for meetings, virtually under the noses of the Gestapo.

The villa, already looking a little better for the attentions of the Sixth Army and hard work by Fanny and Jules, was rented out in summer 1947 complete with the Churchill paintings. The tenant, who described herself as 'half Cherokee', Rosita Winston was the wife of Norman Winston (her second husband), who had made an estimated forty million dollars from mass housing. Rosita was keen to use some of those millions to capitalise on the villa's short but illustrious history to make her own reputation as a party-giver.

In a report about the post-war Riviera, *Life* magazine recounted how the willowy Rosita 'swept in' driving her custom-built black Packard Cabriole, 'wearing a simple cotton dress that cost $275 if it cost a dime', her mop of frizzy hair bound up in a flame-coloured scarf. After she proceeded to fling a good portion of her husband's millions around, Rosita quickly became a fixture on the social scene.

By the end of that summer, although the Château de l'Horizon was still looking somewhat the worse for wear, it was once again the place to be seen. Impoverished British and European noblemen – anyone with a title had an open

invitation – together with society divorcees who were temporarily between husbands, were once again able, according to
Life, to enjoy 'an adequate diet of caviar, Scottish grouse and
vintage champagne', while 'lounging against the soft cushions
of the terrace around the blue-green pool',[2] all thanks to 'the
Winston Plan'.* Lunch for twenty was inevitably followed
by dinner for thirty on seven days a week. Protests by over-
worked staff were settled with offers of increased pay, bonuses
and bottles of champagne, which were handed round to rehy-
drate the kitchen workers.

The food bill alone was 100,000 to 150,000 francs a
week[†] – literally a fortune to hard-pressed local people still
struggling to feed families with inadequate post-war rations
on 150 francs a week. The ever-present queues that straggled
down the streets outside the butchers' shops in Juan-les-Pins
and Antibes were testimony to the fact that the local population was suffering the same uncertainty, privations and
inconvenience as war-weary people all over Europe. The daily
bread allowance in Provence was 250 grams, and when this
very poor product was threatened with a reduction of 50
grams, hundreds of indignant housewives pushing babies in
pushchairs demonstrated, carrying home-made posters bearing slogans such as '*Amélioration de la qualité du pain*', and
'*Maintien de la ration de pain a 250gr!*'

For the rich though – mostly Americans in the post-war
years, along with a good sprinkling of Belgians and those
from neutral countries such as Switzerland, Sweden and
Argentina, who had profited in various ways – those who

---

* A joke at the expense of the much-publicised Marshall Plan, which would allocate
over twelve billion dollars to rebuild and modernise Western Europe.
† $1000 to $1500 (now $13,345–$20,020).

found their way back to this small sliver of opulence in the gigantic poorhouse that was Europe for a decade following the war, there was no hardship and nothing that could not be obtained on the black market. The Hôtel du Cap was fully booked for months ahead, and you needed to 'know someone' to get into the two most popular restaurants,* where the selection of hors d'oeuvres was greater than that at the Dorchester or Claridge's. The journalist Charles J.V. Murphy, writing a long article about the Riviera in 1947 for *Life* magazine, attended a party at the Casino in Cannes, where the orchestra played Cole Porter numbers in the moonlight and he was informed by a woman guest 'that there were at least two dozen Paris gowns on the dance terrace which had cost 100,000 to 150,000 francs each'. He wrote succinctly: 'Wealth never disappears. It only changes hands.'[3]

One thing he noticed particularly was the absence of British aristocracy. 'The most striking thing,' Murphy wrote, 'was the virtual extinction on this coast of the once-swarming British peer – a phenomenon so startling in scope as to recall the famous disappearance of the passenger pigeon.'[4] He heard one middle-aged habituée of Eden Roc asking in irritation, as she looked around the crowded tables, 'Who are these people? Where do they come from? I do not know a single one.' The reporter thought this was a bit rich since he had already spotted in the last forty-eight hours Greta Garbo, Doris Duke (once the richest girl in the world, and in Antibes on honeymoon with her third husband), the ice-skater and movie star Sonja Henie, Woolworth's heiress Barbara Hutton, Maurice Chevalier, Orson Welles and Eva Perón. Still, he understood

---

* The Bonne Auberge and Château Madrid.

what the woman meant: those who before the war were the *ancien régime* – the old rich families who owned the big villas behind Cannes and Antibes, or in Monte Carlo, who took suites in the Hôtel du Cap or the Carlton – were mostly missing. Only a few stalwarts such as Willie Maugham and the Windsors crept back to their villas to represent the old crowd and attempted to revive the villa life they had previously known. The new Riviera set – some felt – truly lived up to the old description of the Riviera, 'a sunny place for shady people'.

One former l'Horizon denizen who was not to be seen on the Riviera after the war was Doris Castlerosse. Following her divorce from Valentine, and Margot Flick Hoffman's – after a remarkably short marriage – from her husband Dick, Doris and Margot had based themselves at Doris's Palazzo Venier dei Leoni in Venice for a year, before going to California in 1938.

During his final trip to the United States before the war began, Randolph Churchill had met Doris in New York. By then she had 'broken up' with Margot and was at a loose end. Randolph thought she was not her usual high-spirited self, and some months later he mentioned this to his former adversary, Valentine Castlerosse. Valentine never stopped loving Doris: he couldn't live with her, nor could he live without her. Since they parted he had kept a scrapbook into which he pasted every press cutting which mentioned her.

By the time America entered the war at the end of 1941, Doris was at a low ebb, quite possibly suffering from mild depression. Her looks were fading and she was struggling financially; she had begun to pawn her best jewels in order to maintain her lifestyle. Early in 1942 Doris wrote to Valentine suggesting a rapprochement, and she subsequently received a cable from him, which led her to believe he would welcome her return. Berths on transatlantic crossings were severely restricted but with the help of influential friends in New York, one of whom was Franklin D. Roosevelt's trusted adviser Harry Hopkins, Doris was able to see the President, and it appears she persuaded him that a very senior member of the British government wished her to return to England – possibly she used the magic name of Winston Churchill, who had recently been staying at the White House, or perhaps it was Beaverbrook's name that was invoked. In any case, Doris was provided with a priority-passage document.

Valentine met the boat train at Waterloo station. It was *Private Lives* all over again. Doris was dressed in the glamorous clothes of America that were not available in Britain, and wearing perfume – a product almost unobtainable outside black-market suppliers. In the darkness of the station Valentine was thrilled, and in the initial rapture of their reunion it seemed that they might indeed be able to recapture some of the romance of the early days of their marriage. But it was too much to hope for. By the end of dinner at the Dorchester both knew there was no going back. He was put off by the changes in her appearance; ten years older than when they divorced, she was no longer the old carefree Doris, and it showed. Doris quickly realised she had lost her power over him. When they parted at midnight Valentine put an end to any possibility of a reunion when he told her that he was on the verge of marrying Enid Furness, once rich and now dubbed 'the penniless peeress' by the press.

When Doris crossed the Atlantic she had not been allowed

to bring any money or valuables with her, and after Valentine departed she took stock of her situation. She had hoped they might remarry but now, without the possibility of Valentine's financial support, she needed money to live. There was no question of raising any cash on the palazzo, for not only was it in occupied territory but after their break-up Margot had somehow tied up the deeds.* The following day Doris sent a telegram to New York enquiring about selling her jewellery, which she had pawned some time before her departure, and suggested an arrangement where she could get the cash for it through a London associate of the jeweller.

That evening as she walked along a hotel corridor she came face to face with an old acquaintance, an earl with whom she had once had a dalliance, who cut her dead but muttered aloud as they passed that she was a traitorous bitch. She was very upset about this incident, but worse was to come.

Her telegram to New York had been intercepted by the Censor's Office, and the next day Doris received a visit from two detectives, who pointed out to her that what she had done – effectively attempting to bring money into the country by subterfuge – was illegal, and under wartime legislation she could be arrested and jailed. She was very open with them about what she intended and what she had done, never dreaming that she had broken any laws, but after they left she panicked and telephoned friends, asking for a loan of five hundred pounds. Cash was in short supply in spring 1942, one of the darkest times of the war, but after she broke down sobbing one friend, a bookmaker, offered to lend her

---

* The property eventually reverted to Doris's estate and was sold by her heirs to Peggy Guggenheim in 1948.

two hundred pounds and send it the following morning by messenger.

When the messenger arrived at the Dorchester Doris did not answer her telephone or her door. Eventually the door was opened with a master key and Doris was found in bed, unconscious. There was an empty pill bottle on the side table. She was rushed to hospital and lived for a few days, with Valentine remaining at her bedside for most of the time. When she died he was distraught, blaming himself because he had refused to marry her. He went to stay with his biggest supporter; Beaverbrook thought that Doris was more likely to have been distressed by the visit of the detectives than by Valentine's rebuff, but felt unable to tell his friend about this because of wartime security laws. Valentine blamed himself for the rest of his life for Doris's suicide, after an inquest ruled she had died by her own hand from barbituric acid poisoning.

The loss of former habitués did not unduly concern the flood of new visitors to the Riviera who, having come through the dark war years into the sunshine of peace, seemed determined to live by the motto 'If you have money, why not enjoy it?' They had come to eat lotus. Movie stars and would-be starlets flocked to the South of France, and many such as Tyrone Power found their way onto the terrace at Château de l'Horizon. The constant partying at the villa became too much for Norman Winston. He packed up and left Rosita to her guests. Thereafter, he was to be found each day lunching alone at Eden Roc. 'It is not that I find it difficult to eat with 20 or 30 strangers,' he complained. 'And it is of no importance, probably, that I don't know who they are, or my wife hasn't the faintest idea who they are or how they got invited.

The trouble is that they all know each other so damn well.'[5]

Perhaps it was no surprise to find that Rosita had consulted a team of Riviera old-stagers regarding her guest lists: Elsa Maxwell, Sir Charles Mendl and 'Scrap' Schiaparelli were among her advisers, and they were some of those most frequently to be found, once again, at the Château de l'Horizon. But the greatest coup of the summer season was all Rosita's own work. When the US aircraft carrier *Leyte* dropped anchor in Golfe Juan, she smartly despatched a motor boat out to the ship, bearing invitations for the admiral and senior officers to a series of lunches and dinners to introduce them to local society. For the ten days of their stay every day was a gala and in the evenings the tropical white naval uniforms lent an air of distinction to the cosmopolitan gatherings on the pool terrace overlooking the moonlit sea. Rosita's reward was not only her increasing popularity, but access to an unlimited store of scarce American cigarettes, smooth white bread baked aboard the ship and American ice cream.

In turn, her American visitors were thrilled to be introduced to Prince Pierre of Monaco, who wore his jacket like a hussar's cape across his shoulders. He was not *the* Prince of Monaco, of course – he was formerly Count Pierre de Polignac – but had attained his title when he married Princess Charlotte, only daughter of the Prince of Monaco, in 1920. It was a very romantic union but after a dozen years the marriage ended unhappily and his father-in-law told Pierre in undiplomatic language that if he ever set foot in his principality again he would call out the Monegasque army to deal with him.

The handsome, slender and charming Pierre was not the only former prince to attend Rosita's parties – the Duke of

Windsor was seen one evening, although he was perhaps not treated with quite the same deference as in Maxine's day. Nor was Pierre the only scion of the de Polignac family haunting the Riviera. Princess Ghislaine, wife of Prince Edmond de Polignac, was a frequent guest and became a close friend of Rosita.

In the previous year Ghislaine, a long-legged, vivacious, blonde Parisienne, had met Duff Cooper, by now British ambassador to France, who was already involved with several mistresses.* This was clearly no obstacle to a new liaison, and Ghislaine was also involved elsewhere – with the Russian ambassador to France, in fact. After their first tryst Cooper had written about Ghislaine in his diary: 'She is a girl after my own heart, good company, a formidable appetite for pleasure and no nonsense about love. She is 26 – has had four children, feels that she has done her duty, and is now determined to enjoy herself.' One can sense him leering as he ends lasciviously, 'I have no doubt she will succeed in doing so. I shall do my best to help her.'⁶

Rosita took an instant liking to Ghislaine, who 'knew everyone', and invited her to travel home with the Winstons for Christmas and New Year and stay at their New York home. Rosita even paid for Ghislaine's first-class cabin on the transatlantic crossing and bought her a wardrobe of Dior clothes styled in the New Look, which earned much notice in society columns. Unfortunately, Mr Winston also took a liking to Ghislaine, and on New Year's Eve, when Rosita

---

* Among them the socialite Gloria Rubio Alatorre and Louise 'Loulou' Lévêque de Vilmorin, Countess Pálffy. Diana Cooper knew about her husband's serial affairs, and once when asked by her son if she minded she replied that she did, but that they were just the flowers while she was the tree.

returned home from the beauty shop where she had been preparing for a party, she found her husband and Ghislaine *in flagrante delicto*. The party went ahead as planned and Rosita regaled fellow guests with how she had pulled Ghislaine out of bed, kicked her out the door and told her to go back to France. Not surprisingly, the story got into the gossip columns with rumours that the Winstons were divorcing. Some days later Rosita found a note on her pillow which read 'Are we, or are we not, living together?' There was no divorce, but Rosita was quickly showered – according to Cecil Beaton – with 'a great block of stocks, a platinum mink cape and some emeralds'.[7]

At this point Maxine's nieces decided that they would never be able to regard the Château de l'Horizon as home – it had been Maxine's place and they felt it would be too uncomfortable for them to give orders in their formidable aunt's house. So when the Winstons' lease was up (the Ghislaine episode having ended their plans to buy) the villa was put up for auction. Before the auction could be held, however, it was bought in a private treaty sale by an agent operating through the Bank of England on behalf of anonymous bidder.

The price paid was sixty-five thousand pounds,* and the buyer was Prince Aly Khan.[8]

---

* Now £2.3 million, but houses of a similar size in that location fetch £10 million and more.

12

Prince Aly Khan

Château de l'Horizon was sold more or less as Maxine left it, discounting the wartime depredations. Before the sale Aly Khan, accompanied by his long-time chauffeur and bodyguard Emrys Williams, had gone looking for 'a cottage near the sea' and had looked over a number of suitable properties in what was then a buyer's market. They were shown over Château de l'Horizon by Maxine's former chauffeur, the blond-haired Jules, who on behalf of Maxine's nieces had looked after the villa during the war whenever possible, and ever since. 'He told us some amusing stories about the fabulous parties which had taken place at the château in the pre-war times [and] pointed out a rock,' Emrys Williams recalled, 'where he had . . . seen Winston Churchill at work . . . painting. It obviously gave him pleasure to talk about the past.'[1]

Although the property had been swept of landmines before Rosita Winston had rented it, nothing had been done to tidy the formerly pristine grounds. The rocky garden areas stretching along the coast on either side of the villa, which once had neat little winding paths beneath the umbrella pines, leading to secluded areas to sit on a rock and watch the sea in solitude, had become a haven for feral cats: dozens were living among the overgrown shrubs, weeds, detritus and litter left by a company of Polish soldiers who occupied l'Horizon for a few months after the Sixth Army moved out. The swimming pool had been cleaned, but was unused for a massive crack had appeared in it. The white marble in the hall had, inexplicably, been covered with brown paint by the Germans, and in many of the bedrooms the walls were flaking or peeling, and covered in mildew after rainwater had seeped through the damaged roof.

As Aly Khan toured the property and the problems revealed themselves Emrys Williams assumed that it would be rejected because of its poor condition, but strangely Prince Aly seemed unconcerned. Instead, he 'grew more and more excited', Hughes recalled, as his employer went from room to room. 'It's wonderful. Wonderful!' he said. 'I didn't realise how beautiful it was. I'm going to buy it ... Just think how marvellous my pictures will look in this house. The Matisse – the Murillos – the Dufy, and the Picassos. It's the perfect home for them ... I've made up my mind. I must have this place.' Emrys Williams, who could see only the amount of work needed, wrote that he could hardly believe his ears.[2] He was right to be wary – it would ultimately cost the Prince more than the purchase price to refurbish the villa.

As soon as the sale was finalised Aly and Williams began by removing most of Maxine's furniture. Helped by Jules and a few of Aly's friends who were shanghaied into a work party, the men scrubbed the hall with caustic soda to remove the brown paint from the marble. When they had cleaned everything to Aly's satisfaction a team of thirty Italians was hired to redecorate, and to repair all the walls and the roof. Step by step the villa began to come back to life. A set of 'everyday' crockery was made to Aly's own design at the Vallauris Ramie pottery (famous for Picasso's input). From the gardens at Maisons-Laffitte,* where his wife Princess Joan was living with their two sons,† a statue of Hercules was brought to Cannes and sited on a mount to the left of the drive so that it could be viewed to advantage against the clear Mediterranean sky. Furniture was acquired from all over Europe in a mad spending spree. With almost limitless funds – or at least limitless credit – Aly was intent on creating a perfect bachelor residence.

The Louis Quinze table which graced the dining room in Maxine's day was replaced with a 15ft slab of flawless polished Carrara marble set on gilded supports. The old English School paintings were auctioned and replaced with Aly's treasured collection of Impressionists. Most visitors who saw l'Horizon at this point described it as 'fabulous' and 'luxurious', but at least one regular guest thought that despite all the comfort it was rather 'a funny house, very big and like a hotel in that there is nothing lying about – no sign of an owner's mark on it'.[3]

*

---

* The seventeenth-century Château Maisons-Laffitte is located about ten miles northwest of Paris. It is also known for its racecourse, which is often compared with that of Newbury, England.

† Aly married the divorcee Joan Guinness (née the Hon Joan Yarde-Buller) in May 1936. The bride converted to Islam and took the name Tajuddawlah. The couple had two sons, Karim (now Aga Khan IV) and Amyn, but by 1947 had been living apart for several years.

Aly had seen little of his father during the war because the Aga Khan had moved to Switzerland in 1940 with his third wife, the Princess Andrée, and their son Sadruddin. It was a luxurious haven for them, of course; the Aga already owned a huge chalet in Gstaad and the couple spent winters at St Moritz, where he took half of one of the floors of the prestigious Palace Hotel. There was an apartment for himself, with quarters for his valet and male secretary, and another suite of rooms, known as the family apartment, for Andrée and six-year-old Sadruddin. Various additional rooms accommodated their entourage. The Aga never entered the family apartment, which was the equivalent of harem quarters: Andrée always came to him when they met. Sadruddin – known as Sadri – saw his father every morning for English conversation and to play games such as backgammon and chess. It is impossible not to notice how different Sadruddin's childhood was from that of Aly, with Sadruddin given so much attention by his father. In the summer, the Aga spent his afternoons playing golf and enjoying whatever social life he could find. It was not what he wanted – he enjoyed politics and hobnobbing with world leaders – but it was the best arrangement he could manage given the times.

Born in Karachi in the days of the British Raj to a family regarded as feudal Indian royalty, he had succeeded his father in 1885 at the age of eight to become the third Aga Khan and forty-eighth Imam. He was descended, in direct bloodline, from the Prophet Muhammad through the Prophet's daughter Fatima. This made him the world leader of the Nizari Ismailis, the second-largest branch of Shia Islam, a non-radical sect whose fifteen million followers in twenty-five countries believe that the Imam has the spirit of God within him and is therefore a divine personage.

His Persian mother ensured that he was educated as a prince, with a thorough knowledge of his oriental background augmented by a Western gloss obtained at Eton and Cambridge. Knighted by Queen Victoria, and given a lifetime pension from the Crown at the age of twenty, he thereafter travelled the world to meet and receive the homage of his followers, and to consult with world leaders on matters that affected Ismaili Muslims. His roots were Indian, and this is where the largest section of his followers lived, but there were also sizeable communities in Arabia, Africa and elsewhere. In 1906, in an attempt to improve the lot of Bengali Muslims who were the core of his followers, he founded, and headed as president, the All India Muslim League (which fostered fair relations between Hindus and Muslims and would eventually lead to the founding of Pakistan in 1947).

Notably, Ismailis contribute a tenth of their income to the Imam, whose role it is to oversee the welfare of his followers with personal guidance and financial assistance, and to arbitrate in matters of strife among them. In effect this equates to an income worth hundreds of millions of pounds a year which is at the Aga's own disposal. He had, however, no country or state to rule over – he was a prince without a kingdom, and from the end of the First World War until his death the Aga would unsuccessfully attempt to be made a Prince Regent for the British in one or other of the countries in which his followers resided, or else be given some territory to create a state for his people.

Friends on almost equal terms with many members of Queen Victoria's family, the Aga Khan was often a guest at royal events such as coronations, marriages, christenings and funerals; he possessed a Royal Household Badge, given to him by the Queen, to guarantee entrance to all such functions. He moved with aplomb among kings and princes, tsars and grand dukes, maharajas and emirs, viceroys, prime ministers and world spiritual leaders, and was so well thought of in political and royal circles that he was frequently consulted on matters concerning India by the Royal Family and successive governments. In 1934 he was made a member of the Privy Council, and Vice-President of the League of Nations (an organisation of which he would later become President). At a personal level he considered himself a British subject, and kept a permanent suite at the Ritz for those times each year when he needed to reside in London, on the grounds that it was less expensive than keeping a house and staff there.

The Aga Khan had enormous personal charm, and this – together with his personal leanings – enabled him to venture outside his royal milieu to mix with actresses and beautiful society women, racehorse trainers and jockeys, golfers and entertainers. He loved popular theatre, the ballet and the opera; he was obsessed with horse breeding and racing, and golf. He adored music and Impressionist art, and had as a younger man known such luminaries as Stravinsky, Puccini, Diaghilev, Nijinsky, Dame Nellie Melba, Sir Henry Irving, Ellen Terry, Forbie Forbes-Robertson, Edith Wharton and Marcel Proust – just a few names from a list too long to detail – and he could recount fascinating anecdotes about his encounters with all of them, making him a charming dining companion.

He had known Lord and Lady Randolph Churchill well, and he first met Winston at Poona in 1896 while the latter was serving in India with the 4th Hussars and had been introduced as a 'promising polo player' who had come to look at

the Aga's horses. In a subsequent encounter they had discussed
FitzGerald's translation of the *Rubáiyát of Omar Khayyam*
which Winston could recite from memory. The Aga was not
only impressed but taken aback, since Persian was his mother
tongue and he regarded Khayyam as only a minor Persian poet.
During their talk young Winston had remarked flippantly that
he admired the poet's philosophy that 'it doesn't greatly matter
what we do now – it'll all be the same in a thousand years'.
The Aga was scandalised. 'What you do now may be of little
account in a thousand years,' he told Winston, with what now
seems remarkable prescience. 'But certainly events a hundred
years hence will very much be the direct results of our present
deeds and misdeeds.'[4]

The Aga tried, genuinely, to live up to this concept,
investing much of his vast income from his followers into
an investment trust for helping Ismailis in need. He was a
pioneer in providing education and medical facilities, especially midwifery. He founded universities and attempted to
abolish the veil, which he insisted 'did not exist till long after
the Prophet's death and is no part of Islam. The part played
by Muslim women at Kardesiah and Yarmuk the two most
momentous battles of Islam next to Badr and Honein, and
their splendid nursing of the wounded after those battles, is
of itself a proof to any reasonable person that purdah, as now
understood, has never been conceived by the companions of
the Prophet. That we Muslims should saddle ourselves with
this excretion of Persian custom, borrowed by the Abbassides,
is due to that ignorance of early Islam which is one of the
most extraordinary of modern conditions.'[5]

In short, the Aga – fabulously rich, intelligent, supremely
well-connected, urbane and charming – occupied a unique

niche. Despite the fact that his devoted Ismaili followers regarded him as divine, he had a colourful personal life. His first marriage, which had been arranged by his mother, ended in an amicable divorce; his second marriage, for love, was to an Italian ballet dancer, Theresa. The Aga was attending the coronation of George V in London in 1911 when he heard that Theresa had given birth to his son and heir. In fact, she delivered two sons within a year but only one survived: Prince Aly Khan. Theresa died suddenly in 1926, aged only thirty-seven, of a blood clot following an operation. Three years later the Aga married his third wife, Andrée Carron, a French dressmaker he met in Paris and who thus became Her Highness the Begum Aga Khan. The couple had a house on Cap d'Antibes where the Begum spent most of her time, while the Aga continued his almost continuous world travels. This house made them neighbours to Maxine, and in 1933 when the Aga first visited the Château de l'Horizon he had just become the proud father of a second son, Sadruddin.

Correspondence at the India Office makes it clear that one of the reasons the Aga did not achieve his principal aim to be made a regent in one of the British protectorates in the Middle East was the behaviour of his son and heir, Prince Aly Khan, to whom officials at the India Office and the Foreign Office took exception. 'The young man has a doubtful reputation and was recently mixed up in a divorce case of a somewhat sensational kind,'[6] wrote one.

The Aga did not return immediately to the Côte d'Azur when the war ended, but Princess Andrée – as she always preferred to be known – did, and she lived quietly as before in Villa Jean-Andrée with Sadruddin. She had the same circle of mostly women friends but people could not help asking the question, where is the Aga? Initially it was not known that the Aga and Andrée had parted. She had expressed shock when her husband announced in 1943 that he wanted a divorce so that he could marry his social secretary Yvette Labrousse. The sixty-six-year-old Aga had always had mistresses, that was the norm for him,* and Andrée accepted it; they lived separate and complaisant lives connected mainly by their son. But tall, leggy Mademoiselle Labrousse – thirty years younger than the Aga and ten years younger than Andrée – was somehow different.

Born near Marseilles, the daughter of a tram driver and a seamstress, Yvette grew up in Lyon and was apprenticed to a dressmaker there before she became a beauty queen as Miss Lyon and ultimately Miss France, which brought her many rich admirers. The Aga met Yvette in the mid-Thirties in Cairo, where she was living as the mistress of a wealthy Egyptian, and he became besotted with her. Soon after he left for France she followed him. There is a well-told story that soon after her arrival in France the Aga visited Yvette, who was staying with her mother. He brought with him a small attaché case which he placed on the table and opened to reveal that it was packed with large-denomination notes totalling a million francs. He told her that it was hers whether or not she became his mistress, but that if she came to him there would be lots more to follow.

Andrée believed that Yvette had strengthened her hold over the Aga when she expressed a desire to convert to Islam. She

---

* Although the Aga was, under Islamic law, allowed four wives, he subscribed to monogamy. However, Islam also allows 'temporary marriages', a convenient arrangement to cover mistresses.

heard this when the Aga began to build Yvette a sumptuous villa, romantically called Yakymour,* high on the sun-baked hills above Cannes, near the small village of Le Cannet. Yvette had helped to design and furnish this villa in Californie, although it was unfinished when it had to be abandoned to its wartime fate. It was not too unusual for the Aga to build houses for his favourite mistresses, so probably forty-five-year-old Andrée was not overly concerned about Yakymour, even though it was virtually on her doorstep, some ten kilometres away. Living in luxury at Antibes, Andrée had her own lifestyle and friends, and often made the top three in lists of the world's best-dressed woman; she had long ago adopted a complaisant attitude to the Aga's other women and it was even rumoured that she had a discreet relationship or two herself.

The uncontested divorce was granted at Christmas 1943 on the quaint grounds of 'mutual dislike and diversity of characters' and custody of Sadruddin was awarded to his father, although the boy was at boarding school in Switzerland and for practical purposes invariably stayed with his mother at Antibes during post-war school holidays. The couple agreed on a generous settlement, to be effected when the Aga regained access to his money and properties, and it was also agreed that after the war Andrée would have the family house at Aix-les-Bains, an apartment in Paris and the Villa Jean-Andrée, as well as a suitable income for her position.

Until the divorce Yvette lived quietly in her own apartment in Geneva, and the Aga travelled regularly by train to be with her. Although he missed terribly his old annual routine of

---

* His pet name for Yvette was Yaky, and he combined this with the last four letters of the French word for love (*amour*) to come up with Yakymour, by which name it is still known. The villa is still in the family of the present Aga Khan.

spring in Paris and the Riviera, summers in England doing the season and winters in India, he still had golf and horses, his closeness to Sadruddin and the diversion of Yvette. So the war years were not too difficult for the Aga, even though in his memoirs he remembered them as the unhappiest time of his life. After waiting ten months for the sake of appearances, he married the statuesque Yvette in Vevey, near Lausanne, on 9 October 1944.

Aly Khan had met his new stepmother briefly before the war and the two had instantly taken a deep dislike to each other, so he decided he would simply ignore her. The news of the marriage depressed him for he suspected it would make his relationship with his father even more remote than it already was. But then, by chance, just as the war was coming to an end and German surrender was inevitable, something occurred that would create a new bond between the two men and restore some of the Aga's respect for his son.

In the spring of 1945, when almost everyone else was anticipating the end of the conflict with relief, Aly realised that the end of the war would leave him rudderless. His marriage had effectively ended; Joan blamed his womanising, and undoubtedly that contributed, but the truth was they had grown apart. The war years had been hard, and dangerous at times, but Aly had found them deeply fulfilling. For the first time in his life he had been accepted for himself, not as the son of his famous father, but for what he was and what he could offer; he had forged some deep friendships and earned the respect of men he admired.

During the ten months leading up to the end of the war Aly was based at the Sixth Army's headquarters at Heidelberg, and by spring 1945 he was seriously considering volunteering for further service with the American army in the Far East, along with Henry Cabot Lodge, Jr. Then an unexpected opportunity to help his father came along; one which also promised the sort of adventure Aly enjoyed.

Besides his impeccable royal and noble connections, the Aga Khan was chiefly known in England and France for his interest in horses. He was a leading racehorse owner and by the end of his life had achieved an enviable record of five Derby winners and sixteen Classic winners. He was also the British flat racing champion owner thirteen times. In 1926 he had begun a tradition by presenting the Aga Khan Trophy to the winners of the premier international team show-jumping competition at the Royal Dublin Horse Show.* In the Thirties the Aga's stables in Newmarket, England, the Curragh in Ireland and Normandy in France were among the best in the world. It had been a huge tragedy to him when in 1940 more than a hundred of his beautiful horses, many of them from irreplaceable bloodstock lines, were looted from the Normandy yard as spoils of war and sent to the German national stud at Altefeld in Bavaria.

From his Swiss haven, the Aga had continued whenever possible buying, selling and even running his horses in Britain by telephone, through his racing managers. Towards the end of the war he issued a statement that all of his win-nings would be donated to the Indian Army Fund.† This

---

* Still going strong, this cup is hotly contested each year. Any team winning for three successive years wins the magnificent trophy outright and a new trophy is presented thereafter. In its ninety-odd year history, the Aga Khan Trophy has been won outright five times: by the Swiss in 1930, Ireland in 1937 and 1979, and Great Britain in 1953 and 1975. The present trophy is the sixth one.

† More than forty thousand pounds was donated – not equal to his pre-war winnings, but the prize money was much smaller for wartime racing.

may have been, at least in part, a move to counteract adverse publicity earlier in the war that the Aga had been invited to Paris with the Begum and had dined there with Hitler and Nazi leaders. It was entirely fictitious – the Aga had never left Switzerland. However, he did go to see Hitler and his chiefs in August 1939, in a well-meant but naive attempt to try to prevent war, and furthermore his Parisian house *was* a venue for meetings of highly placed Nazis, on account of it having been occupied by the Germans. This sort of gossip had a habit of clinging, even when untrue, and he was anxious to revert to being 'the good old Aga', favourite of British racing crowds.

Having been brought up with horses and racing, Aly Khan had a marvellous eye for a horse, was a naturally gifted rider and a successful amateur jockey. That spring of 1945 he wangled a precious forty-eight-hour leave in order to fly to Newmarket* to watch Dante win the first post-war Derby at odds of 100/30.

Like many dedicated horse-lovers Aly could recognise individual horses on sight, much as he might recognise a person, and it was apparently by sheer chance that he was out with a patrol which arrived at Berchtesgaden shortly before VE Day. As they drove through mountain pastures Aly saw a group of thoroughbreds in a field and stopped his jeep to take a look. To his shock he recognised some of them, so he left his vehicle to walk round the adjoining fields, where he was able to identify twenty mares that he knew belonged to his father. Making his way to the stable yard nearby he found a favourite stallion. It was coincidence that he had come across them,

---

* The Derby has been run at Epsom in all years except during the world wars. From 1915 to 1918 and from 1940 to 1945 the Derby was run at Newmarket Heath.

and he quickly realised that it was important to get them back to France before all German assets were parcelled out, appropriated, or simply disappeared after the official surrender.

While he was still looking round a man came out of the feed store with his hands in the air. It was the groom responsible and it turned out to be Robert Muller, who had been assistant manager at the Aga's Deauville yard in 1939. Muller had been captured while serving with the French army and transported to a prison camp in Poland. His record came to the notice of Ribbentrop, who had Muller brought to Altefeld and reunited with his former charges. Muller's importance in the care of these valuable horses earned him no favours, however, and he was quite badly treated, but he had his revenge: he managed to steal a gun and hide it, and just before Aly's arrival, when he learned that the Americans were a few miles from the town, he shot six German soldiers based at the stud because he believed they intended to kill his horses before the Allies could liberate them.

Muller told Aly he knew where most of the other stolen horses were too, and he helped identify the most valuable mares in the fields. Muller's family home was at Metz, in northeastern France, some twenty-six miles from the German border. On the spot the two men cobbled together a plan whereby Aly would arrange for Muller to return home and locate a suitable stable yard where the horses could be held safely under guard for a short time pending their return to Normandy, then return to help Aly with their transportation.

Meanwhile, Aly returned to base and confided in his commanding officer. He was able to arrange the necessary paperwork for Muller's travel permit, as well as a leave of absence for himself and Major Gordon Grand, an officer friend with whom he sometimes rode and who agreed to assist him. Together they put together some spurious paperwork stating that Lieutenant-Colonel Prince Aly Khan was responsible for transporting General Eisenhower's charger back to France. It was signed with one genuine signature and one forged one.

Aly then hitched a lift on a military flight to Geneva, where he met his father for the first time since 1939 and was able to tell him about the remarkable discovery and events of the last two days. Together they had various yards in France alerted to receive the rescued horses. Aly knew that moving irreplaceable horses which effectively belonged to the occupiers as war loot around a country ravaged by war, where gasoline was like gold dust and where there were Allied road blocks every few miles, would be no easy task. He also knew that what he proposed was illegal, and was even more difficult because of the speed with which it had to be effected. Apart from his CO, who lent his informal support to the venture, the Aga and the few who physically assisted Aly in the operation, no one else knew of this personal mission to rescue horses which were worth then close on a million dollars. But it seemed to Aly that the risks were justified.

He somehow acquired a scruffy two-horse trailer that he could tow with his US Army jeep. They loaded up the stallion and one of the most valuable mares and Aly set off alone for Normandy, a distance of over five hundred miles. Muller stayed to guard and care for the rest of the horses until Aly's return, when Muller immediately set off for Metz where he stayed to receive the succession of horses that Aly and Major Grand delivered to him. Grand helped with the feeding, catching and loading in a series of exhausting back-to-back

250-mile trips in a series of twenty-hour days, until Muller had two dozen precious horses in his possession. He then personally escorted them through France to the Normandy stud in more comfortable vehicles and with the help of the Aga's staff. Needless to say, Muller stayed with the Aga for the remainder of his career.

Aly went on searching and rescuing for some time after that: the sense of adventure and slight danger in the missions appealed to him. His energy was inexhaustible and he would drive all day and night to get the horses back to Metz, or – occasionally – directly to Normandy.

Their love of horses was something that the Aga and his son shared, and the Aga was absolutely overjoyed to recover irreplaceable horses, whom he had believed lost to him. When in August 1945 Aly was demobbed, he was rewarded by becoming the Aga's legal partner in the horse-racing business and the chairman of the farms, studs, stables and horses. It was a significant enterprise worth about five million dollars of which some three million dollars was the value of the horses, and the remainder included four stud farms in France, and seven in Ireland. Wartime advances in technology had made transatlantic air travel almost safe enough to be commercial, albeit for the very few, and for the next few years Aly flew constantly between Europe and the United States buying and selling bloodstock and nominations while the Aga, who had almost forty years' experience of racing (though always claiming it was for him 'merely a hobby'), made all the decisions about breeding.

It was almost impossible to go to the cinema in the late Forties without seeing on Pathé Pictorial newsreels a clip of the famous Prince Aly Khan, usually described by the narrator as 'the millionaire playboy', driving expensive sports cars such as Bentleys, Lagondas and Delahayes; winning horse races (he won dozens of races riding as a 'gentleman jockey'); boarding his own aeroplane, the twin-engined De Havilland Dove, named *Avenger*; relaxing on a sunny beach; having drinks with a famous beauty of the day; or dressed in romantic Arab clothes, riding in the desert. He was also termed a Casanova, and he did not bother to deny the description, loving all that life had to offer and draining the dregs from every minute.

He was not only a playboy, though. He took seriously his role as the heir apparent of the Ismaili faith, travelling for three months of the year to visit followers scattered throughout Asia, Africa and South America. He was often mobbed, and worshipped as a living deity, and he told friends that he found this so exhausting that he trained for his tours as if he were about to ride in an important race. Having his own aeroplane made an otherwise impossible schedule feasible, and though he had obtained his private pilot's licence in 1937 he did not have a twin-engine rating, nor have the time to learn and practise good instrument flying, so he employed John Lancaster, a highly qualified former RAF squadron leader, to manage and fly the *Avenger*.

Lancaster recalled how on their visits to the village of Salamiyah, the largest Ismaili community in Syria, their car would be swarmed over by young men who wanted to kiss their leader's hands and feet.[7] Aly was in his element as he made speeches, inspected schools and mosques, headed meetings of village elders, resolved problems, attended naming ceremonies of babies and marriages. At night they mounted sure-footed desert horses (which Aly had introduced to Salamiyah a few years earlier) for a ten-mile ride to their desert camp, tribesmen carrying swinging lanterns and firing muskets that had been used in the Crimea – the flashes lit their way across the stony steppes and the reports echoed from the hillsides. As they passed through hamlets the villagers would be waiting for God to pass, and when he did there would be much shouting and firing of guns, along with clapping and high-pitched ululation from the women. Aly would return to Salamiyah many times, and eventually chose to be buried there.

Aly also took his partnership with his father in the racing business very seriously, and within three years the combination of his buying and selling and the Aga's canny breeding policy proved unbeatable. The Aga's horses (he always led the winners in) won a number of Class One races including the Irish Oaks and – the icing on the cake – the 1948 Derby. It was the Aga's fourth Derby victory and the French-trained My Love, which started outsider at 100/9, won by a length and a half over the British favourite. The occasion was only marred for Aly by the presence of the hated Yvette, who towered over both him and his father.

That evening the Aga and Begum were in Paris at a celebration dinner party thrown by Daisy Fellowes. Nancy Mitford was there too and she wrote of the event in Daisy's dining room, which was 'the prettiest modern room you ever saw, like a pink and white sugar sweet'. She met the Aga and his 'lovely new Begum' and was impressed by Yvette's 'wonderful jewels'. She found the Aga 'extraordinary just as one had always heard', and he told Nancy, 'Your grandfather was a great friend of mine.' But when she looked at the dignified and bejewelled Begum Nancy could not dismiss from her mind what her lover, Gaston Palewski, had told her: 'the Aga does the most dreadful things to the Begum'.[8]

Two years earlier, in March 1946, a feature on Pathé Pictorial had stunned glamour-starved cinema audiences with a spectacle which established the Aga Khan in the public consciousness as a truly exotic personality. He was just short of his seventieth birthday and already famous for, in 1937, on the fiftieth anniversary of his accession, having been publicly weighed and presented with his (not inconsiderable) weight in gold by his adoring followers. Now it was his sixtieth anniversary as leader, and he was to be given his weight in diamonds at Bombay's Brabourne Stadium before an audience of over a hundred thousand Ismailis. Unfortunately for British cinema-goers, the newsreel was in black and white, so they missed the spectacle of thousands of multi-coloured silk saris and brightly coloured umbrellas (providing shelter from the midday sun), the vibrancy of national costumes and uniforms of the Aga's followers from all over the world: Arabia, East Africa, various islands in the Indian Ocean, and Asia.

The Aga and Aly were gorgeously dressed as rajahs in silk jackets and turbans but it was the beautiful Begum Yvette who caught all eyes, in a white sari glittering with diamonds which had been liberally sewn all over it. The Aga weighed in at more than 234 pounds and the value of the diamonds in the counterweight was said to be in excess of three million dollars. One stone alone was worth one hundred thousand dollars. There was inevitable press criticism of such an overt display of wealth, but few journalists bothered to report that once the celebration was over the diamonds were returned to a London diamond merchant and most of the monetary equivalent was placed into a well-managed trust for education, housing, general charity and a cooperative organisation which provided, among other things, loans at low interest rates to Ismaili businessmen. In the UK, post-war rationing was stricter than during the fighting, and even for those who had managed to emerge from the war with some money there was very little to buy, except through the black market. The exotic spectacle of excess, colour and noise and the sensational wealth of the Aga Khan awed its cinema audience.

Although Aly was considered to be the heir to all this pomp and riches, the title lay not in primogeniture but his father's gift, and despite their successful cooperation in the racing business the Aga deplored his son's way of life. It was not so much the women (he had probably bedded as many himself, but was extremely discreet about it), or the fast cars, or the ostentatious use of money – it was the fact that he could hardly open a paper or go to the movies without his son's flamboyant antics being aired, and for the most part he hated the type of woman that Aly seemed drawn to. He had never been close to Aly; in fact, he had been much closer to Aly's wife Joan and the couple's two boys, Karim and Amyn (known to their contemporaries as 'K' and 'A'). Now, although he and the Begum lived at Yakymour, a mere twenty minutes' drive from the Château de l'Horizon, he still saw little of Aly, or Joan and the boys who were living in Paris.

The Aga openly disapproved of Aly's indiscreet behaviour which he felt did not befit a religious leader, but there is also good reason to believe that the Begum, who disliked Aly as much as he disliked her, missed no opportunity to drip poison into her husband's ear. One of her attributes was her well-known ability to make the Aga laugh, but, as he told a friend, she was also the only person who could make him cry. (This, it was said, was after she placed him on a strict diet and restricted his champagne intake.)

The Aga had no complaint about one woman friend of Aly's. Pamela Churchill became such a frequent house-guest at Château de l'Horizon (as well as Aly's house near Paris) in the late Forties that it was widely rumoured she had become its chatelaine. Having parted from Randolph, she had enjoyed a wartime romance with Averell Harriman (whom she met at one of Emerald Cunard's parties at the Dorchester) and a deeper five-year relationship with the acclaimed radio journalist Ed Murrow, to whom Harriman had introduced her. Both men were married, and though Murrow had asked her to marry him he later returned to his wife. Pam had been an immature nineteen-year-old when she married Randolph but her two grown-up relationships, plus a successful stint as *éminence grise* at the Churchill Club in Westminster,* had witnessed her metamorphosis into a sexually aware young woman, confident in her beauty and her power over men. Her young son, 'little Winston', was well cared for by a nanny, and it would not be unfair to say that in the matter of their son's divorce, Winston and Clementine's sympathies lay with Pamela.

Perhaps because she knew everyone in society and in politics – she was a frequent guest at Chartwell, and beloved of the Churchills – and was so adept at persuading men to tell

---

* A wartime club for visiting officers in London, which Pam had hosted for several years.

her news, gossip and even secrets, Beaverbrook added Pamela to the staff of 'Londoner's Diary' on the *Evening Standard*, for which she received a generous salary.

Pam met Aly Khan when, following Royal Ascot in 1947, she and her then best girl friend, Kathleen 'Kick' Kennedy (the sister of Jack and Bobby and the widow of the Marquess of Hartington, heir to Chatsworth and the Duke of Devonshire),* went on with a circle of friends to the races in Paris. Three weeks earlier Aly had acquired a chestnut colt which he named Avenger II, and to everyone's surprise the 33/1 outsider obliged by romping home in spectacular style to win the prestigious Grand Prix de Paris at Longchamp.† Aly then hosted the first of what would become a sensational annual society event, his famous summer ball at a prestigious restaurant in the Bois de Boulogne. The sea of floral decorations and massed balloons in his racing colours of green and red‡ filled the room with colour and scent. Each of the invited guests received a favour – for the women a trifle such as the new perfume, Yla, that he had financed, or an Hermès silk scarf featuring horses; for the men Cuban cigars or silver cigar cutters. Magnums of pink champagne flowed like waterfalls, and several orchestras ensured there were no breaks in the entertainment and dancing.

When she danced with Aly at his first summer ball, Pamela received the full force of his dynamism; after all, the daughter-in-law of the most famous man in the world was a

---

* William 'Billy' Cavendish, Marquess of Hartington, had been killed in military action in September 1944.
† Ridden by English jockey Charlie Smirke, who was retained by the Aga Khan.
‡ A green jersey and cap, with a red sash. It was probably no coincidence that they are also the colours of the Ismaili flag: that is a red diagonal stripe on a green background with the Ismaili coronet in the top right-hand corner.

good connection for him. She agreed to meet Aly for dinner in London the following week. She told Kick about it later and was warned off in no uncertain terms: Aly Khan was seriously bad news, a womaniser of the most blatant type and someone to steer well clear of. Pamela ignored Kick's advice; if anything, the warning acted as a spur to her interest, and during the next weeks she flew back and forth between London and Paris with Aly in *Avenger* for a series of intimate dinners. The attraction was mutual – he was rich, handsome, dangerous and fun. She was beautiful, well-connected, loved for him to drive fast and, having hunted all her life, was as good a rider as he was. It wasn't long before he invited her to come and stay at the Château de l'Horizon.

Fair, with fine translucent skin, red-haired Pamela received an almost literal baptism of fire at the villa. Unused to the Mediterranean sun (it was her first visit) she did not realise its power. On the first day she fell asleep on a sun lounger after lunch and was burned badly enough to require hospital attention. This might have spoiled the holiday, but Aly was so kind and solicitous while she was recovering that he earned her gratitude.

Aly's biographers all state that as a teenager he was sent to Cairo to be taught *Imsák* by a Persian *hakim* and that as a result he was famed for turning his sexual technique into an art form. The Aga Khan himself had supposedly undergone the same teaching, which apparently enabled a man to restrain his sexual climax almost indefinitely in order to ensure the total satisfaction of his partner. The practice was said to have origi- nated in India, land of the *Kama Sutra*, and was also supposed to have been mentioned by Richard F. Burton in the infamous 'Terminal Essay' to his acclaimed translation from the original of *The Arabian Nights*, and one or other of the various sex manuals he translated.* Pamela's two biographers claim that she was captivated by this ability of Aly's to prolong love-making.

Although far from being the only woman in Aly's life, during the winter of 1947–8 Pam was the one that visitors were most likely to find in residence at the Château de l'Horizon. Kick and her fiancé, Peter Fitzwilliam,† were among those invited to stay at the villa over the Whitsun weekend in May 1948. Kick had recently flown to America to tell her parents of her wish to remarry. On her return to London on 12 May she lunched with Pamela to tell her what had happened. She said the family talks had not gone well; the biggest problem for Kick's parents was that Peter was not only a Protestant, but that in fact he was still married (his wife was an incurable alcoholic). Her mother had threatened to disown her if she married Peter, but Joseph P. Kennedy had quietly taken Kick outside and offered to go to the Vatican and try to arrange a Papal dispensation. Kick and Peter were to fly to Paris that afternoon to meet her father, before dining with Max and Jane Aitken‡ in the evening. They would then fly down to Cannes the following morning. 'Come down with us,' Kick suggested. Peter had chartered a De Havilland Dove, almost identical to Aly's *Avenger*.§

It was a tempting offer but Pamela dithered. She had a

---

* I have a number of Arab friends, none of whom appear to have any knowledge of this so-called practice, and nor – as a Burton biographer – do I particularly recall it in Sir Richard Burton's writings.
† 8th Earl Fitzwilliam (1910–48). His family seat Wentworth Woodhouse, near Rotherham in South Yorkshire, is possibly the most palatial stately home in England at twice the size of Buckingham Palace.
‡ Son and daughter-in-law of Lord Beaverbrook.
§ The aircraft G-AJOU was chartered from Skyways at Croydon and had a pilot and a navigator. However, Peter Fitzwilliam was himself a pilot and Debo Devonshire believed he might have been at the controls when the crash occurred. All occupants were killed.

number of commitments that would have to be broken, had already arranged her transport to leave for Cannes in a few days, and she hadn't even begun packing. All these things considered, she decided not to join them, but she drove Kick to Croydon airport and watched as the Dove took off. On the evening of the following day she heard that they had flown into the side of a mountain in a violent thunderstorm near the town of Privas in the Rhône Valley, some five hundred kilometres south of Paris. They were both killed instantly.

No members of the Kennedy family attended the funeral at Chatsworth, but Pamela joined the grieving Devonshires – who had really loved their former daughter-in-law – and they erected a headstone for Kick which read *Joy she gave, Joy she had found*. Had their eldest son not been killed in the war, Kick would have been the next Duchess of Devonshire.

A week later, deeply affected by the sudden death of her friend, Pamela collected little Winston from school and they were flown to Cannes by John Lancaster in the *Avenger*. Pam was to stay at l'Horizon for most of the summer and the villa was filled to capacity with Aly's friends, including a polo team that he had formed and was sponsoring, a number of beautiful women who came and went, and the usual Riviera society crowd who came for lunches and dinners or an overnight stay. Pam and Aly had become friends as well as lovers by now; they were not in love per se, but had a happy and uncomplicated 'open' relationship that suited them both. Pam enjoyed acting as unofficial hostess for Aly and excelled at running a grand house, which was without any curbs on expenditure for all bills were sent to the Aga. She was not especially devastated when it became obvious that a new woman had come into Aly's life. A woman who would change everything.

13

Rita Hayworth

Elsa Maxwell had met Aly Khan for the first time a year earlier, in New York, and was especially interested in him now because she knew that he had recently purchased the Château de l'Horizon and was living there. Maxwell had spent the war years in the United States, but as soon as she could get a passage across the Atlantic she returned to France and her house on the Riviera. She owned a pretty three-bedroom Provençal farmhouse at Auribeau, midway between Cannes and Grasse, which she and her companion Dorothy 'Dickie' Fellowes-Gordon had purchased in 1933 and renovated. They had employed a gardener to grow all their produce and it was here that Elsa repaid her entertaining obligations. The house was ten kilometres from Cannes and tiny, set in a hollow and surrounded by tall trees which made it dark inside, but many famous visitors were happy to drive from the coast to an invitation given by the supreme party-thrower of the age. She found the house had been looted during the war, but this was a mere irritation to the indefatigable Elsa, who was content that it had survived and soon had it repaired and repainted. She noted a sense of demoralisation of the local people added to shame over the Vichy collaboration, but she refused to allow this to affect her plans to carry on partying.

Within days of her arrival Elsa received an invitation from the Windsors to dine and stay at La Croë, following which she was a frequent guest there. It seems an unlikely friendship, but the Duke and Elsa both enjoyed playing and singing for fellow diners after dinner – popular songs such as numbers from musicals and jazz numbers – and they were good performers, despite neither having a good singing voice. Elsa had the edge in piano-playing ability, but the Duke undeniably won the day – after all, how often was one serenaded by a former king?

At home, whenever possible Elsa entertained on the terrace of her garden, where a huge millstone served as the table and the waterfall, for which the house was named, provided a soothing background. One surviving photograph of a typical al fresco lunch includes guests Tyrone Power, Daryl Zanuck, Jack Warner, the Duke and Duchess of Windsor and Clark Gable, some looking distinctly awkward about where to put their knees, which would not fit under the millstone table.

Not for nothing was she known as Elsa 'Let's-Have-a-Party' Maxwell in the press, and although luxuries were still scarce there was no shortage of commissions for Elsa to organise large, flamboyant events. In one of her many autobiographical books she explained how on 3 July 1948 she was involved in the preparations for an Independence Day party for Admiral Sherman at the glamorous art deco Palm Beach Casino in

Cannes. She had been given *carte blanche* for the guest list, and as she believed that this was half the success of any party she set about gathering a rich mixture of Riviera names.

In a memoir she recalled that she contacted Aly Khan to add some sparkle to the guest list, and knowing the Prince's penchant for beautiful women she set her sights on another potential guest to partner him. Rita Hayworth was at that time regarded as one of the most beautiful and famous women in the world, mentioned in the same context as Vivien Leigh and Elizabeth Taylor, and she happened to be in Antibes while waiting for her divorce from Orson Welles to be made final. It was not Rita's first visit to the Riviera: she had been at the first post-war Cannes Film Festival in 1946 and had loved the atmosphere and climate. This time she was convalescing from minor surgery following a botched abortion in Paris, and was staying on the Riviera to recover her health, accompanied by her secretary/companion Shifra Haran.*

Known the world over as the Love Goddess since *Life Magazine* in November 1947 featured her as its cover girl and described her repeatedly in those terms following her award-winning depiction of a smouldering *femme fatale* in the smash-hit movie *Gilda*, Rita was distinctly unenthusiastic at the invitation delivered in person by Elsa. Film posters ('*There never was a woman like Gilda . . .*') served to emphasise a racy reputation – but in fact Rita was nothing like the characters she played. Crowds frightened her; she preferred a quiet life. She was depressed because she had not wanted the divorce

---

* Shifra Haran had formerly been Orson Welles's secretary and transferred to Rita Hayworth when the couple parted. She is quoted extensively in biographies of the couple.

from Orson, and was still in love with him, but he had grown away from her. She was miserably sure it was because she was not intelligent enough for him, saying self-deprecatingly, 'Men go to bed with Gilda and wake up with . . . me!' They had been known as 'beauty and the brain' in Hollywood, but when Orson had an affair with Marilyn Monroe and Rita retaliated with a romance with the recently widowed David Niven their marriage was over.

Elsa recalled that when she visited the Hôtel du Cap on that morning of 3 July 1948, she found the star in the doldrums and tried to chivvy her along. Rita initially declined the invitation to the party at the Casino, protesting that she had come away in a hurry and had nothing appropriate to wear for such a function, but she was no match for Elsa, who gave her the address of a good dress shop in Cannes and 'talked her into it' (bullied might be more accurate), suggesting that Rita buy something really spectacular, preferably white. 'Arrive late and really make an entrance,' she instructed. 'It'll be good for your morale.'

Elsa recalled that she was speaking to Aly when Rita obediently arrived at the party half an hour after everyone else. Wearing an exquisite off-one-shoulder white dress, she caused a sensation and looked, Elsa wrote, 'more beautiful than the law should allow'.[1] She also noted how Aly stiffened like a pointer suddenly scenting a quarry as he exclaimed, 'My God, who is that?'

According to his chauffeur, Aly Khan was already addicted to Rita Hayworth movies. In Cairo in 1941 he had notably sat through three back-to-back performances of *Blood and Sand*. More recently he had seen a private screening of *Gilda*. In London he had been to see *Cover Girl* and *You Were Never*

Lovelier (in which she partnered Fred Astaire and demonstrated that she was as good a dancer as any of his regular partners). So if he really asked 'Who is that?' it was probably a reflex action, for by then Rita was one of the most recognisable women in the world. Elsa told Aly that Rita had been invited as his dining partner, and with that she felt her work was done.

Aly turned the full beam of his charm on Rita. The couple left Elsa's party at midnight and he drove her to the California nightclub in the hills above Cannes, where spectacular sweeping sea views stretch from Antibes in the east to the Esterel mountains in the west. At night, the view is especially romantic when the lights along the coast appear like jewelled necklaces, and the balmy temperatures, the perfumed air of Provence and the throbbing of crickets combine to create an atmosphere resembling a backdrop from one of Rita's movies. The prince and the movie star drank champagne and danced on the small paved dance floor under the trees. Aly could hardly have chosen a more apt setting to woo Rita: he often remarked that this was one of the best views in the world.

In her autobiography Elsa believed that Aly had taken Rita home from the party early since he had told her he intended to be in Ireland for a big race next day and that he had ordered his plane to be standing by ready to leave in the early hours. Emrys Williams told a different story.

When Aly arrived back in the early hours he burst into Emrys's room and told him about 'the most marvellous evening', saying, 'I've never been so excited in my life. I feel like I'm walking on air,' and Emrys sensed that this was something different from the dozens of girls the Prince normally entertained. He was asked to collect Rita from her hotel* the next day and bring her to Château de l'Horizon for tea. When Emrys rose next morning he found Aly was up unusually early and was fussing about ordering flowers and fancy iced cakes. 'I shall dance with her all afternoon,' he told Emrys, requesting him to get hold of all the latest records. 'Have we got a gramophone? ... I want everything to be absolutely perfect.' Rita was expecting to be collected at one o'clock, he said.[2]

When Elsa telephoned Rita that same morning and asked her what she thought of Aly, she received the careless answer that he was 'a nice little fellow'. And it seems Rita was not particularly impressed by the Prince, for she kept Emrys Williams waiting in the foyer of the Hôtel du Cap for three hours while she lunched with an Argentinian millionaire, Alberto Dodero. In the previous week she was reported as dining with Aristotle Onassis, lunching with the Shah of Persia, who was also staying at the Hôtel du Cap, and meeting her estranged husband, who had checked in. The couple dined together and when Orson leant across the table and kissed her the other patrons burst into spontaneous applause. But Rita's reawakened hope that they might get back together was doomed when Orson left suddenly the following afternoon to return to his mistress in Italy. He had only come to check on the arrangements concerning their three-year-old daughter Rebecca, who at that point was in California.

---

* In his memoir (written many years later) Emrys Williams recalled that he had collected Rita from a Villefranche hotel, but contemporary newspapers confirm that Rita was staying at the Hôtel du Cap in Antibes on this date. Some weeks later she transferred to La Reserve at Villefranche, from where Emrys Williams would have chauffeured her several times.

Emrys Williams was still standing at the reception desk as four o'clock approached. He was unsure whether to wait any longer, but then Rita finally appeared. As he saw her coming down the stairs he was surprised that she had made no attempt to look good for the Prince:

My first impressions were not very favourable. She was well turned out, wearing those informal summer clothes that one expects to see in the South of France on a hot day. Primrose coloured shorts, and a white blouse – a smart enough outfit. It was her looks that disappointed me. She had no makeup on her face. He skin was a sallowy yellow shade and her hair had been dyed black for a film. I could hardly credit this was the glamorous Rita Hayworth I had watched on the screen. I'd seen many girls on the beach who were much more attractive. But as she came up to me she switched on a gorgeous smile. I couldn't make up my mind whether it was real or false.[3]

Emrys discovered the reason for Rita's insouciance in the car. Since the previous evening she had been told that Aly was 'just a playboy' who collected women as trophies. This was substantially correct, but Emrys loyally spent the journey to Golfe Juan explaining to her exactly who Aly was, about his religious and business interests and generally talking up his employer. 'He's rich and good looking,' Emrys concluded. 'Newspapers only write up the sensational side of his life but that's what happens to notabilities [sic], isn't it Miss Hayworth?' He wrote that Rita was the only woman in the world who ever kept Aly Khan waiting for three hours and got away with it.[4]

The Prince was irritated when they arrived. He smiled warmly at Rita, but as he led her away into the salon he turned to look at Emrys over his shoulder and bared his teeth at him. Most of the villa's house-guests were either out or having the traditional afternoon siesta, so Emrys sat alone on the terrace under the pines and listened as music from the gramophone drifted out of the open French windows of the salon, and looking up from his book occasionally he caught sight of Aly and Rita dancing cheek to cheek. He suspected that he was going to be seeing a lot of Rita from then on.

It was three weeks before Elsa saw either of them again. Aly invited Elsa to lunch on the well-remembered pool terrace of Château de l'Horizon and she noted that Rita was among the milling guests but did not think this signified much because she knew the villa was generally crowded with all comers, just as it had been in Maxine's day. She also knew that those who arrived following Aly's casually offered invitation to call in any time but found him away were generally entertained in his absence by Pamela Churchill. Aly did not appear to be especially attentive to Rita, as he normally was when infatuated with a new woman, and he told her he was leaving for America in two days, to attend the top yearling sales at Saratoga. Elsa had also heard that Rita was moving from Antibes to Villefranche, and so she concluded that her attempt at matchmaking had been unsuccessful.

She could hardly have been more wrong. There was no trip to Saratoga. Aly had courted Rita assiduously after their first meetings, sending her huge boxes of red roses every day, to the extent that her hotel room was crowded with vases of blooms. He bombarded her with invitations to lunches, drives to beauty spots, romantic moonlit dinners in the mountains, an evening at the Casino in Monte Carlo. At the International Sporting Club Gala Ball, three weeks after fellow diners had applauded Rita and Orson kissing across the table, Rita and Aly were welded together for the entire evening.

Before this, feeling panicky about Aly's attentions and also those of the press who followed her everywhere, Rita had fled to the Hôtel La Reserve, a small luxurious hotel at Beaulieu-sur-Mer, to distance herself. The extra hour's drive between l'Horizon and Villefranche proved no barrier to Aly. He eventually did what she said she was worried about: he wore her down. A 'Gypsy fortune-teller' who had called on Rita some days earlier and foretold that she was about to embark upon the most important relationship of her life and that she must give in to it utterly, was almost certainly sent by Aly. But Rita was very superstitious and believed the woman, and when Aly invited her to bring Miss Haran and stay at l'Horizon – where, he persuaded her, she would be less available to the journalists who frequently bothered her – she accepted.

Having agreed a date, Aly wanted everything to be perfect. He set in train some changes to prepare the villa for the arrival of the two women, and left with Emrys for Paris to hunt down master chef, René, who had once worked for his father. René was duly traced, recruited to work at l'Horizon and instructed to go to the various family houses in Normandy to collect whatever he needed in the way of kitchen equipment, plate, crystal and china, and get them down to Cannes as quickly as possible. Aly then went on a colossal buying spree in Paris and London. Most shops still had little to offer for sale but he somehow managed to buy some good china and pieces of furniture. When they arrived back at l'Horizon a few days later, Emrys Williams recalled, 'it was like a lunatic asylum'. René was already there unpacking his crates, helped by Pamela Churchill and Elizabeth, Lady Sudeley.* Pieces of furniture brought from other houses were lying about waiting to be placed. Elsa Maxwell had dropped in to offer advice and Aly rushed around giving orders and supervising the alterations he had set in motion before his departure.

At last all was ready and Rita and her companion were duly collected. Aly had organised a large party for that day, and Rita was somewhat shaken to find that among the women were several whom she knew to be former consorts of Aly's – including Pamela and Elizabeth, who were still there in semi-permanent residence and, what is more, still seemed to have the ordering of Aly's staff. Shifra Haran told Rita's biographer that it wasn't jealousy of Pamela and Elizabeth that bothered Rita, but the fact that they were sophisticated European women whom she felt were constantly watching her to see what she wore and how she behaved. Aly somehow convinced her to accept this unusual state of affairs – they were simply old friends, he insisted – and Rita had to agree that it was more private at the lovely villa than at the hotel, where she was constantly hounded by journalists and watched by other guests.

Technically, neither Aly nor Rita were free agents. Rita's divorce from Orson Welles would not be final until December that year, and although Aly had been parted from Joan since the early years of the war they had never bothered to divorce. That arrangement had suited Aly. His life consisted of travel, beautiful women, spontaneous decisions about where to go,

---

* Widow of the 6th Baron, who had died in 1941.

instant parties that lasted until dawn, and a complaisant wife in the background who made him 'safer' from gold-diggers. Now besotted with Rita, his marriage was a problem. Rita was an insecure person who needed to feel loved and cherished; Aly's reputation as a great lover was not enough; her other needs – a stable home, security and family life – were more important to her. He realised that without a major compromise by one of them the relationship was doomed.

At first, though, the strange ménage seemed to work. Rita's daughter and her English nanny came from California to live with them, and for a while life was a series of golden days. The staff and most of the visitors loved Rebecca and were happy to play with the child while Rita and Aly, by now very much in love, went off into the hills dressed in casual old clothes to have lunch and explore. They were seldom recognised and this gave Rita an impression of security. When she asked if they could have a holiday in Spain to visit her relatives (she had Spanish grandparents, uncles and aunts) the footloose Aly was only too happy to oblige her. He ordered a new Cadillac for the trip and Emrys Williams went to Paris to collect it. He was instructed to drive the car to Biarritz and meet the couple off the *Avenger* – that would be enough, Aly felt, for them to get into Spain incognito.

The trip began as planned, but became a nightmare. They crossed the border and were not recognised by a sleepy customs officer who did not bother to look at Mr Khan and Mrs Welles sitting in the back of a limousine wearing sunglasses. The problems began when Aly took the wheel of his new car. He habitually drove at high speeds and it wasn't long before he rounded a corner into a village too fast and ran into the back of a horse and cart. There was no serious damage done, but while the Prince was compensating the owner, a crowd gathered. By the time they reached the Ritz in Madrid a hundred journalists and fifty photographers were waiting outside the hotel. Aly managed to avoid the front entrance and slide round the block so that he and Rita could enter through a side entrance.

Thwarted, the press settled down to wait and the couple found themselves besieged – imprisoned in the Ritz in two adjoining suites. They did not use the restaurant and Emrys was placed on duty outside the rooms; all meals were brought to him first so that he could vet the waiters and check for hidden cameras. Aly arranged by telephone for them to be smuggled out in a Daimler from the back entrance and go to a friend's private residence. They managed to get away from the hotel, but soon saw through the rear window that they were being pursued by nine taxis, each full of journalists and photographers.[5] The local chauffeur who knew Madrid well did his best to shake them off, but it was hopeless and rather than lead them to his friend's house Aly ordered the man to return to the Ritz.

Eventually they organised a better plan: their luggage had all labels removed and was loaded casually in small batches into taxis which went off to wait in a pre-arranged rendezvous on the outskirts of Madrid. Then by a series of subterfuges the Prince got away. Rita made her exit in disguise through the hotel kitchens and jumped into the Cadillac driven by Emrys, who was waiting with the engine running – they were pursued by 'a screaming crowd who realised they had been cheated of a glimpse of the famous film star'.[6] Eventually they shook the followers off and reached the home of Aly's friend, where they stayed for some days undiscovered by the press.

Having got away, it would have been sensible to lie low, but Rita had set her heart on attending a bull fight. They got into the arena in Toledo without being noticed; however, as they took their seats wolf whistles started, and the band struck up the theme to *Gilda*. The entire stadium, now alerted to Rita's presence, began chanting 'Gilda! Gilda! Gilda!' while stamping their feet rhythmically. The noise was deafening and Rita's inclination was to flee, but Aly gripped her arm and told her to sit. All went well until the matador slew the bull and presented Rita with the bloody ear. Emrys Williams said he nearly vomited, but Rita behaved as though she was acting a part in a movie: she stood up and formally received the trophy. Emrys recalled the dramatic moment: 'Her eyes were shining with a sort of fierce pride. Her whole body was taut and I could see the muscles quivering in her outstretched neck. She held her head high with her chin tilted upwards. It was obvious that all her Spanish blood had warmed to the traditional drama of the bull ring.'[7] This was a signal for hundreds of people to rush towards Rita and Aly, and it became a mad stampede as the crowd stood in the ring looking up at them, chanted and threw their hats in the air in a wild crescendo of noise. Rita was terrified, and even Aly began to look alarmed. They got away with the help of a posse of Guardia Civil, drove into the countryside and stopped at a small hotel. The ancient receptionist took one look at Rita and said to Emrys 'Gilda? Gilda *señor?*' The chauffeur felt there was no escape for them.

They drove on to Seville, where Rita's relatives lived, and were swamped at every turn by excited crowds and the press. On the day that her ninety-two-year-old grandfather Señor Cansio visited the city Aly and Rita decided to take her entire family out to lunch. The restaurant was quickly surrounded by crowds, but the police and Emrys kept interlopers out of the walled garden. Rita was happy and relaxed, and after the meal various elderly aunts and uncles danced to show how accomplished they were. As a climax Rita's grandfather – who had taught her the flamenco in California – got up to dance for them. 'Grandpa was a sensation,' Emrys wrote, amazed that such an old man could be so spirited and lithe. 'At last Rita herself took the floor,' Emrys recalled. 'Hollywood hadn't taken the Spanish blood out of her veins. She danced like a real Spaniard – not like the film star ... her skirt had wings as she spun round and her long loose red hair floated above her shoulders. The dance and the night were hers.'[8] Everyone stood and cheered and shouted 'Olé! Olé! Olé!'

Prince Aly watched this and then took his chauffeur by the arm, whispering in his ear: 'I'm getting a divorce ... I'm going to marry Rita.'

14

'A Marriage has been Arranged'

From Spain Aly and Rita travelled to Portugal and then flew to America, where Rita was due to start rehearsals and costume fittings at Columbia Studios prior to filming her latest movie. During the time they were in Hollywood Rita worked every day at the studio and Aly, who was virtually unknown on America's west coast, enjoyed the novelty of being able to go anywhere he liked without being recognised. He also made friends with Rebecca, and was a big hit with the child, which went a long way in changing Rita's attitude towards him. He became her rock when the studio made demands on her and upset her, and his love-making consoled her need for security and reassurance. They spent an idyllic month together, when they were not disturbed and Aly devoted his entire time to her. Rita glowed with happiness.

The script for the film was late and the couple decided to take a holiday in Mexico, only to endure similar attentions as in Spain. They flew to Cuba, where the same thing happened.

In the end they returned to Hollywood for Rita to start filming and it is clear during all these trials that Rita had become more and more dependent on Aly.

When she finally got to see the film script, she hated it. It was not the sort of part she was known for and she turned the film down on grounds that it was not in her best interests. The studio boss Harry Cohn – almost certainly a former lover of Rita's and still jealous – decided to take his revenge with press releases which stated that she had failed to turn up for work, thus endangering a costly production and hundreds of jobs. She was portrayed as a typical Hollywood diva too lazy to work and Rita, who was actually one of the most hardworking of Hollywood stars, was hurt at being described as spoilt and indolent. It was bad publicity, especially as her divorce was finalised at the same time. Aly, who wanted to return to the Riviera, capitalised on her angry insecurity and was able to persuade her to go back to France with him, bringing Rebecca.

Rumours of a marriage between Aly and Rita swirled across two continents and they were the hot topic in every newspaper as they returned to Europe. When they arrived at the Château de l'Horizon they were again besieged for weeks. Photographers sneaked in by fishing boat and climbed the steps beside the swimming-pool chute, or crept along the railway bridge after dark to wait for the gate to open, then charged in and hid in the shrubberies. They even managed to smuggle in a well-known Cannes prostitute and took a photograph of her by the front door of the villa, as though she had been visiting Aly. Finally, they organised a combined attack: a convoy of taxis drove over the bridge and a fleet of boats came in by sea, coordinated to arrive at the same time, all crammed with reporters and photographers bent on getting a story for their editors. Aly and his staff had no way to repel this force, and it was only ended by Emrys Williams brandishing his service revolver and threatening to shoot someone. There was a stand-off and eventually, realising that someone had to compromise, Emrys told them that if they left at once the Prince would give them a statement the following day. They left the grounds but hung around the gate. It was hardly surprising that these journalists – many from international capitals who had been sent to cover the Aly and Rita circus – refused to leave. Who was going away tamely to tell their editors they hadn't been able to get a story? Emrys told Aly that he would have to do something: give them a story, or this situation would never end.

That evening Aly and Rita were smuggled out lying under blankets in the back of the gardener's old station wagon and driven up into the hills to Yakymour, to tell the Aga Khan that they were to be married. Emrys Williams, meanwhile, drove out at high speed in the Cadillac and as he intended, was followed. He led the fleet of press cars on a chase to Monte Carlo, where he lost them in the narrow side streets, and when Aly and Rita later returned to the villa there was no one to be seen. The next morning the Prince met the press corps alone, saying that Rita had flu and could not join him. He announced that he and his wife Joan had divorced, on the grounds of having lived apart for more than three years, and that His Highness the Aga Khan had given permission for his marriage to Rita Hayworth to go ahead.

For a time the reporters vanished, the staff at the villa were left in peace to make their arrangements and Aly threw himself into planning a sumptuous event. His tailors flew from

London to fit him for his suit. The couturier Jacques Fath came down to Cannes accompanied by several of his mannequins to model styles, with bales of material and a retinue of assistants to fit Rita for her wedding dress and trousseau.

Chef René hired dozens of staff, not only to help with the forthcoming wedding breakfast but for the guests who came from all over the world and called at the villa in the weeks and days preceding the wedding. All the hotels in Cannes and Antibes were booked up and the event was billed as the wedding of the century. Certainly it was the forerunner of several other weddings of the century, such as that of Prince Rainier and Grace Kelly in 1956, in that for a while it seemed to capture the interest of the whole world.

Months earlier, when Rita and Aly went to Spain, Pamela Churchill had been left more or less alone and in charge of the villa. She had developed a pleasant daily routine, driving into Cannes after breakfast to visit the hairdresser or to shop and meet a friend or two for lunch or coffee. In the afternoon she would swim and play with young Winston or chat to any visitors, and then dine in one or other of the neighbouring villas or with other friends along the Côte d'Azur. One afternoon she was alone, sunbathing on the pool terrace, when she heard the engine of a powerful motor boat switch off close by and realised someone had arrived at the l'Horizon jetty. She looked up as the most beautiful man she had ever seen emerged into view from the pool steps.

Tall and slender, hard-muscled and tanned with dark curly hair, he introduced himself as Giovanni ('Call me Gianni') Agnelli. From the tittle-tattle of Riviera social life Pamela could hardly *not* have known who he was: the twenty-seven-year-old grandson and heir of the founder of the Fiat empire, and one of the richest young men in Europe – and certainly the richest man in Italy. He lived in a seventeenth-century palace in Rome and his fortune was then rumoured to be about three billion dollars.* With his sports cars, yachts and private aeroplane, he was hardly ever out of the gossip columns. He gambled in the casinos with stakes that were more than a year's salary to most people, night-clubbed with beautiful actresses and models, and ran with a fast crowd of men which included Porfirio Rubirosa,† Aly Khan, Darryl Zanuck and Errol Flynn (both Zanuck and Flynn famously prowled the Mediterranean on their respective luxurious yachts), the Marquis Alfonso de Portago‡ and the Brazilian playboy Prince Francisco 'Baby' Pignatari.

Pam was twenty-eight, and at the height of her physical beauty. Although usually drawn to older men, she was instantly attracted to Gianni, and the magnetism operated both ways.

There were many who said that Pam was drawn to Gianni because of his money and her two biographers were certainly at pains to point this out, claiming that everything she did during the five years they were together was financed by him. It was Gianni, they wrote, who paid for the fabulous homes in Rome, Turin and London, and the lease every summer of Château de la Garoupe on the Cap d'Antibes,

---

* Before it turned over its manufacturing process to cars at the end of the Second World War (when few had a car, but everyone wanted one) Fiat had manufactured trucks, tanks and military vehicles in both world wars, but especially benefited from lucrative commissions through Mussolini.
† A diplomat of the Dominican Republic, he was a racing driver, polo player and noted playboy jet-setter.
‡ The Spanish racing driver.

for the purchase of La Léopolda, the old palace that had formerly been the home of the Belgian King Leopold II, for the designer clothes Pam wore when featured in fashion and society magazines such as *Vogue*, for the costly jewels he gave her, and for the superb apartment in Paris which became her base for many years as she flitted constantly between Turin, London and the Riviera.*

Pam's brother Eddie was convinced, however, that whatever she got from the relationship with Gianni, Pam 'truly adored him',[1] and despite agreeing to terminate a pregnancy in the first year of their relationship, she always thought and hoped that the relationship would eventually lead to marriage. He believed that Gianni behaved as any rich husband in love with his wife would do, happily accepting the bills she ran up to make their various homes, and herself, beautiful for him. Pam had been raised as an aristocrat in an English country manor house, and now she filled Gianni's properties with designer furnishings, works of art and banks of beautifully arranged fresh flowers fit for entertaining the world's leaders. Girls of her class at that time were educated to look after and entertain men, and run their homes, and that was what Pam did with great style. As a move towards marriage she converted to Catholicism and had her marriage to Randolph Churchill annulled, pleading that she had been very young at the time, and that her initial doubts had been overcome by Randolph's persuasion. Coincidentally, Gianni made a

---

* Young Winston was removed from Gibbs School in Queens Gate, London, and sent to Le Rosey, the exclusive Swiss boarding school attended by Aly Khan's sons. This move was not looked upon kindly by his grandparents, until they met the English nanny recruited by Pam, and were promised that the child could spend summer holidays with his father (who was about to remarry). Then they knew all would be well.

very large donation to the Church at the time this papal annulment was granted, but with hindsight, although he had certainly considered marriage it seems clear that Gianni could never have married Pam because of ferocious opposition from his family. His parents were dead but he had four sisters, all of whom insisted that their brother must make a happy marriage to an Italian virgin. They considered Pam to be a sort of red-haired she-devil.

During those five years when Pam was wife to Gianni in all but name, it was certainly not a one-way street because, indisputably, she was a social asset to him. Pam knew everyone worth knowing in English, European and American society and politics, partly through her own family connections, partly as the beloved former daughter-in-law of Winston and Clementine Churchill, and partly through her former intimate relationships with several influential Americans. She was polished and confident, and spoke fluent French without an accent. Many of the numerous guests who visited Gianni over the years – some of whom became invaluable contacts for him – he met through Pam. In short, they were a good partnership, who were widely regarded as a permanent couple and treated as such. She did not merely live with him as his mistress, but ran his various homes, furnished them and managed the bank accounts allocated for the purpose as though she were his wife. Gianni was never happier, and although his sisters refused to formally receive Pam* her family welcomed him as a valued friend and he was a frequent visitor to the Digby home at Minterne Magna for the rest of his life. Nothing else pleased Gianni half as much

---

* They did meet once, accidentally.

as the weekend Pam took him to Blenheim Palace to stay with the Duke of Marlborough, or when she introduced him to Winston Churchill at Chartwell. Still, although socially adept even Pam needed help when asked a tricky question for a party at Beaulieu-sur-Mer. Who took precedence, the Aga Khan or the Duke of Windsor? She knew whom to ask, though, and the response from Duff Cooper was very precise: 'His Highness the Aga Khan is regarded as God on Earth by his many million followers. But an English Duke, of course, takes precedence.'[2]

By the time Aly and Rita returned from Spain, the Pam Churchill and Gianni Agnelli partnership was in full bloom. They had even been on a short cruise together, mainly to avoid a threatened visit by Randolph, who was bent on persuading Pam to remain married to him. This new relationship came as a relief to Rita, for Pam had been one of the women at the villa who had made her feel inadequate, and although this was not intended by Pam there was some understandable initial competitiveness.

After Gianni came on the scene Pam and Rita became good friends and would remain so for the rest of their lives.

15

Wedding of the Century

On 27 May 1949 the Château de l'Horizon was the focus of world press interest. At dawn an army of trucks snaked along the road and across the railway bridge as they lined up to unload tons of fresh food, huge baskets arranged with long-stemmed roses, cut flowers by the hundredweight and scores of ornamental trees and shrubs. Two set pieces, each fifteen feet long and containing thousands of white carnations and roses, picked out the initials A and M, for Aly and Rita (her baptismal name was Margarita); mounted on pontoons, they were floated in the swimming pool into which – as the first guests started to arrive – ten gallons of eau de cologne were emptied, filling the air with exquisite fragrance. Aly had made all the arrangements himself.

In the days leading up to the 27th wedding presents arrived by the hundred, along with thousands of telegrams from all over the world. Aly read them all, but he was unimpressed with the diamond earrings sent to Rita by the Aga and the

Begum as their gift to the couple – he had rather hoped for a large cheque, in the region of a million dollars. The wedding cake, made in Paris in great secrecy, had been flown to Cannes on a private plane and collected by Emrys Williams. The vehicles in Aly Khan's garage were kept so busy that when the Prince departed to dine at La Croë with the Duke and Duchess of Windsor all his cars were occupied with pre-wedding errands. At the last minute he sprinted across the bridge to stand on the main road and flag down a passing taxi to take him to Cap d'Antibes.

Two days before the wedding there was a private screening in Cannes of Rita's latest film (probably the first screening in France), *The Loves of Carmen*,* attended by Rita, the director King Vidor, a number of wedding guests and staff of Château de l'Horizon. In the film, which follows the story of the opera *Carmen*, Rita plays a dishonest and tempestuous gypsy girl who seduces an innocent soldier, Don José, and leads him to commit murder for the love of her. The male lead was played by Glenn Ford, who had starred with Rita in *Gilda*, and this was the first film chosen and co-produced by Rita's own production company, the Beckworth Corporation, which gave her a say over the content of the production (indeed, she was co-producer). She hired her father and uncle, both professional flamenco dancers, who had taught Rita to dance from the age of six, to choreograph the traditional Spanish dances. The scene in which she first meets Don José and dances to

---

* During the making of this film, soon after she and Orson Welles parted, Rita had a brief love affair with the millionaire Howard Hughes and became pregnant. Made aware by the studio of the effect on her image of having a baby out of wedlock she agreed to an abortion. She was still recovering from the effects of this abortion when she met Aly at Cap d'Antibes.

attract him is a cinema classic, and Aly's chauffeur believed that it was this dance that she recreated when she danced in Spain for her family and Aly, and precipitated his decision to marry her.

Following the private screening Rita and the wedding guests had arranged to drive into the hills for an al fresco dinner at La Terrasse restaurant in the village of Le Cannet. Outside the cinema, however, a crowd had gathered to see Rita leave, and she was mobbed. Rita was helped into the limousine by Emrys Williams, but by the time he got into the driver's seat she had almost been pulled out of the other door. She found this crowd adoration a nightmare.

In French law a civil marriage service must be conducted in public, but the couple knew from experience that their wedding might provoke chaotic scenes. Having been briefed by the Duke and Duchess of Windsor about their success-ful application twelve years earlier to be allowed to marry in a private residence, Aly had applied to the French Minister of Justice. However, his application was refused a few days before the wedding. There was nothing for it but to fall back on the contingency, which was to hold the four-minute civil service in Vallauris, to which the owner of Château de l'Horizon paid its land taxes.

By 1949 Vallauris had already become known as the home of Picasso.* But the mayor and chief of police were well aware what this wedding meant in terms of favourable publicity for the little town, and played it to the hilt. A red carpet was bor-rowed from Cannes and fresh paint applied to the *mairie*. Not

---

* He had worked occasionally in one of the potteries at Vallauris since 1946, but had bought a house in 1948 and lived there after that date. Prior to 1948 he lived in Antibes and Californie.

only were the bride and groom a major security issue but the guest list, many hundreds strong, read like an international edition of *Who's Who*. Over a hundred policemen in uniform and almost the same number in plain clothes were drafted in. Aly arrived an hour before the time of a quarter past one specified on the invitations, hoping to persuade the mayor to restrict the number of reporters allowed inside the building. His request was sweetened by a donation to the town of a million francs, the notes wrapped up in newspaper – suggesting the idea came from his father, who often made gifts and donations in precisely the same manner. The mayor said he was obliged by law to leave the doors of the room open for the public service, but he had been able to arrange for it to be held in a small ground-floor room for the sake of the Aga Khan, who could not climb stairs. Having done all he could Aly, looking tired, greeted his guests while he waited for his bride.

Rita, escorted by police cars and motorcycle outriders, was driven to Vallauris at fifteen miles an hour in the new white Cadillac convertible that Aly had bought for the purpose. Every foot of the road leading into the hills was lined with people, who had begun waiting in the early morning. As soon as the Cadillac passed they fell in behind and followed on foot to the town. The streets were soon *en fête*, but as the room provided at the *mairie* was so tiny only thirty guests were able to attend the service. Chief among them were the Aga Khan and the Begum, Princes Sadruddin, Karim and Amyn, three important Ismaili clerics and King Vidor. Just as the ceremony was about to get under way a group of journalists caused a vociferous disruption, protesting that, by keeping them out, the wedding was being illegally conducted in private. Twenty of them, but no cameras, were allowed in, to stand against the wall of the little room. After the brief exchange of vows the mayor made a speech about the honour paid to the town, to be sure of his moment of glory.

Rita, now formally Her Highness Princess Margarita, wore an ankle-length Jacques Fath dress in ice-blue chiffon, with long sleeves and a matching picture hat in swirls of organza which haloed her face. On the third finger of her left hand, beside her wedding band, she wore a twelve-carat diamond, which was only out-dazzled by Rita's smile. She looked radiantly happy and few would have guessed she was two months pregnant, and had such cold feet that a few days earlier she had sent for Orson Welles and begged him to remarry her. Against his better judgement Orson persuaded her to go through with the wedding on the basis that if it didn't work out she could divorce Aly. Later he would say that he had done so with qualms; in his heart he knew that Aly was one of the most promiscuous men in Europe, and though generous and charming he was not right for the emotionally needy Rita. Nor were her misgivings lessened when Rome* publicly declared that her marriage could not be recognised by the Church.

The formal proceedings over, half-blinded by flashbulbs, the newlyweds were cheered through Vallauris by the townsfolk and showered with petals. Their small convoy – the Aga Khan and the Begum followed the Cadillac in their Rolls-Royce convertible (one of only a handful in the world at that point) – was cheered and pelted with flowers all the way back to l'Horizon. Safe inside its high walls, the couple

---

* Rita was a Catholic.

were greeted by their guests; Rita later said she did not know many of them, but that quite a few of the women had been lovers of her new husband. Aly had hired a hundred security guards to keep press and paparazzi out, and two motor boats patrolled the shore, but clearly the villa was infiltrated for in one report some photographs appeared of the couple's bedroom.

At the time, it was easily the most grandiose wedding ever held on the Riviera – covered from beginning to end by newsreel photographers and relayed to cinemas all over the world within days. In Europe the audiences had hardly recovered from the war: the occasional pair of black-market nylon stockings was the ambition of most women in terms of glamour. Mass television lay in the future and a weekly visit to the cinema was one of the chief forms of entertainment available to them. Millions watched and were thrilled by the fairy-tale wedding, with the beautiful bride and her handsome prince celebrating in the sunshine on the terrace of their swimming pool, the Mediterranean Sea in the background, surrounded by flowers and with rich, beautifully dressed guests drinking champagne and a newly created cocktail,* eating caviar while being serenaded by Yves Montand backed by a full orchestra dressed in white tuxedos. They were able to watch the bride cut the huge 120-pound three-tier cake with Aly's gleaming ceremonial sword. On the screen were the bridegroom's father, the Aga Khan – the man who'd been given his own weight in diamonds in India in 1946 – and his wife, a beautiful woman dressed in a blue and gold sari.

---

* The Ritaly cocktail: two-thirds whisky, one third vermouth, two drops of bitters and a cherry.

There too was Rebecca, the child of Rita's previous marriage to Orson Welles, dressed in a pretty organza dress, presenting her newly royal mother with a posy of flowers. This dazzling event was manna to an audience starved of colour and experiences; a Hollywood fantasy come to life.

Readers of newspapers learned the following day that the guests enjoyed more than six hundred bottles of champagne, at least fifty pounds of caviar and forty lobsters, as well as groaning buffet tables of food lovingly created by René and his small army of chefs. It was excess taken to the maximum possible, but not everyone wholly enjoyed it. The Aga wrote his opinion of it in his memoir, deprecating the 'clamorous publicity such as we had never before experienced in our family ... This was a fantastic, semi-royal, semi-Hollywood affair; my wife and I played our part in the ceremony, much as we disapproved of the atmosphere with which it was surrounded.'[1]

After six hours the pregnant bride was exhausted. Hollywood gossip columnist Louella Parsons sniped that Rita looked anything but happy and was trying to lose herself in the crowd, but that may have been mere pique, for Parsons's arch-enemy Elsa Maxwell took line honours, having introduced the happy couple. Eventually Rita slipped into the salon to join her father-in-law at the dining table, where he had ordered a calming cup of tea after sampling the delicious food on offer. 'Too much caviar, Rita,' he muttered. 'Too much caviar.'

On the following morning the only sound at l'Horizon was of the packing up and removal of the wedding furnishings from the terraces, and the inevitable cleaning up. Inside the villa, though, another marriage service was being held – in total secrecy. It was an Islamic ceremony conducted by the Ismaili mullahs who had attended the civil ceremony the previous day, and witnessed by several dozen Ismaili nobles and their colourfully dressed wives. Here, Aly promised Rita a dowry which included a house of her own, and the oaths were given and toasted in fruit juice.

Not a word of this secret ceremony ever reached the newspapers, nor the fact that Rita was subsequently instructed in the Islamic faith by a mullah. Aly also hired a tutor to teach Rita French, because as his wife she would need good French for all the politicians she would meet and entertain, and an etiquette coach to teach her all the things that Pam Churchill had learned at her mother's knee. This curriculum had to be fitted into a constant round of junketing.

At Epsom that summer Rita fainted when the crush to see her became too much. The same thing happened at Longchamp, and again at the Festival of Stars at the Tuileries in Paris when a crowd of autograph hunters gatecrashed the dining room and mobbed her. Maurice Chevalier, sitting at a neighbouring table, was very put out when his new suit was soaked by the contents of a fallen champagne bottle and he complained bitterly, but maybe he was aggrieved that it was Rita the mob were after, and not him. There was a failed hold-up when thieves tried to snatch Rita's jewels in Paris, and an attempted kidnapping of Rebecca at Gorizia, Aly's palatial house at Deauville, which was foiled by her attentive nanny and the faithful Emrys Williams.

To forestall possible adverse publicity, when Rita's pregnancy became obvious Aly announced that the birth of their child was expected in February. However, in November they slipped away to Switzerland and took the largest suite at the Palace Hotel in Lausanne, where Rita had booked into a clinic much favoured by European royalty. She went into labour on 28 December and gave birth to a girl, Princess Yasmin, delivered by Caesarean. Aly was a model husband: he stayed with her all night dozing by the bedside in a chair, and for the next few months, in the Gstaad house belonging to the Aga, they lived the quiet family life that Rita had always dreamed of.

It was probably the happiest time of her life, for Aly appeared to be the husband she wanted. Not only did he seem quite content playing with little Yasmin and Rebecca, but his two sons from his first marriage came to stay and there was no evidence of his former womanising, even when he made a few hasty business trips to Paris. He devoted himself to making Rita happy. This idyll lasted about three months, by the end of which Aly was showing increasing signs of restlessness. 'I've been around this place too damned long,' he complained to his chauffeur. 'I'm bored stiff.' To burn off some of his excess energy he took to the slopes. Aly had always been something of a daredevil skier and had broken his leg twice; now he became a demon on the most challenging runs, almost as though determined to break his neck. He almost did so when he took a nasty fall, breaking his right leg in seven places. 'I guess I'm being paid out for all my sins,' he told reporters, smiling to hide the seriousness of his injury – doctors were unsure at the time whether they would be able to save the leg.

Rita was happy to nurse her Prince; indeed she welcomed the opportunity to prove herself the devoted wife, but Aly was a bad patient, bored and fretful. His entire leg was in plaster from toe to thigh, and as soon as he became even slightly mobile, with the aid of crutches, he clamoured to be taken to the Château de l'Horizon, where, he insisted, he would make a faster recovery in the mild climate of the Riviera.

A flying ambulance was arranged and Aly was duly taken to Cannes. Had she been able to look into the future, Rita might have fought harder to keep him in Switzerland.

16

Marital Troubles

When Rita returned to the Château de l'Horizon with the children some weeks later she felt Aly had reverted to the old life he had known before their marriage. The villa – her home – was constantly invaded by hordes of friends and visitors who had to be entertained and amused, and Aly began to behave like a bachelor again. Among the constant stream of visitors were many beautiful women to whom Rita thought Aly was far too attentive for a married man and the couple began to row over trivialities. She was not deft; after a dinner at La Croë Rita put her household staff into the same black and white maids' uniforms that the Duchess of Windsor's staff wore. One girl, who refused to wear such outdated clothes, was fired and promptly wrote an exposé for the newspapers.

Soon, Emrys Williams recounted, the couple were having regular arguments and even fights. Rita, who was so quiet when in company, had a fiery Latin temper which sometimes erupted into wild rages, and one occasion Emrys wrote about occurred when Aly wanted them to move to England for the racing season. Rita was determined to stay at home with the children and Emrys, who was helping his employer to walk at the time, became an unwilling spectator as the quarrel erupted:

> The dispute became very bitter. Rita's rage boiled over. Never before or since have I seen such fury in a human being. She was flaming mad. And flaming – for once – is the right word. Her eyes were alight. Her face and cheeks were flushed a deep crimson. Loose red hair floated round her shoulders like a cloud of fire. 'I'm sick of this!' she screamed. 'I'm going back to America.'[1]

Aly's quiet response, observing that she had been drinking, incensed her even further. She picked up two photographs in heavy silver frames and hurled them at him. A series of books followed the photo frames. Finally a tray of glasses of orange juice was flung at Aly, who was struggling to remain standing on his crutches. At last Rita had finished; she collapsed on the sofa in sobs as Aly hobbled over to her. Emrys slipped out of the room as his employers began a tender reconciliation. But it was doubtful that any marriage could survive such onslaughts for long, and like the rest of the staff Emrys was unhappy to have to work in such a miserable atmosphere. Devoted to his employer, Emrys knew only too well that the Prince was not an easy man to live with, but when the couple had a violent argument in public over whom he was going to drive home (they had arrived in different cars) he threatened to leave them unless they stopped fighting.

Unfortunately this had become the pattern of the marriage, and it became the talk of the Riviera that they argued about everything from him using her money to the attentions he paid to other women.

Among the women visitors was Debo Devonshire,* the young Duchess of Devonshire and the youngest of the Mitford sisters. She had met Aly at a party in London before his marriage to Rita, and often thereafter at the races in England and France. They became friends and she was a regular guest at both the Paris house and the Château de l'Horizon. She recalled that Aly's chief characteristic was his overwhelming charm, and that he was the easiest of company. She first met Rita at Ascot shortly before the birth of Yasmin, but her favourite memory of them was on another occasion at Royal Ascot, as Rita and Aly walked arm in arm through the paddock behind Harold Macmillan and the crowds cheered and clapped Rita. Macmillan, then Housing Minister (and Debo's uncle by marriage),† assumed they were cheering him – and though it had never happened to him previously, he took it as a sign that his work was appreciated and he courteously removed his top hat and bowed to his audience.

Debo was bowled over by Rita's appearance. In a memoir she wrote that Rita was one of the four most beautiful women she had ever seen.‡ 'Her features were perfect, her mass of truly auburn hair sprang straight from her forehead and cascaded down to her shoulders, and she moved like

---

* Sister-in-law to the late Kick Kennedy, Debo died in October 2014 while this book was being written.
† Harold Macmillan was married to Dorothy Cavendish, aunt to Debo's husband Andrew, the 10th Duke of Devonshire.
‡ The others were Elizabeth von Hofmannsthal, Madame Martinez de Hoz and her sister Diana Mosley.

the dancer she was.'[2] But the two women got on well. Debo spoke very little French so she and Rita were fellow sufferers at the Château de l'Horizon where the lingua franca for conversation at the dinner table tended to be French. She remembered that the guest list was impressive: 'You never knew who you were going to meet at Château de l'Horizon, Aly's house on the sea near Cannes, where fellow guests ranged from beautiful women friends to international racing people, with a sprinkling of showbiz thrown in.'[3] One day Aly arranged for her to dine with his father and the Begum at Yakymour. The Aga, whom Debo's sister Nancy referred to as 'Father Divine', 'made me feel as though I had known him all my life'. As she was taking her leave he gave her a book 'to read in bed' – she half expected it to be an Islamic tract, but it was a romantic novel. At 2 a.m., when she was fast asleep, her telephone rang and she fumbled to answer it only to find it was the Aga asking how she was enjoying the book.

Rita always attempted to show a smiling face to visitors but the noisy quarrels, mainly about Aly's playboy behaviour and his spending (too often of her money), continued. After Christmas 1950 the couple left France for a three-month official tour of the Ismaili communities in East Africa and stopped over in Cairo to attend a New Year's Eve party. Here, Rita stormed out during one of their public rows. Already upset over missing Yasmin's first birthday because she had agreed to accompany Aly, she said he was neglecting her and paying too much attention to others. Aly smoothed things over. On arrival in Kenya, highly anxious about the part she was expected to play in meeting the wives of the Ismaili groups when she did not understand them, Rita appeared

28. & 29. The Château de l'Horizon; built by Maxine on the French Riviera
between Cannes and Antibes

CHATEAU DE L'HORIZON

LIKE A PALACE OF AN
ENCHANTED DREAM

SCENE OF PINE TREES, RAMBLER ROSES
AND THE SEA

30., 31. & 32. When the new King rented the villa from Maxine it was described as
'like a palace of an enchanted dream'

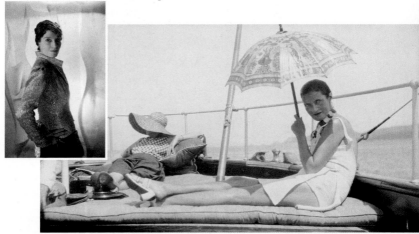

33. & 34. Daisy Fellowes on her yacht the *Sister Anne*, and (inset) showing how well she
wore 1930s fashions

35. The Churchills were among the first visitors to Maxine's villa, but Clementine did not care for the people she met there

36. Winston with Doris Castlerosse (back to camera) and an ageing Maxine

37. Winston on the famous chute into the sea. There is a video online of him clowning on this slide

38. 'Naughty Lady C': Doris in her signature micro shorts

39. Maxine in the swimming pool at Château de l'Horizon in 1939

40. Noël Coward visited Maxine shortly before her death, 'looking more beautiful than I had ever seen her . . . I knew I should never see her again'

41. Maxine's grave in the Protestant cemetery, Cannes. She had always knocked years of her age so the date of her birth is wrong, and due to the war no one checked the carving. Her name is also misspelled

42. The Second World War on the Riviera. Occupation, first by Italian and then by German troops, meant extreme hardship for local residents

This is the Gin
Gordon's

The Daily Telegraph
and Morning Post

LONDON
LATE
EDTN.

LANDINGS IN SOUTH FRANCE

BEACHHEADS EXTENDED & WIDENED, SAYS H.Q.

ALLIED TROOPS SEVERAL MILES INLAND

TANKS & SUPPLIES POUR ASHORE

43. Report of the Allied landing on the Riviera, August 1944

44. Allied ships off St Tropez

45. Entertaining went on at the Château de l'Horizon as before, regardless of cost, when Rosita Winston rented the villa after the war

46. Prince Aly Khan. Women found his warmth, charm and energy irresistible

47. Aly's private plane, a De Havilland Dove named *Avenger*

48. Aly, dressed in tribal robes at Salamiyeh, Syria. A first-rate horseman, he was revered as a godlike figure in Syria and chose to have his tomb erected there

49. Rita Hayworth as the eponymous move heroine Gilda – but the passionate Gilda was not Rita. Rita wanted a quiet family life. 'Men go to bed with Gilda,' she said ruefully, 'and wake up with me!'

50. When Elsa Maxwell arranged an introduction between Rita and Aly she advised, 'wear something white, arrive late and really make an entrance'

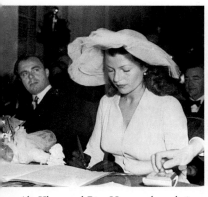

51. Aly Khan and Rita Hayworth at their civil marriage ceremony, Vallauris, France

52. The newlyweds leave the *mairie* to return to the Château de l'Horizon

53. Huge floral arrangements of their initials, A (Aly) and M (Marguerite – Rita's real name), floated on the pool, to which gallons of perfume had been added to scent the air

54. Rita cuts the wedding cake with Aly's officer's sword

55. The newlyweds at the reception

56. After the marriage to Rita Hayworth ended, Aly fell madly in love with Gene Tierney but dropped her when his father threatened to disinherit him if he married another movie star

57. Aly and Bettina. They were engaged and she was bearing his child when he crashed his car in Paris a few weeks before their planned wedding

58. Aly's death on a Paris backstreet in a car crash made headlines

IKE STILL PLANS SUMMIT, RUSS TRIPS

Los Angeles Times

FINAL

ALY KHAN KILLED, GIRL FRIEND HURT IN CRASH

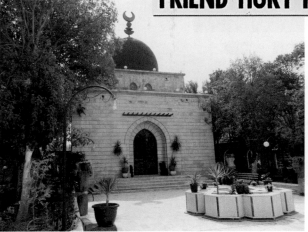

59. Prince Aly Khan's mausoleum in Salamiyeh, Syria. Still cared for despite over five years of civil war as this book is published

content, at first, to allow Aly to go off alone on various trips to Mombasa and Zanzibar to fulfil his obligations to his followers.

They had agreed to make a luxurious safari at the end of the trip, but after Aly departed Rita did some thinking and concluded that life with Aly was never going to be any different, and that his playboy lifestyle was not the life she wanted. The next day she sent Aly a note to say she was returning to Cannes and wanted to go to America with the children. He quickly returned to her and they quarrelled again. In the end she insisted on at least returning to Château de l'Horizon alone, and he agreed on the understanding that she would wait for his return before the proposed trip to the United States. He was adamant on one point: she must not take his daughter to America without his permission.

Emrys Williams was on a rare leave in London when he received a worried phone call from one of the servants at the Château de l'Horizon. The Prince was still in East Africa and the Aga was due to return from a holiday the following day. Rita had packed and flown to Paris with the children and their nurses, and now she had apparently boarded a liner at Le Havre, bound for New York. From her packing and luggage it looked as though she did not intend to return. Emrys telephoned the Aga, who was deeply upset. Aly was also alerted. Chartering a private plane, he flew directly to France to try to stop Rita from leaving, but he was too late for the ship had sailed by the time he landed. As she boarded the ship Rita announced to the newspapers she had left her husband and intended to instigate divorce proceedings from America.

Aly flew to California and, using all his charm, talked Rita into a very brief reconciliation, but it did not last. And this time the fairy-tale marriage was well and truly ended.

While all these events had been occurring, the other fairy-tale romance – that of the Windsors – had also very nearly hit the rocks in nearby Antibes.

After having spent the war years in the Bahamas, where the Duke was Governor, followed by some time in Paris, the Duke and Duchess had moved back to the Riviera in 1947. A year later Winston and Clementine Churchill spent their fortieth wedding anniversary at La Croë. This was surprising, in view of Clementine's dislike of the Riviera and what she considered to be the louche crowd it seemed to attract. She did not like Wallis either. But Winston loved the climate and could take or leave what he wanted of the people he met. Clementine stayed only a few days, returning home alone and leaving her husband to paint, write and relax.

He had already begun work on his series of books about the Second World War which would make him financially secure for the rest of his life, but of course in 1948 he was not yet aware of this so an invitation to spend some time in the overwhelming luxury of La Cröe was welcome. Even so, despite his loyalty to his erstwhile monarch Winston seems to have, at about that time, come to agree with his wife that the Duke would not have made a good king and Wallis would not have made a good queen.[4]

After he left La Croë in 1948, and again during 1949, Churchill stayed with Beaverbrook at his magnificent villa La Capponcina at Cap d'Ail, which looked across the bay to Monte Carlo. Just as he had always done at Maxine's villa, immediately he arrived Winston plunged into the sea and swam like a schoolboy. During the second visit, at dinner on the veranda, he gazed at the lights and said wistfully how much he wished he could go to the Casino, but he had promised Clementine he would not. He kept to his old routine of dictating his book in the morning and bathing or painting in the afternoon. Fellow guests invited by Beaverbrook to keep Churchill amused were amazed by Winston's fluency as he spoke and clowned and held the table in his spell; 'It was as though,' said one, 'he were raised to the highest pitch of his life and genius in one glorious peak of exultation before the climax.'[5]

The Duke and Duchess of Windsor joined them one evening. The Duke had included in his book some things about Churchill's part in the abdication and wished to discuss this with him before submitting the manuscript to a publisher, for there was a general election looming. Later Winston played rummy with Wallis, and after the Windsors left he continued to play for some hours. As he climbed the stairs to bed he complained of cramp and an 'odd sensation'. On the following morning his doctor examined him and confirmed that he had suffered a mild stroke. At Winston's insistence this was kept secret, and he left for Chartwell as scheduled after two weeks of complete rest. Churchill would often meet the Windsors in the South of France in future years, but he would never again stay with them.

Following the war, La Croë was the only home of significance left to the Windsors: they had not owned their Paris house in Boulevard Suchet, and the owner declined to renew the lease. Fortunately, they were able through Sir Charles and Lady Mendl to obtain an affordable lease on a house on the

Bois de Boulogne which became their Paris base,* and were allowed to draw on rations from the British Army because of the Duke's military position, which enabled them to entertain. But Paris was changed from the city of frivolity and light that it had been prior to 1939. Extreme food shortages and daily power cuts made life difficult for most residents, although there were plenty of diplomatic social events at the British Embassy after Duff and Diana Cooper took over. There, expats of the right sort could meet and, while drinking champagne, at least pretend all was as before. Noël Coward saw the Windsors at an embassy party in the winter of 1946; he wrote that the Duke was still deeply in love with Wallis, but he was able to believe that, at last, Wallis seemed to love the Duke. Lady Diana Cooper, as wife of the ambassador, adopted the practice of dropping a royal curtsey to Wallis, which was frowned upon by the Foreign Office – but who was going to tell the daughter of a duke how to behave? Having been given an official lead, most ladies could happily follow her example, which pleased the Duke, who still smarted over his family's treatment of his wife.

The couple had made a low-key visit to England in the autumn of 1946, staying privately at the house of the Duke's former equerry Sir Dudley Forward, Ednam Lodge near Sunningdale in Berkshire, and having no contact with the Royal Family. The Forwards obligingly moved into Claridge's

---

* The owner, Paul-Louis Weiller, millionaire owner of Air France, also owned and financed Le Petit Trianon, the exquisite house in Versailles occupied by the Mendls. In fact, he owned dozens of houses and apartments in Paris and was known for helping displaced and exiled royals and others, who in return made his place in society by attending his parties. He was said to be so boring that if he had not done this no one would have ever accepted his invitations; he is known as 'poor Louis' in the published correspondence between Diana Cooper and Evelyn Waugh.

while the Duke and Duchess occupied their home but the hope that this private visit would not attract any press notice was doomed when Ednam Lodge was burgled one evening while the Windsors were out to dinner. The thief – or thieves – got away with priceless uncut emeralds given to Wallis by her husband, which were said to have once belonged to Queen Alexandra, plus all of Wallis's jewels apart from those she was wearing – the value was estimated at a sum that would be thirteen million pounds today. Nothing else in the house was touched: not even some Fabergé eggs. Only the Duchess's jewellery, locked in a trunk in her bedroom, was taken. A thin trail of dropped baubles – gold, diamonds, sapphires, emeralds and pearls – led police across the nearby golf course, but the perpetrator was never found.* This incident, together with the grim austerity of England, the widespread depression caused by even more harsh rationing than during the war years (even bread was rationed now) and the Labour government's attitude to inherited wealth, helped the Windsors to decide to return to Antibes. The England over which the Duke had reigned seemed to have vanished.

Thanks to various official contacts, many items of value from their Paris and Antibes properties had been rescued and stored during the war. The Château de la Croë had been abused, like most other properties belonging to expats, but it suffered less damage than most others. Axis forces had turned the garage into a mini headquarters, had cut down sheltering trees in order to improve visibility to the sea, and the sea frontage and grounds had been mined. The château itself

---

* The police saw how the burglary had been effected and suspected a well-known local cat burglar, but they were unable to find sufficient evidence to make the charge stick.

had not been lived in, although a bomb had landed outside and blown in all of the windows, admitting adverse weather for months. The Duchess soon had it all in hand and within weeks had employed a staff of twenty-two, with the women house servants all dressed in the classic black with white frilly aprons so admired by Rita Hayworth. Wallis wrote to her aunt that outside of foreign embassies it was probably the only house in France that was still maintained in such a manner, possibly in England too.

By the start of the Fifties the Windsors had been married fifteen years and felt they had been shunted into a siding in life. The Duke was deeply offended that they had been excluded from the wedding of his niece Princess Elizabeth to Prince Philip of Greece in November 1947, an insult which had caused headlines in England. Very occasionally the Duke paid a visit to his mother, and in February 1952 was a senior mourner at the funeral of his brother King George VI, but he always went alone and his family pretended Wallis did not exist. His frequent attempts to obtain some sort of official position – his personal objective was the governorship of Canada – were all firmly rejected.

Both the Duke and Duchess had loathed the war years in the Bahamas, regarding it as a sort of exile – Wallis called it their Elba – though millions living in Europe envied them. They had been able to escape on occasion to the United States for short holidays, such as in April 1941 when, on leave in Florida, they were invited to lunch at Palm Beach with Jessie Donahue. Jessie was one of the three daughters of Frank W. Woolworth, founder/owner of Woolworth's stores, who inherited between them a billion dollars. The Windsors met Jessie and her family again that autumn in New York, and when

Jessie sailed to Nassau that winter they were able to repay her hospitality.

For at least a decade thereafter Jessie Donahue showered the Windsors with invitations. She was one of the richest women in America and the cost was nothing to her; association with this gilded couple was a pinnacle of social achievement. For the Duke of Windsor, always concerned about money (except when commissioning extravagant new jewellery for Wallis), it was a way to enjoy the lifestyle he enjoyed without affecting his income. Through Jessie the Windsors were able to enjoy such benefits as vacations in Palm Beach mansions, cruises on huge yachts, a long lease on a Long Island estate which included a twenty-five-room château overlooking a golf course, and all for free or at a peppercorn rent.

From time to time Jessie's son, the playboy Jimmy Donahue, would put in an appearance. Born to such wealth that he knew from childhood that he would never have to work and would hardly have time to spend what he would inherit, he decided on a life of self-indulgence and degradation worthy of a latter-day Roman emperor. Along with his more famous cousin Barbara Hutton, who was also among his best friends, he discovered drugs early and was already hooked on Seconal* by the time he was expelled from the Choate School, where he had been a contemporary of John F. Kennedy. He openly admitted his sexuality when being gay was shocking to most people, but shocking people – or, as he called it, 'making mischief' – was Jimmy's stock in trade. His father had also been homosexual and had committed suicide after being jilted

---

* A barbiturate known as 'seccies' or 'red dolls' by recreational users. Judy Garland's autopsy found she had overdosed on Seconal.

by his sailor lover. Multilingual and a qualified pilot, Jimmy could play the piano, sing and dance, and was a raconteur.

Most of his 'pranks' were repellent. At a low level they were simply distasteful, such as when he purchased a cow's udder and minced down Madison Avenue with one of the teats hanging out of his flies, but they also included the group rape of a kidnapped waiter and the castration of a victim who refused his advances, which provides some sort of scale of his conception of 'mischief'. With the willing connivance of a group of largely male prostitutes and other disreputable hangers-on it amused Jimmy to abuse – both physically and mentally – various helpless victims, knowing that anyone who complained about him would be paid off by his doting and worried mama. Whenever his more infamous and sordid behaviour looked like reaching the newspapers a team of public relations men countered with stories showing Jimmy with a beautiful woman on his arm, dining and dancing *tête-à-tête*, or helping veterans and old ladies. Despite his intrinsic nastiness, Jimmy was able to make himself appealing in society, and evidently he charmed the Duke and Duchess of Windsor in 1950 when they all found themselves crossing the Atlantic on the *Queen Mary*.[6]

From that date onwards, this unlikely trio were seemingly inseparable. Encouraged by his mother Jimmy bankrolled the Windsors, paying for Wallis's purchases at Mainbocher and other world-class fashion houses, buying her a collection of fabulous furs, paying the couple's air fares, always picking up the bills after evenings at smart places such as the Stork Club or the Twenty-One Club, and chartering private yachts for cruises in the Mediterranean. Loathed by many in the British upper classes and American polite society, Jimmy Donahue's presence in the ducal train frequently raised hackles and eventually some top houses were denied to the Duke and Duchess if Donahue was in attendance. Elsa Maxwell – still going strong in her late sixties and still throwing her incomparably smart parties – was so disgusted by Donahue that she openly criticised the relationship and warned Wallis that it would not enhance her reputation. As a result, the two women did not speak to each other for some years.

A number of books and newspaper articles have been written about the relationship between Wallis and Jimmy Donahue, which is sometimes purported to have been a sexual one. In some of these a good deal has been made from little actual evidence and the conclusions reached appear to be based mainly on supposition, more with an eye to increased book and newspaper sales than any need to verify facts. It would make far more sense had it been claimed that Jimmy had an affair with the Duke, for some of Donahue's gay friends have said that – initially at least – it was the Duke in whom Jimmy was interested. However, that story seems unlikely, for as far as Wallis was concerned the Duke wore his heart on his sleeve until his death.

Did Wallis have an affair with Jimmy Donahue? The answer is that we don't – and can never – know the truth. According to several of his male lovers, Jimmy Donahue was physically revolted by women. Some writers on the subject, determined to prove the unprovable, have inevitably claimed that while there was no actual penetrative sex, Wallis – totally obsessed in her flirtation with a younger man – had performed oral sex on him. Jimmy apparently boasted of a 'blow job' from Wallis – and this, whether true or not, is perfectly in line with his character. But it would still appear to infringe their differing sexual orientations for which, at least in his case, there is plenty of substantiation. The interior designer Nicholas Haslam, the son of a diplomat, was then a young member on the fringe of the same social set and knew Wallis and Donahue, and his comments to Wallis's biographer seem to have a credible bearing on the matter: 'I can't think he would have touched any woman, let alone one as rigidly un-undressable as Wallis.'[7]

Wallis was naturally flirtatious and her upbringing as a belle in America's south was deeply ingrained. She also appears to have enjoyed heterosexual sex, for as well as her several marriages there is incontrovertible evidence of her having enjoyed a liaison, most probably a sexual one, during the period when she was still married to Ernest Simpson and was also being pursued seriously by the then Prince of Wales. The relationship was detailed by the Special Branch of the Metropolitan Police, who had Wallis under surveillance from the time that the Prince's inclinations towards her became obvious. Her lover, Guy Trundle, was the rakish son of a vicar, employed by Ford Motors to market their cars to the trade. He was described in the police report as 'a very charming adventurer, very good looking, well-bred and a good dancer'. The pair often met openly at social events but made 'secret assignations' when – it was alleged by the surveillance officer – 'intimate relations take place'. This statement would seem to be confirmed by Trundle's subsequent open boasts about his relationship with Wallis, and his assertion that she had made him presents of money and expensive trinkets. Her latest biographer regarded this behaviour by Wallis as 'part of the flirtatious and promiscuous pattern which provided her with continuous reassurance of her attractiveness to men'.[8] She also openly enjoyed the company of many gay men, including Noël Coward, Barry Dierks, Cecil

Beaton and Somerset Maugham, to name a few who were among the regular guests at Windsor entertainments.

Of course there are those who hint darkly that the androgynous-looking Wallis was really a man (and this despite the fact that she had a pregnancy terminated in her youth, and it is a matter of record that in 1951 she was diagnosed with, and treated for, cancer of the womb). Just as she was supposed, as a young naval bride posted to the Far East, to have studied 'Chinese' sex techniques and used these to ensnare her prince. But such outrageous claims aside, why would the ambitious and level-headed fifty-four-year-old Duchess risk everything – especially as she must, surely, have known how unreliable he was – for a one-sided relationship with Jimmy? It makes intriguing gossip, but somehow it doesn't totally add up. Many women will have experienced the very special charm of a personable gay man flirting with her, each knowing there is no danger involved. Even accepting that sexual morals among this particular set of people were often loose (to say the least), it seems most likely that for Wallis this *was* merely a flirtation, because Jimmy, a fellow American, was free from stuffy European protocol, and quipped endlessly with salacious, camp tittle-tattle. He made her laugh, and he made her feel young and carefree again. The Duke had slowed down considerably, no longer wanting to carouse until the early hours and often returning home before his wife, or allowing her to go out alone, especially when he was working on his memoirs.* Also, ironically, she may have felt safe from adverse gossip when with him, because Jimmy was so openly gay.

---

* *A King's Story* (1951). The Duke was not the 'onlie begetter' – he was assisted by a ghost writer, Charles Murphy, who later wrote his own version with additional information he had gleaned during his work.

A member of the Windsors' personal staff* recorded in her diary what appears to be the crisis caused by Donahue's relationship with the Duchess. Wallis habitually returned home late from her solo evenings out on the town with Donahue, humming a tune and smiling. One such evening she went into the Duke's bedroom as usual to say goodnight, little knowing that since her departure someone had told him, 'in his own interests', of the unfavourable gossip about his wife and Jimmy. Wallis was told by a jealous and tearful Duke that whatever relationship she had with Jimmy must stop, not because she was the Duchess of Windsor but because no man would accept such behaviour in a wife. Wallis's response was not heard by the eavesdropper, but when she came out onto the landing 'all her gaiety [was] gone – walking slowly with her head bent, her face submissive, her eyes blue & bewildered ... She was very quiet and submissive for a long time afterwards. She telephoned immediately cancelling whatever arrangement she had made with the young man.'[9]

The Windsors continued to meet Jimmy Donahue socially but as the scales fell from their eyes they became increasingly disillusioned with him and began to find fault. It started with small things: the Duke was irritated by the smell of Jimmy's breath after eating garlic, and the Duchess would correct Jimmy's stories. She was, after all, a frequent dining companion of world leaders and some of the most powerful men on the planet, and Donahue sometimes spoke nonsense. Things

---

* Anne Seagrim, personal secretary to the Duke of Windsor from 1950. Later she was secretary to C. P. Snow and latterly administrator of the Winston Churchill Trust. She admired Wallis as 'charming, witty ... and very intelligent ... There was nothing of the grasping harsh scheming woman one heard so much about.' See *Daily Telegraph* obituary, 19 August 2011.

came to a head at a spa in Baden-Baden in 1954, when they were dining together. Wallis disagreed with something Jimmy said and he retaliated by kicking her ankle under the table, so hard that he drew blood and she cried out in distress. The Duke threw down his napkin and helped his wife to a nearby sofa before coldly turning to Jimmy. 'We've had enough of you, Jimmy,' he said firmly. 'Clear off.' And Jimmy did. They never saw him or Jessie Donahue again.

Twelve years later, aged fifty, Jimmy Donahue was found dead in his apartment, having choked to death on his own vomit after a session of drink and Seconal. The only pictures in his bedroom were a dozen framed photographs of Wallis.

The Donahue incident was the nearest thing to a rift between the Duke and Wallis, and it was soon healed. They sold La Croë to Stavros Niarchos shortly before the Baden-Baden incident, having decided to make Paris their main domicile. Thereafter, their stays on the Riviera would be in rented villas. Soon after their move to Paris, on their eighteenth wedding anniversary, the Duke told Gaston Palewski that he doubted a happier couple existed than he and the Duchess.

17

Changes

The break-up of Aly Khan's marriage, along with the disappearance from the Côte d'Azur of Rita Hayworth and – effectively – the Windsors, marked the changing dynamics of Riviera Society in the Fifties. There were other losses too, of personalities guaranteed to liven a dinner table such as Duff and Diana Cooper.

Duff had spent three highly successful years as the first post-war British ambassador to France, when he and Diana were parodied fondly but mercilessly by their friend Nancy Mitford in her novels about society life in Paris. The post had earned Duff a knighthood in 1948, and he spent the next six years writing. His biggest success was his autobiography, *Old Men Forget*, and in 1952 he was created Viscount Norwich for his political and literary work. His wife, saying that the title sounded too much like 'porridge', advertised in the newspapers that she wished still to be known as Lady Diana Cooper.

*

Winston Churchill, back in power since 1951, had weathered several strokes since the first at Max Beaverbrook's Villa La Capponcina in 1949. The worst of these – again kept secret from the British public – occurred in London in June 1953, shortly after the coronation of Queen Elizabeth. In September that year Winston again stayed at Cap d'Ail where, apart from a few trips to Monte Carlo, he did very little other than work on an important speech. Once again the Riviera climate worked its magic and he slowly regained his health.

Beaverbrook allowed Winston to treat the villa as his own and invite whomever he wished. These were mainly old friends such Daisy Fellowes, widowed now, for her husband – Winston's fun-loving and extraordinarily complaisant cousin Reggie – had died in 1953 after years in a wheelchair following a stroke, nursed admirably by Daisy. The couple had suffered a deep trauma in the post-war years. Daisy's daughter from her first marriage, the Princess Jacqueline Marguerite de Broglie, had worked for the French Resistance, and in 1941 married an engineer called Alfred Kraus following a hasty wartime romance. Kraus was subsequently found to have been an important Abwehr agent, and in 1945 was accused of betraying members of Jacqueline's cell in order to protect her. He was interned before eventual repatriation, but Jacqueline was apprehended by a mob and had her head shaved as punishment. Daisy's self-confessed feelings of shame over this did not change her habits: she continued to throw impressive parties in Paris and entertain on the Riviera at Les Zoraides where the luncheon menu seldom varied – Churchill's secretary noted that even in August it was 'vodka, more vodka, caviar and grouse'.[1]

Winston was understandably most comfortable with old

friends around him, but he found few survivors now from the old Maxine days. His friend Consuelo Balsan – née Vanderbilt, and the former wife of Winston's cousin and best friend of his youth, Sunny, the Duke of Marlborough – now owned a hilltop mansion in Provence and adored Winston's occasional visits. And Willie Somerset Maugham was still around for luncheons with stimulating conversation. It all helped his recovery, and on his return to England in November 1953, Winston delivered an uplifting speech to the Conservative Annual Conference at Margate. He even injected some off-the-cuff humour, and showed no sign of reduced faculties. Throughout the summer there had been considerable press speculation about his health and capability to continue in office, but his dazzling rabbit out of the hat performance at Margate put an end to it; Winston was nearly eighty, but he was able to demonstrate that he was still a force to be reckoned with, and he also knew that in a matter of weeks he would be back in the warmth of his beloved Côte d'Azur.

New personalities had appeared on the Riviera to replace absent friends. The Greek shipping magnate Aristotle Onassis became a prominent face; he based himself in Monte Carlo and entertained grandly on his yacht. His wife Athina (Tina) was the daughter of the ship owner Stavros G. Livanos, a Greek traditionalist who disliked Onassis and his business methods, and they had two children, Alexander and Christina (for whom he named his yacht).

The *Christina O* was the most luxurious yacht on the Riviera. A converted Canadian wartime frigate with a top cruising speed of eighteen knots, she carried a twin-engine amphibious plane as well as several pleasure boats for guests to use. Air-conditioned throughout, she boasted gold taps shaped like dolphins, her own hospital and laundry, telephones in every stateroom, and a swimming pool tiled with a fresco copied from the Palace of Knossos in Crete that could be emptied and the base hydraulically lifted to provide a dance floor. The beautifully appointed salon boasted an El Greco* as well as one of Winston's landscapes, and there were valuable works of art dotted throughout the ship. Few people ever refused an invitation to cruise on the *Christina*, including Winston Churchill and Aly Khan.

After Rita Hayworth's departure, Aly regularly featured in newspapers escorting a chain of beautiful women including Joan Fontaine. At a ball thrown by Jacques Fath he danced with Pam Churchill for the entire evening. Rita had started formal divorce proceedings and she went on record in the newspapers announcing that while she loved Aly he didn't understand family life and thought only of gambling, horse racing and big-game hunting. 'He is a playboy,' she stated, 'while I work all the year round in Hollywood.'[2] When she got home after work, Rita continued, she didn't want to have to share it with eighty of Aly's friends 'of all kinds, coming and going'. She neglected to explain her chief complaint, that they were mostly women friends, or that during the Cannes Festival that year his visitors had regularly included Gina Lollobrigida, Yvonne de Carlo and the Greek actress Irene Papas. Irene Papas once said that her affair with Aly had set her career as a serious actress back by ten years.[3]

---

* Tina divorced Ari in 1960, citing his multiple infidelities, but it was widely rumoured to have been following her discovery of her husband and Maria Callas *in flagrante* on the white leather sofa beneath the El Greco. Tina then married the Duke of Marlborough.

Aly did not sleep with every woman who visited the villa, of course, but he never turned down an opportunity either. And it must be said that the women he invited to stay were often long-legged and spectacularly lovely. He was coupled that year with the Folies Bergère star Mistinguett, and Zsa Zsa Gabor who was in Paris that year (1954) to make the movie *Moulin Rouge*. There was considerable press interest in his relationship with Lise Bourdin, a gorgeous French actress and singer. The ingénue Lise assumed that staying at the Château de l'Horizon and sleeping with Aly meant she was engaged to him. Indeed she announced this in a press statement, but she was speedily disillusioned.

Debo, the young Duchess of Devonshire, spent a few weeks each year at the Château de l'Horizon in Aly's time, usually accompanied by one of her female friends as a chaperone because the Duke was working as part of Princess Margaret's train. Half a century later Debo would recall that Aly was frequently absent during these visits, but that his house-guests were free to wallow in the luxury he provided, supervised by his 'sweet' Italian uncle, a secretary and an excellent chef. Debo wrote home to her mother about her trips in a series of letters, several of which have been compressed here:[4]

Aly has got a lovely new boat, we spent the day in it yesterday and went to St Tropez ... This house is ... so quiet after Cannes which is stuffed full of [tourists] with huge cars. Here we have the sea under our windows and the pool as well; one can bathe in the night – it's all so lovely and warm ... it's a sort of dotty dream world here, with everything almost too easy ... I do love the change of food and company, but I couldn't stay up so late for very long. One needn't get up in the mornings though, so it comes to the same thing in the end ... one might as well throw away one's watch – the disregard of time is something chronic ... Everyone is incredibly late; we sat down to lunch today at a quarter to 3 and dinner is out at a restaurant at about 10 p.m. – we go to bed at 3 or 4 in the morning but as the restaurants and night clubs are all out of doors it isn't half so tiring as when one's eyes are filled with smoke ...

The Château de l'Horizon was invariably filled with an eclectic mixture of visitors and callers which amused Debo: 'A lot of frogs have come this morning to make a bit of a film,' she wrote one day. 'I can watch it from my balcony, all taking *hours,* with the star sitting looking cross in a hairnet.'

During a March 1954 visit she wrote that there was 'a very odd collection of people ... a Frog general, [an] Irish Stud manager, and some of the Marquis de Cueva's ballet dancers, all very nice, but all complete opposites and yet they all seem to get on all right, even though the ballet ones can't speak English.'

Debo was often provided with one of Aly's sports cars to enable her to shop in Cannes, visit local gardens to get ideas for Chatsworth or to tour the area. When Aly was in residence he took her to the ballet, or sometimes to the Casino in Monte Carlo which didn't appeal to her, or to Yakymour to see his father:

We've twice been to the Aga's. Goodness he is sweet. The Begum is a giantess, quite friendly, with a ghastly common secretary-companion ... I want to laugh every time she speaks ... Oh ... the *Aga!* The utter sweetness, I worship him; I will become a Believer ... He tells gossip of 50–60 years ago, and says [about Debo's long-dead grandfather and uncles] things like 'he was in the 4th, or was it the 10th?' and expects one to know, although the person has always been dead for at least 40 years. Aly and the Begum can't stick each other, one can see.

The old Aga was very unhappy with Aly over his frequent appearances in the newspapers with 'unsuitable' women; he felt very strongly that this was not the right image for a man widely regarded as heir presumptive to the title of Imam of the Ismailis.

Aly had by now become deeply involved with another beautiful screen goddess. This time it was Gene Tierney, whom he had met while on a bloodstock buying and selling trip in Argentina, where she was making the movie *The Way of the Gaucho*. Gene had a string of successes behind her and was best known for her portrayal of the character Laura in the film of the same name. She was nominated for a Best Actress Oscar in *Leave Her to Heaven* and had starred in a series of other well-known and still-loved movies such as *Heaven can Wait*, *The Ghost and Mrs Muir* and *The Mating Season*. Her high cheekbones were somehow emphasised by the shadows created by black-and-white movies and gave her an ethereal, aristocratic look. She and Aly fell for each other at their first meeting and, as always, Aly quickly monopolised her.

The Aga and the Begum looked upon this latest of Aly's exploits with deepening disproval. At Aly's flamboyant New Year's Eve party held in Cannes the Aga was horrified to find that a pile of cotton wool balls were provided on each table for guests to soak in champagne and throw at each other. Aly had never been allowed to get as close to his father as young Sadruddin, and when he stood and laughingly pelted the elderly nobleman with soaked 'snowballs' he was evidently unable to see his father's distress. At midnight Aly publicly demonstrated his affection for Gene Tierney with a passionate kiss in the middle of the dance floor, and the Aga was heard to complain to the Begum that he – who had been the friend of Queen Victoria, who had dined with every crowned head and world leader in the twentieth century – was now subjected to this vulgarity by his son.

The Aga Khan had had his own *affaires du cœur* – quite a few of them, in fact – but all his ladies were dealt with according to a strict set of belle-époque rules and rewarded appropriately when the affair ended; some were regarded as old friends. Even after he married the Begum, he enjoyed the odd dalliance, but discretion was his watchword. Few if any of these romances ever reached the newspapers.

There was an immense charm and an old-world courtly manner about the Aga, which Debo witnessed and was captivated by. He was a kind and gentle man with a wonderful magnetism. His attitude towards the opposite sex was that of a man who adored women, and he invariably treated them as though they were special, fragile, beloved creatures.

Perhaps this characteristic is best illustrated by the story of Heather Manchester,* who met the Aga in the early Fifties, when he was in his seventies. She was twenty and only recently married when her husband was sent to a Swiss

---

* A pseudonym.

clinic for the treatment of acute bronchitis. She had gone to stay at the Hotel Royal in San Remo, a venerable old Riviera hotel, much patronised in its heyday by European royalty. It was just across the Italian border and located where Heather could easily visit her husband if needed. She was nominally chaperoned by her aunt and uncle who, however, preferred the much livelier social scene at Nice's Hôtel Negresco some twenty miles away, so Heather was left alone at the Royal, which in the off-season was almost empty and very quiet.

Wishing to let her mother know she had arrived safely, she dressed quickly in the clothes she had worn while travelling the previous day and went down to the reading room to write a postcard. 'Consequently,' she said, 'I looked like a ragbag.' There was only one other occupant of the reading room and she recognised him instantly as the Aga Khan, famous to her as the owner of numerous Derby winners. With the confidence of youth she pretended not to know who he was, or to withdraw, and a relationship developed between them. After that, they met in the reading room every morning for about a month, and spent from breakfast until lunchtime chatting and laughing, he teasing her gently.

He was multi-lingually fluent, and for a man who had had four wives, and was reputed to have several mistresses, he seemed remarkably unsure of himself with a woman ... Initially I think he was shyer than I was. He always referred to me as '*La petite madame*' but within a few days we had drawn closer to each other than I have ever felt to anyone in my life. When I left him I was always fizzing. I have never felt anything like it before or since.[5]

319

Curiously, she had already met Aly, while on honeymoon in Paris. Heather and her bridegroom had gone out to dine on a stormy winter night at an exclusive new restaurant and found only one other couple dining – it was Aly and Rita, and Aly, his leg in plaster after his skiing accident, suggested they might like to join them. 'I remember how this couple literally glowed with love for each other,' she told me, 'and I was impressed by the size of Rita's ring, which had a stone the size of a postage stamp.' They never met again, but one morning in San Remo Heather saw a story about Rita splashed across the headlines and she found the Aga grumpy and agitated. She wrote:

I recalled that lovely glowing Rita, and I knew the Aga disliked this sort of thing for we had spoken of it. Rita was arguably the most famous woman of her time – a bit like Princess Diana became later. During the war we had Vera Lynn and Churchill; the Americans had Rita Hayworth and Roosevelt. Artillery shells used to come off the production line and were adorned with messages such as 'with love from Rita Hayworth'. She was a household name and her marriage to Aly Khan had been on every cinema newsreel and in every newspaper ... I knew the Aga thought such publicity was demeaning. I listened for a minute and then told him reasonably: 'She doesn't have to <u>do</u> anything to make these headlines; she just has to <u>be</u>,' and he calmed down at that, because he had himself experience of excessive press intrusion and when I asked him once if he minded people always looking at him, he thought about it a little and told me 'You get used to it. And you know that when people stare at you it is not mere curiosity; they get pleasure from seeing you.' My point about Rita had been made and he appreciated it.

They spoke every day for hours; he told her of his love for his family and his pleasure when he watched Aly ride in races ('He has no fear ... is as brave as a lion'), his admiration for Aly's eye for a horse and his concern at the way Aly drove ('He drives like a *maniac* ... he will kill himself one day.'). He also spoke of his youngest son Sadruddin, who was a contemporary of Aly's son Karim, and how close those two boys were – they were 'more like brothers'.

There was never any impropriety, and as far as Heather was concerned age and physical intimacy were irrelevant: 'We existed for each other in the moment, and we were both absolutely fully aware of what we had together. It seemed perfect just as it was.'

After more than a month she received the phone call from Switzerland telling her that her husband was to be allowed to leave hospital, and although she had always known this moment would come, and part of her welcomed the news, the suddenness of it shocked her. She raced through the foyer, late for her meeting, and cannoned into the Aga, who had come to look for her. It was their only physical contact. He held her in his arms saying with a smile, 'Ah *petite madame* – at last I have you.' But as he looked into her face and saw her distress he must have guessed the reason, and released her gently. Heather, drowning in the moment of intimacy, glanced up at the hotel reception staff as she and the Aga walked to the reading room; they were open-mouthed at the incident. 'I didn't care: I was too unhappy. Meeting this wonderful man and falling in love with him had been like coming into the sunlight.' She knew he took as much pleasure in their relationship as she did.

On the following day – her last at the hotel – while she was

lunching with her aunt and uncle the Aga walked purpose-
fully to their table and bowed deeply to her. '*Merci bien*,' he
said quietly. The dining room was agog for the Aga never
dined publicly; her aunt was suspiciously puzzled but Heather
had nothing to reproach herself for and did not feel obliged to
explain. She saw the Aga only once more as she left.

> He looked at me with such overwhelming tenderness in his
> eyes, he could see that despite the tears in mine, my face
> was full of love for him. The concierge came for me, and
> we bade each other a formal goodbye. That was the last
> time I ever saw him. I read about it in the papers when he
> died in Geneva about seven years later. But he is with me
> still.

As well as his racing successes, the Aga was famous for having
been weighed in gold and diamonds for his jubilee celebrations. What could he do for his seventieth anniversary in 1954
to top this? It was called his Platinum Jubilee Observance,
and there was no precedent for such a ceremony, which would
be held in Karachi. He asked Aly to accompany him and the
Begum, and Aly – as well as many Ismailis – believed that
in his post-ceremonial address the Aga would formally name
Aly as his successor. It was all Aly had ever dreamed of; he
regarded it as his birthright to be leader of their people. And
it would be fair to say that most of them openly venerated
him as the natural heir.

The gorgeously spectacular ceremony in Karachi was duly
held and afterwards the Aga gave the address for which Aly
was waiting. But nothing was said about who was to be his
successor, a position which was in the Aga's own gift. Aly was

deeply humiliated and distressed, but only allowed Emrys Williams to see his tears of frustration. He continued the considerable amount of work he carried out on behalf of the Ismailis because he felt it was his duty, but also he still hoped that his father would one day name him as his successor.

Aly was now free again, Rita having obtained her divorce,* and he transferred all his attention to Gene Tierney. She had spent the spring of 1954 in England, shooting the final scenes of the movie *Personal Affair*. During this time Aly flew in his own plane, sometimes several times a week, to see her and they spent weekends in Ireland and Deauville. Gene was pictured with him at the Derby and at the Oaks, and when she had to return to Hollywood for a new movie Aly recalled his experiences with Rita and arranged for them to rendezvous quietly in Mexico.

He slipped incognito into Mexico by flying in from Canada, and they booked into a luxurious beach hotel on the Baja peninsula just twenty minutes from the border with California, which enabled Gene to be back in Hollywood within a couple of hours' drive. That meant she could report to the studio quickly, without raising any suspicions. The relationship with the exquisitely beautiful Gene flourished; she was a far better match for Aly's lifestyle than Rita had ever been. For a start Gene spoke fluent French and had attended – as Aly had – a boarding school in Switzerland. She had grown up among a smart set of people who lived in New York and spent weekends in second homes in Connecticut, and she was never intimidated by the people Aly introduced to her. She

---

* She immediately married fellow actor Dick Haymes, which was to prove another deeply unhappy marriage for her. See Postscript.

rode well, and Aly was considerably impressed when, given a hot horse to ride, Gene managed it with total aplomb. When staying at the Château de l'Horizon she usually played tennis with the Carlton Hotel coach Tommy Burke, who rated her ability very highly.[6] Unlike Rita, Gene was happy to stay out late, enjoying the pace of Aly's life, loving his fast cars and the way he drove them, and she took an interest in the running of his homes in Cannes and Deauville, although Aly did not care for her attitude towards his staff, which he thought imperious compared with his own relaxed attitude. When she stayed at the villa in the late summer a fellow guest was Lise Bourdin, which might have been awkward, but Gene weathered it gracefully. Lise dropped out of the picture. To his friends Aly looked much happier and behaved more quietly than he had for some time. And yet Gene undeniably came with baggage.

Discovered in her teens and put under contract by Columbia, she had warded off the amorous advances of Howard Hughes, who nevertheless became a lifelong friend. She then met Oleg Cassini (later the internationally famous fashion designer) and eloped with him in the face of her parents' disapproval. While entertaining troops in Hollywood she contracted German measles from a fan during the first trimester of her pregnancy and as a result Gene's daughter, Daria, was born prematurely with severe mental and physical damage. Daria spent her life in a series of expensive institutions in California, always lovingly cared for, and most of these costs were met by Howard Hughes. Several years later Gene met a fan seeking an autograph. The woman told her that she had served in a women's corps of the Marines, and was quarantined with rubella on the day of Gene's only concert in Hollywood. She bragged that she was so desperate to see her idol that she sneaked out to see her and shake her hand. Gene later wrote that she had stared silently at the woman, realising immediately what had happened, then she had turned and walked away. Twenty years later this exact scenario was used – almost word for word – as part of the plot in Agatha Christie's novel *The Mirror Crack'd from Side to Side*.

Perhaps the stresses of this sad occurrence contributed to the collapse of Gene and Cassini's marriage after several periods of living apart, although the couple had two more daughters before they eventually divorced. Gene had met the young veteran John F. Kennedy on the set of *Dragonwyck* and began a serious romance with him, only to part painfully after a year when he told her firmly that he could never marry her because of his political ambitions. She and Cassini reconciled, parted again, then remarried and divorced for a second time in 1952,* a year before Gene met Aly in Rio de Janeiro. She had occasional bouts of depression but seemed well able to cope with any personal demons during the time she was with Aly. One further problem was Gene's mother. Manipulative and ambitious, she had once unsuccessfully sued Gene and Cassini for a share in Gene's earnings from movies, claiming that Gene was part of the family business. Aly seemed able even to charm Mrs Tierney, who admitted she liked him, but no one would have wanted someone like Mrs Tierney in their lives.

The Aga could not see *any* beneficial aspects to Aly and Gene's relationship. What he mainly recalled was the

---

* They remained friends until Gene's death in 1991.

vulgarity of that New Year's Eve party in which Gene had appeared to revel in Aly's behaviour, and even encourage it, and he squirmed at the constant newspaper gossip about them. Furthermore, having already lived through the trauma of Aly's marriage to and divorce from Rita, the old man simply did not want his position, or his family, or his followers, tarnished by yet another marriage to a Hollywood screen goddess. He had taken Aly's divorce badly, had despised the sensational media coverage (his own had always been handled with such discretion). He had actually come to like Rita and he adored the granddaughter, Yasmin, who had resulted from the marriage. Now he never saw Yasmin, which was a source of great sadness and bitterness to him as his health deteriorated. He sent for Elsa Maxwell and asked her to go to Aly with a message from him. The message was that if he married Gene Tierney 'my door will be closed to them both'. He would not, he concluded, allow Aly's indiscriminate marriages to destroy their family heritage.

In the autumn of 1955 Winston Churchill again visited Beaverbrook's villa, La Capponcina, where he spent two months working on his *History of the English-Speaking Peoples*. He returned to England for Christmas and then, as arranged, went back to the Riviera as the guest of his literary agent, Emery Reves, and Reves's beautiful mistress Wendy Russell,* a Texan former fashion model who had been a cover girl for *Vogue* and *Harper's Bazaar*, at Roquebrune-Cap-Martin.

---

* They would marry in 1956. Even before their marriage, Churchill always referred to Wendy as Mrs Reves.

Their impressive villa had been built for Coco Chanel in the early Thirties after she purchased a five-acre plot that had originally been a lavender farm, set among wild olives and citrus trees, at about the same time Maxine Elliott built Château de l'Horizon. The villa's new name, La Pausa, is said to reflect the old legend that Mary Magdalene paused at the spot after leaving the Holy Land following the crucifixion of Christ. The building, which cost in excess of six million francs, a good proportion of which was spent on white Carrara marble, was mainly financed by Chanel's lover Hugh Grosvenor, 2nd Duke of Westminster, and was famous for its all-white minimalist decor, apart from some massive pieces of antique oak furniture sent from various homes of the Duke in England.

Sited at an elevation of 600ft on the sunny hillside of a promontory, La Pausa has a panoramic view over Monte Carlo some six miles to the west, and eastwards to the Italian frontier and Italian Riviera resorts. In Chanel's day the villa was visited by strings of eminent guests including Stravinsky, Picasso, Salvador Dalí and Luchino Visconti, and while standing apparently empty during the war, it had been utilised to advantage by the French Resistance. The villa's architect, Robert Streitz, established a hideout in a cellar with a secret exit onto the garden. Here he hid a radio and also, from time to time, a number of Jewish refugees who were in the process of being smuggled to the Italian border.[7] Chanel had a high-ranking German lover so her house was not badly affected by occupation, and the couple made several visits to it during the war without ever realising its covert use.

Emery Reves, a Hungarian Jewish refugee, had purchased La Pausa from Chanel in 1953, having made a post-war fortune as sole distribution agent for – among other things – Churchill's six volumes of *The Second World War*.* He spent almost two years renovating the villa with Wendy's able help until it was a treasure house of pictures, statuary, furniture, carpets and *objets d'art*. 'The effect was breath-taking . . . [and] the breadth and richness were extraordinary,' Churchill's secretary reported.[8] It was not a huge house, but it was well-proportioned and surrounded by jewel-green lawns and simple landscaping. Once inside, the iron gates were locked to create an utterly private world. Every male visitor to La Pausa had the soles of their shoes cleaned by the major-domo as they entered the house, and women had to take their shoes off.[9] It was a perfect setting for a world-class collection of more than seventy important Impressionist and post-Impressionist paintings and Spanish works of art which had been started by Emery, but Wendy was also knowledge-able on the subject and helped to establish the collection and hang the works to advantage.

Churchill had accepted the invitation with alacrity. His doctor, Lord Moran, noted how much improved his patient's health was after a spell in the South of France, and especially the lift in Churchill's spirits after his visit to La Pausa.[10] This was to be the first of many extended visits, of up to a third of a year at a time, to Roquebrune, following Winston's retire-ment as Prime Minister.

An entire floor was set aside for Winston to make his own quarters; it included a sunny bedroom suite for him, an office for his secretary (Anthony Montague Browne) and a

---

* Connected with Churchill since the early 1930s, Reves had distributed overseas rights to Churchill's pre-war writings, but Churchill did not make serious money from his books until after the war.

separate room for Clementine for the occasional times that she visited. Clementine never lost her dislike of the Riviera and the crowd it attracted. She was even unhappy about Winston's liking for it. 'It epitomised to me,' she once told Montague Browne, 'the shallowest side of his nature.'[11] And even though the Churchills had by now escaped the threat of relative poverty thanks to the success of his books, and they would never again feel the pinch of money shortage which had always terrified her, Clementine remained afraid of the siren attractions of the Casino which called to Winston. As a matter of fact, Emery and Wendy also disliked the Casino, so that was one point – perhaps the only one – in their favour as far as Clementine was concerned. Always a jealous guardian of her husband's public image, when invited to fly down to the Riviera and join him in a cruise on the Onassis yacht she responded pointedly that she had no desire to become beholden to 'this rich and powerful man' and for it to appear in newspapers. She said she felt the same about the Reveses, though to a lesser degree.[12]

Winston always hoped, however, that she would join him at La Pausa at some point and assured her that Reves only ever invited people he (Winston) wanted to see ('and none that I don't').[13] Meanwhile, various members of his family joined him there from time to time.

As a personable couple, Emery and Wendy might have attracted a similar calibre of visitors anyway, but there was an undeniable pulling power in having Churchill as a long-term house-guest. Wendy had known Princess Grace of Monaco as an actress in Hollywood, but it took Churchill's residence at La Pausa to bring forth an invitation to lunch at the Prince's Palace at Monaco in early June. It was the first formal luncheon the Prince and Princess had given since their spectacular marriage six weeks earlier, which had captivated the world. Winston later said that when people asked him about the royal couple he gave both 'a good character'. The Prince and Princess made several visits to La Pausa after that, but always when Winston was in residence. The Windsors also came to several lunches and dinners whenever their time in the south coincided with Winston's visits. The Duke was deaf now, and perhaps because of this was very quiet at table. After one such occasion Winston told his secretary that the Duke had become 'an empty man'. He had shown extraordinary promise, Winston continued, but it had only been 'Morning Glory'.

There was also a fair sprinkling of international stars who were invited to La Pausa, among them Greta Garbo (whom Winston first met at Les Zoraides while lunching with Daisy Fellowes), Errol Flynn and Clark Gable. He once met Frank Sinatra, but that was accidental. Winston was standing at the entrance of the Casino in Monte Carlo waiting for his car when the singer appeared, grabbed his hand and shook it, saying 'I have always wanted to do that' before departing. Winston, who hated to be touched, took a moment to recover from this effrontery before bellowing 'Who the hell was that?' He was not much wiser when told.

One of the first visitors, though, that January, was Daisy Fellowes, who dropped Winston a note to tell him that she had suffered a thrombosis in the previous July 'and nearly went to the Bon Dieu – but he did not want me'. Now she longed to see Winston again and so invited him and his hosts to lunch. Later she came to La Pausa, bringing her 'young man' (her last lover), looking twenty years younger than her age, Winston wrote, and keeping them all agog with her funny stories and gossip. Winston's secretary thought it very questionable, when there was still such visible poverty nearby, that a woman of her age would spend two thousand pounds on a single gown. He was equally scathing of her morals, and suspected she was responsible for spreading mischievous rumours that there was something beyond friendship between Winston and Wendy.

Just as Maxine Elliott had once done, Emery and Wendy took 'endless pains', according to Anthony Montague Browne, for Winston's comfort and entertainment in what were to be his final productive years; Montague Browne described the time at 'Pausaland' as lotus-eating days in which the entire establishment revolved around Winston and his wishes. Inevitably, whenever the great man ventured out of the confines of the villa he was quickly surrounded by crowds of admirers, or the frankly curious. So unless he was invited to the homes of friends nearby he preferred to stay at La Pausa, sitting quietly under a large parasol smoking a cigar and admiring the lovely views, or chatting with his host and hostess in the lavender-scented gardens. He still worked each morning on his writing and correspondence, painting in the afternoon when the mood took him. He enjoyed playing bezique and being educated in serious music by his host. Emery Reves was a talented classical pianist and Winston always enjoyed listening to him play after dinner. These periods of rest and contentment were, Winston would later recall, 'among the brightest of my life'.[14]

Wendy openly stated that she adored Winston, but it was a love born out of admiration for his achievements, a genuine affection for the old man and a sincere gratitude for what his association with Emery had done for them both. Winston was certainly extremely fond of Wendy, unusually so, in fact. His letters to Clementine were full of praise for his hostess and he often mentioned how charming, agreeable and kind she was – usually in an attempt to lure his wife to join him at La Pausa. He even admitted that his plans to buy or lease a house of his own somewhere close to La Capponcina and La Pausa (which horrified Clementine) had now been put off because he was made to feel so welcome by Wendy and her insistence that he stay as often and as long as he wished.

Noël Coward was one of the many high-profile and entertaining guests invited to La Pausa that year – along with the couturier Edward Molyneux, with whom Coward was staying, and Somerset Maugham – all with the aim of keeping Winston amused and stimulated. Coward wrote in his diary: 'to Roquebrune to lunch with Emery Reves, Wendy Russell, the most fascinating lady, Winston Churchill, Sarah [Churchill] and Winston's secretary'. Winston, he noted, was 'absolutely obsessed with Wendy Russell. He followed her about the room with his brimming eyes and wobbled after her across the terrace . . . I doubt if . . . Churchill has ever been physically unfaithful to Lady Churchill but, oh, what has gone on inside that dynamic mind?'[15]

There was more, which doesn't need repeating, but it added up to an unusually spiteful implication that it was an old man's last sexual fling. Anthony Montague Browne, who always enjoyed the luxurious visits to La Pausa, later suggested that Noël Coward's rumour-mongering was no more than bitchiness because Coward believed (incorrectly) that Winston had played a part in his consistent omission from the honours list. Or it might have been a riposte to Winston's off-the-cuff remark about another homosexual, that 'buggers can't be choosers'.[16] Montague Browne agreed that there was a form of love and affection between Winston and Wendy, but one which owed nothing to the prurient insinuations of Noël Coward. However, Diana Mosley and Nancy Mitford, Beaverbrook and others in their circle firmly believed that Winston *was* infatuated with Wendy, and even Winston's doctor noted in his medical record the 'uplift' in Winston's spirits whenever he visited La Pausa.

Probably, Winston did fall in love with Wendy in a way, and his feelings were reciprocated. But it was never a sexual relationship. It never affected Wendy's happy relationship with Emery, or Winston's visceral love for Clementine, except in so much as it kept the Churchills apart physically because he so enjoyed himself at La Pausa, where he was spoiled and *never* corrected. Winston was affected with an octogenarian equivalent of a teenage crush, and Wendy with idol worship.

To be fair, the rumours of Winston's obsession with Wendy did not originate with Noël Coward. Coward was staying at the time with Molyneux (who was in love with Coward) at Biot, a hilltop town between Cannes and Villeneuve-Loubet. The two men had first heard of Winston's supposed infatuation in the previous week, when they dined with Pamela Churchill at the Agnelli villa and had been told by her that the matter was causing some concern within the family. The rumours quickly swirled into society and appeared, in various forms, in several contemporary letters.

Aristotle Onassis first came to lunch at La Pausa with Randolph Churchill, who had been staying on the *Christina* while Randolph's daughter, niece and sister were staying with the Reveses. Such was Churchill's reputation that Onassis was uncharacteristically nervous of offending, but his ability and strength favourably impressed the great man.[17] After Winston accepted an invitation to visit the yacht he stated that it was the most beautiful structure he had ever seen afloat.

That was to be the start of a long and unlikely friendship, and thereafter there would be frequent day cruises along the coast in the incomparable yacht with its master and crew dedicated to one aim: ensuring Churchill enjoyed himself, no matter what the cost. Onassis thought nothing of shipping an entire orchestra along to play while they cruised. Winston called him Ari and was always the cosseted guest of honour. Onassis 'never took his eyes off him', watched out for his needs and personally served him with drinks, or fetched a blanket if he thought Winston might be cold on deck. Lord Moran noticed how, noticing a hair on Winston's collar, Onassis hurried off to find a clothes brush. Once when Winston was unwell he fed him tiny teaspoons of caviar 'as one feeds a baby',[18] and learned to play bezique in order to partner his hero. Moran thought Onassis a kindly man, and a lonely soul for all his great wealth.

The Reveses did not like Onassis, whom Emery regarded as vulgar, any more than they liked Daisy Fellowes, but they nobly continued to invite both into their home for Winston's sake.

Robert Boothby may have been in at the very start of the enmity between Daisy and Wendy, recalling in his memoir a luncheon party at a private villa to which Churchill, Wendy, Onassis and Daisy were invited. Churchill had not been well and after lunch appeared to become unconscious in his chair.

The other guests were obviously shocked and Daisy whispered to their host, 'What a pity that so great a man should end his life in the company of Onassis and Wendy Reves.' Suddenly, to their horror, one eye opened and Churchill said, 'Daisy, Wendy Reves is something you will never be. She is young, she is beautiful, and she is kind.' Then he closed his eye again.[19]

18

Causes and Effects

When Elsa Maxwell delivered the message to Aly from his father saying that if he married Gene Tierney he would be removed from the succession, he and Gene had already agreed to marry and he had given her a ring – a stunning six-carat emerald-cut diamond – which she flashed at reporters, calling it a 'friendship ring'.

Initially, Gene had agreed to keep the engagement secret, since Aly was still contesting the custody of Yasmin, his daughter with Rita, and he wanted no adverse publicity. He knew his father disliked Gene, but this new ultimatum would end his hopes and dreams for the future and he did not know what to do about it. However, as time wore on Gene's situation changed. She had a run-in with the Internal Revenue Service and came off badly due to a retrospective change in tax legislation. Aly was often in Europe while she was tethered to Hollywood, making a series of movies for which she was contracted, and this made her anxious and short-tempered. She constantly forgot her lines and 'dried up' in front of the cameras, and her worried maid reported to the studio bosses that Gene sat in her bedroom vacantly staring into space for hours. Finally, despatched by the studio to a quiet hotel at Rosarito Beach, Mexico, for a few weeks' rest, Gene moved the ring from her right hand to her left and confessed to reporters that she and Aly were engaged, and they intended to marry 'in about six months, in France'.

Aly was in Paris when the story appeared in the newspapers on the morning of 31 March 1954, and when he telephoned Gene to ask what was going on she insisted, to his consternation, that he marry her this year. He explained again that he needed his father's assent, but told her he would fly at once to Cannes to speak to the Aga. To Gene it appeared he was seeking permission to marry her, but it seems more likely that it was a damage-limitation exercise by Aly, who was already only too well aware of the Aga's strong feelings on the matter. Aly and the Aga spoke at great length, but nothing that Aly said would change the old man's mind: he was adamant that if Aly went ahead and married another movie star he would never be Imam.

Aly flew to California and reported to Gene the outcome of his interview with his father, proposing that they continue their relationship as it was, with her as his indefinite fiancée, his wife in all but name. Gene knew that this actually meant permanent mistress; she became hysterical and the couple argued. Bitter quarrels became the pattern of their meetings during his stay in California, until her tantrums became too much for him to take and Aly made excuses not to see her. He flew back to Europe, and after a while he stopped taking her calls. Realising that the relationship was over, Gene's already fragile mental health failed; she suffered a complete mental breakdown and was admitted to a psychiatric clinic in Hertford, Connecticut. She was treated for over a year but she never regained her former mental health. Later she played some minor roles in films but she was no longer a star; the episode marked the end of Gene's glittering film career. Aly never saw her again.

Aly believed that because he had sacrificed Gene his succession as leader of the Ismailis was now guaranteed. This led to another serious quarrel between him and his father over a remark Aly made in an interview, in which he was asked about the succession and he made certain assumptions. When he learned that Aly had spoken on rumours about his future as leader of the Ismailis the Aga Khan was furious. He berated Aly, calling him presumptuous and outrageous, and told him no one but himself had any right to discuss a successor. All Aly could do was make frantic denials about what he had said and he called a number of press conferences to do so. Soon afterwards the Aga suffered a mild heart attack and Aly evidently made some attempt to be more discreet in what he said to the press, but that same year he was linked with a number of women including the popular French actress Juliette Gréco,* Queen Soraya of Persia (who had parted from the Shah) and several others, one of whom sold her story to the newspapers.

Juliette Gréco had initially ignored Aly's attentions, but even she ended up spending two holidays at the Château de

---

* Juliette Gréco, when asked by a reporter whether she had an affair with Aly, replied: 'I don't know who didn't have an affair with Aly!'

l'Horizon after she found Aly's high-voltage charm impossible to resist. There, she found the same old chaotic situation that had so disconcerted Rita: various women 'crying and slamming doors'; American film-makers who drank too much, starting at breakfast; guests of all shapes and sizes breakfasting in pyjamas on the terrace or unable to resist sliding down the famous chute into the sea. Almost everyone rested in the afternoon ('at least, they went to bed,' she wrote)[1] before an evening on the town, and then they would roll back to the villa at all hours. Aly was everywhere, the great charmer, the great seducer who made all women feel wonderful and adored, and that there was never any need for them to worry about anything. 'It was always, "What can I do for you? What do you need?" Airplane tickets, cars, boats: you felt you were on a pink cloud.'[2]

Debo Devonshire experienced much the same thing, and as well as her visits to Château de l'Horizon she often saw Aly at the races in Paris and sometimes she stayed at his château in Neuilly. Although no night owl, Debo found the time she spent in his company unusual and exciting: 'We went to marvellous night clubs and restaurants including Maxim's and turned night into day, sometimes with friends of his, sometimes on our own,' she said, but despite his seemingly ceaseless round of activity she noted that he also took his duties as heir to the Aga very seriously, and nearly always when they returned from these sorties there was a little group of Ismailis waiting patiently in the entrance hall for an audience with him. In February 1955 Debo accepted Aly's invitation to join him as he fulfilled an old ambition to visit Rio de Janeiro for Mardi Gras. She stayed at the luxurious house of Brazilian friends of his while Aly went off on bloodstock buying and selling trips around the country. When Aly returned she often joined him as he partied hard every night and could only marvel that next day he was still able to play top-class polo or ride out with her to explore the local forests – it was as though he had a source of inexhaustible energy. He never slept more than four hours a night and he did everything faster and better than anyone else, as if he had to drain every drop of fun from life.

It was soon after Aly returned to the Château de l'Horizon from the Brazil trip that he became involved with Simone Bodin, a top fashion model in Paris who was known professionally as Bettina.

Bettina had been Jacques Fath's lead mannequin at a time when the House of Fath was considered one of the three dominant influences of post-war haute couture (the others being Givenchy and Dior) and she was one of the most photographed women in France. Following Fath's death she was lured to Givenchy and soon after met Aly at a ball in Paris. It was not their first meeting, but he had hardly noticed her when they originally met on what was to be her initial visit to the Château de l'Horizon: she had modelled wedding dresses for Rita Hayworth while he volunteered his opinions. Bettina modelled for Aly again, in Paris in 1953, but on that occasion the gowns were intended for Gene Tierney. Then, in the summer of 1955, they were formally introduced and within weeks Bettina was acting as chatelaine at the Château de l'Horizon, where the couple spent the summer, and later she presided over Aly's house in the Bois de Boulogne. He once said of her that what immediately drew him to her was the manner she wore an old raincoat as if it were a mink.[3]

By the end of the year it was widely believed that, as soon as Aly and Rita's divorce became legal in France, he would marry Bettina. Importantly to Aly, the Aga approved of Bettina, as did the Begum, who came from the same petit bourgeois French background, and the two women became close friends. For Aly it was a pleasant change to be gathered into the family fold and to feel welcomed at Yakymour for the first time. His friends noted a new air of quiet contentment.

Bettina was passionately in love with Aly, but unlike his other women she did not panic every time there was a picture in the newspapers of him with another glamorous woman on his arm, such as at the Cannes Film Festival in 1956, when Aly was seen almost every night with Kim Novak, whom he had met at Yakymour. Bettina was a pragmatic, very beautiful, intelligent Frenchwoman, quietly confident in her ability to keep her man. She was in Paris when Aly's brief fling with Kim Novak was raging but apparently ignored the press coverage and simply waited for him to return to her. And after a while he did.

Kim Novak recalled in her memoirs that when she was with Aly she felt sorry for all the people around them who seemed only half alive. Like Debo Devonshire, she noted that Aly was a man who enjoyed every minute of life and was not prepared to waste a second. But he was not a free man – Kim knew that – and soon he was back with Bettina, who gave up her modelling career in order to be with him all the time. In summer 1957 they were in London at a party thrown by Mike Todd and Elizabeth Taylor when Aly was given the news that his father had been flown to Switzerland, and he knew at once what it meant.

The Aga always said Switzerland was the only sensible place for a very rich man to die and his careful plans had been in place for some time. Yasmin, who was much beloved by the Aga, was already on her way to France by transatlantic liner to see her grandfather; Aly and Bettina collected the child from Calais and flew straight to Geneva. They were just in time: the Aga died forty-eight hours later, of cancer, on 11 July 1957 at the age of almost eighty.

The Aga's will was removed from a bank vault in London, flown to Geneva and read to all those with a concern in it. And after thirty years of waiting, a stunned Aly heard that he had been left out of the succession, bypassed in favour of his twenty-year-old son Karim, who was studying history at Harvard.

To say that Aly was absolutely crushed by this turn of events would not be an exaggeration. According to a newspaper statement issued by the Aga's secretary, the will read: 'In view of the fundamentally altered conditions in the world in very recent years due to the great changes that have taken place, including the discoveries of atomic science, I am convinced that it is in the best interests of the Shia Muslim Ismaili community that I should be succeeded by a young man who has been brought up and developed during recent years and in the midst of the new age, and who brings a new outlook on life to his office.'

Even further humiliation was to follow when it was announced that the Aga had formally appointed the Begum, Aly's hated stepmother, as Karim's mentor. Aly Khan, who had been universally regarded as the Ismaili heir presumptive, who knew everyone in the Ismaili world, and had studied all his life for the role of Imam, was supplanted even in this lesser function by a woman born an infidel and who had only espoused Islam in mid-life. In public Aly presented a dignified acceptance, indicating that he was content to play a supportive part in his son's new governance. In private he was in agony, raging that the Begum had worked on his ageing and ill father. She was possibly the only woman Aly had never been able to charm.

Following the funeral in Geneva, the Aga's body was flown to Aswan where a beautiful mausoleum had been built, high on a hill on the west bank of the Nile, overlooking Elephantine Island, to house the marble tomb.* When the day came to inter the Aga's remains the Begum overstepped herself by joining the procession to the tomb, accompanied by her women attendants, despite the fact that she had been told she should not. Traditionally in Islam, such events are attended by men only and the Aga's followers were deeply shocked and offended by this display of what they regarded as immodest behaviour. Nothing was actually said, but following this – to Aly's intense gratification – Karim noticeably distanced himself from his step-grandmother.

In the autumn of that year, Winston managed to persuade Clementine to spend a holiday with him on the Riviera. She refused to stay at La Pausa, but agreed to spend two weeks at La Capponcina, after which she returned home and Churchill moved the short distance to La Pausa for the remainder of his long holiday. The files of correspondence between Winston and Clementine for the five years following his retirement from politics in 1955 are full of the excuses she made as to why she

---

* Every day since, a red rose has been placed on the tomb each morning, a convention begun by the Begum.

could not join him at La Pausa. No historian can fail to see parallels for Winston between the dozens of letters he wrote as a small boy to his beloved mother, vainly begging her to visit him at boarding school, and the other end of his life, when he wrote a similar number of letters, also in vain, to his beloved wife, beseeching her to join him.[4] She was not overly fond of Beaverbrook but evidently she found him preferable to Wendy Reves, and it is hard not to suspect that the gossip about Winston and Wendy affected Clementine's attitude.

And the gossip continued. During Churchill's visit in 1957 Wendy was informed by someone she trusted that Daisy Fellowes had recently become friends with Clementine, and had made some very unkind remarks about Wendy to her.[5] Wendy recalled how cold Clementine had been towards her when they last met, and she became deeply upset. Winston was perplexed about the sudden change in the demeanour of his hostess, but it was not until just before he left La Pausa that Emery told him the reason why Wendy was 'unwell'.

As soon as he arrived home Winston lost no time in asking Clementine about the matter. He then wrote to Wendy to tell her that Clementine had dismissed the story; there was not 'the slightest goodwill' between her and Daisy and no foundation for the report that they had become friends, he wrote – they had merely met at the table of a mutual friend. Furthermore, he reported, Clementine was astonished to hear that her manner towards Wendy had been perceived as 'hardened', saying Wendy must have imagined it. Wendy did not have Winston's total confidence in Clementine, and when he asked her to put the matter out of her mind he assumed that she had done so and accepted his assurances. But Wendy could not, and it was a sore that would fester.

Following this awkward event Clementine was persuaded to join Winston on holiday in February 1958 but she did not enjoy her visit and told her daughter that she found La Pausa claustrophobic, for it was situated in a steep hilly area remote from any town or village. The terrain made walking too difficult, which meant that if she wished to go anywhere outside the grounds she had to request a car and driver, which she hated to do. Since Winston spent all his mornings in bed working he was not affected by this restriction, so though she was grateful for the care and kindness the Reveses provided for her husband, Clementine told her daughter that, despite all the smiles, she had little in common with them and that their relationship with her was shallow. She made no such complaint about walking in the hills around La Capponcina, from which an obvious conclusion may be drawn.

Winston's regular visits continued, during which Clementine resolutely took separate holidays. The rumour, gossip and innuendo about Wendy and Winston also continued, and eventually would destroy the happy relationship. Between his visits to La Pausa, the Reveses occasionally visited Chartwell and stayed with the Churchills. After Christmas 1958, however, Winston did not join them at the villa as usual, going to Marrakech with Clementine instead. Some months later Emery suffered a heart attack and was not up to receiving visitors, so during the summer of 1959 Winston spent his visit to the Riviera with Onassis on board the *Christina*, instead of staying at 'Pausaland'.

In the autumn Onassis asked the Churchills to take a Caribbean cruise with him that winter, inviting them to choose their own cruise companions. There had been a number of such cruises in the past two years and Winston had no hesitation in accepting, advising through Anthony Montague Browne that Ari should invite anyone he thought appropriate. However, when he heard that the Windsors had been invited Churchill demurred. It was not that he disliked them, although he no longer felt the same affection he once had for the Duke; the problem was that whenever the Duke and Duchess were around the atmosphere was formal and people had to keep jumping to their feet.[6] Winston felt he could not cope with this; furthermore, he knew that Clementine disliked Wallis. He instructed Montague Browne to phone Onassis and tell him. The Windsors were diplomatically put off with the promise of the loan of the yacht for their sole use at some other time of their choosing.

All seemed well, but what happened next was to have long-term repercussions. Clementine now went to Montague Browne in a state of agitation and told him that she was looking forward to the long cruise with her husband, but she would not go if the Reveses were also aboard, and she instructed him to see to it. In Anthony Montague Browne's autobiography he explained this away as Clementine's not wanting anyone connected with a 'South of France background' on the cruise, but taken together with other correspondence on the matter it is quite obvious that Clementine wanted no contact with Wendy. Nor must it be forgotten that many members of the Churchill family had joined Winston at La Pausa during the past three years. So his children Diana, Sarah, Randolph and Mary, his grandchildren and some close friends of the family – all invited at Winston's request – saw at first hand the relationship between Winston and Wendy which led Pamela Churchill to confide to Noël Coward that the family were perturbed by it. We shall never know exactly what lay behind Clementine's agitation about the Reveses; it might be, as Noël Coward thought, that there was some truth in the rumours, or it could be that as the self-appointed keeper of the flame of her husband's reputation Clementine was not prepared to allow gossip to damage his reputation at the end of his life.

Whatever the reason, it was a tricky situation for Montague Browne to handle. When consulted on the matter Winston said he dearly wanted this cruise with Clementine for her health and his own pleasure, and it seems the treat of a luxurious winter cruise in the benign climate of the Caribbean overcame his common sense. He realised he owed a vast amount of hospitality to the Reveses but he was inclined to think (or wished to believe) that Montague Browne's deep concern about the circumstances that had arisen was making a mountain out of a molehill. He insisted that he valued the friendship of Emery and Wendy, and he would go and stay with them afterwards – everything would be the same, he said. A telegram was duly sent to Onassis, asking him to un-invite the Reveses.

As Montague Browne had feared, the Reveses were deeply offended. They had been looking forward to the cruise and, not unnaturally, they pressed Onassis, who was also a friend, as to why they had been removed from the guest list. With his back against the wall, Ari felt obliged to show them the telegram. The Reveses drew their own conclusions.

This was bad enough, and they were badly hurt, but it appears they initially decided to overlook the slight, since Reves was deeply involved professionally with Winston and they must still be able to work together. But worse was to come. When

Winston disembarked at Monte Carlo after the cruise, instead of asking the Reveses if he could come directly to La Pausa – as they anticipated he would do, since he had intimated as much in his conversation with Montague Browne – Winston moved into a specially renovated luxury suite at the Hôtel de Paris, Onassis's hotel in Monte Carlo. It was a second kick in the teeth for the Reveses and they had had enough.

Several months later, writing from Chartwell, Winston innocently proposed himself as a guest at La Pausa for the coming September. Emery replied in a very long letter that they had been greatly surprised by the request, since Winston had declined their frequent and 'even persistent' invitations since last winter and had gone to the Hôtel de Paris follow-ing the cruise. He said they had therefore concluded he had decided not to visit them again, and continued:

We could understand that cruises had a greater attrac-tion to you than our villa, but we could not interpret your decision to stay at a hotel rather than Pausaland in any other way than that we had done something ... Our, perhaps foolish, dream was that during the years 1956, 1957 and 1958, when you spent about a third of each year at Pausaland, we had become friends ... you cannot imagine how shocked we were when two years ago we suddenly remarked that all kinds of intrigues started destroying this friendship and a few months later we realised that these forces had succeeded in destroying what was a happy and lovely companionship.

It is not possible for me to describe the humiliation and suffering we had to endure which has left deep marks in both Wendy and me ... Wendy has suffered deeply and dangerously with mental depression ... I am fully aware that all of this was not intended [by you] and that you were a victim, perhaps even more than we were.[7]

Wendy had now become a different woman, Emery wrote, she was very wounded and not yet capable of mastering her deep emotional distress over the apparent rejection of the hospitality that they had openly placed at Winston's disposal, 'a home, a garden, a sunny sky, a fireplace, Wendy's devotion'. It did not seem possible for them to resume those happy times, or at least not at present. They were going to the United States in October, but he hoped that if Winston visited La Capponcina 'or some other place on the Riviera' in September he would find time to pay them a visit.

Winston was grieved, puzzled and shocked at Emery's letter, and instead he and Clementine, accompanied by Montague Browne, accepted an invitation by Onassis to stay at the Hôtel de Paris. Clementine wrote personally to Wendy to assure her there were no intrigues, saying that she was deeply grateful for the hospitality they had always enjoyed at La Pausa and she hoped the Reveses would join them for luncheon at Ari's hotel. Winston wrote a short personal note to Wendy from the hotel, saying he was so sorry that she was 'vexed' with him, and that the months he had spent with her were among the brightest in his life. He sent her sincere and warmest thanks and affection.

There were subsequent meetings – Emery still acted for Winston in his capacity as his literary agent – and very occasionally in the following few years, while Winston was still able to travel, the Reveses lunched with him in London and at the Hôtel de Paris in Monte Carlo, or at La Capponcina.

There were more enjoyable cruises with Ari. But the happy days of Pausaland were over, just as finally as those happy days Winston had once spent with Maxine Elliott. They were all losers; Winston told his daughter Diana at about that time that he felt his life was now over, even though it was not yet ended.[8]

One notable absentee from the Riviera scene from 1959 onwards was Pamela Churchill, who had waltzed off the terrace of Château de l'Horizon into the arms of Gianni Agnelli a decade earlier. For five years their relationship had flourished, each happy with their arrangement that they maintained their own homes – Gianni's in Turin, and Pam's in Paris. With the help of Gianni, and possibly Averell Harriman, Pam also purchased the flat in London that she needed to keep in order to satisfy her British residency status, which was important to the custody order of young Winston. She rented the flat to incoming American ambassadors and also to Cary Grant. Later Gianni bought her an apartment in Paris.

In Paris Pam was a star in the firmament of leading expats but she was equally acceptable to *tout le gratin parisien* – the top people in Paris who were normally a closed shop to outsiders. Gianni's position as head of the Fiat empire made it necessary for him to be based in Turin and she mainly flew there to be with him, but when she had to be in Paris for some reason he would fly to France to be with her, sometimes commuting several times a week. From June to the end of September in 1949 and 1950 Gianni rented the Château de la Garoupe, a spacious villa on the Cap d'Antibes adjacent to the Château de la Croë, a short distance from the Hotel du Cap and Eden Roc, and a twenty-minute drive from Château de l'Horizon.* Pam and Gianni spent most weekends and the odd week there, and when Gianni was absent Pamela did not lack for company. She often dined with the Windsors; Pam liked Wallis and the two women shared housekeeping tips.

Unlike Wallis, Pam had grown up in a large country house, which although larger than La Croë, was not so much a stately home as a family residence containing the odd van Dyck among its gallery of Digby ancestors. But Wallis had taught herself much about how to please her lord and Pam learned something from her about 'spoiling'; from this point onwards, visitors to any of Pam's houses were pampered beyond excess. Pam was frequently invited to make up numbers at dinner parties whenever Winston was staying on the Riviera, because his former daughter-in-law was one of the few people he was always happy to see.

Despite a clearly successful relationship, and the fact that in order to be eligible to become Mrs Agnelli Pam had converted to Catholicism and had applied to the pope to have her former marriage to Randolph annulled, as the years went on it became clear to her that Gianni was reluctant to marry her. He was as much a serial womaniser as Aly was, and this

---

* Built in 1907 for Lord Aberconway, La Garoupe looks down a long stairway to Anse Garoupe bay in one direction, and in the other faces a magnificent park with English rose gardens and pergolas. It regularly won prizes for the most beautiful garden on the Côte d'Azur and had famously been visited in 1919 by the Duke of Connaught (son of Queen Victoria). During the Twenties it was leased by Cole Porter and his wife Linda, and was the scene of some of the parties written about by F. Scott Fitzgerald, whose wife Zelda wrote in 1926 that being on the Riviera provided her with precious, transitory times 'when all in one's life seemed to be going well'. Until his death in 2014 this magnificent house was owned by Boris Eltsine Berezovsky, friend of President Putin, one of the many Russian oligarchs who now own most of the Cap d'Antibes. Following his death La Garoupe was seized by the French government in connection with money laundering charges and at the time of writing this, it is still held by them.

had little to do with his feelings for Pamela, just as Aly's emotional involvement with other women when he cheated on Rita did not reflect his love for her. But Pamela was not Rita; if she knew about the affairs (and since gossip thrived in their circle she must have at least suspected) she behaved as most upper-class wives did and turned a blind, if jaundiced, eye as long as matters were conducted discreetly.

In the winter of 1951 Gianni purchased La Léopolda, a palatial villa at Villefranche, an area still considered the *crème de la crème* of the Riviera. It was one of two Riviera properties originally built for King Leopold II of Belgium regardless of cost,[*] although it had undergone some changes since his death and had been used as a military hospital in 1918. The Windsors had once tried to lease it from the American owner, an architect who had spent a fortune restoring it, but the changes they wished to make offended him. It was larger, more secluded and yet more accessible for Gianni from Turin than was La Garoupe; indeed, it still has the reputation of being one of the most spectacular properties on the Riviera. Pamela was given *carte blanche* to redecorate it.

This being a formal home of Gianni it was not considered suitable for young Winston to live there with the lovers. He therefore spent winter holidays with his father, or his grandparents at Chartwell, but during the summer holidays he always stayed with Pamela for a month at Aly's Deauville

---

[*] King Leopold was the founder and sole owner of the Congo Free State, a company he established with the help of the explorer Henry Morton Stanley under the guise of improving the lives of the native Congolese. This was merely a cover for the exploitation of the assets of the Congo, initially ivory, but later – using forced native labour and costing the lives of millions of Congolese – rubber processing. Leopold employed mercenaries to administer a cruel regime which earned him multiple millions. Some of this money he used to construct grand public buildings throughout Belgium, but much went to gratify his own lifestyle, including La Léopolda.

mansion, which Aly loaned to her. Gianni remained at La Léopolda, flying up to see Pam in Normandy regularly, but he was seldom alone when on the Riviera. Pam heard gossip about his womanising in her absence, but she was obliged to – and wanted to – provide a summer home for young Winston and there was nothing she could do but hope that she could rein Gianni in again once her son left to spend a few weeks with his father before returning to school.

When young Winston left for England in mid-August 1952 Pamela returned to La Léopolda to find that Gianni was in Turin and expected to return the following day. That evening she attended a dinner party at the house of friends in Beaulieu-sur-Mer, leaving early since she was tired after travelling. Arriving back at the villa just after midnight she walked into the bedroom to find Gianni there, *in flagrante* with the daughter of a good friend, the Comte d'Estainville.

Pamela had had more than a fair share of lovers, but an important factor about her many affairs was that she was never unfaithful to a man while she was in a relationship with him. In that respect she was just like her favourite ancestor Jane Digby,[9] whose life had always fascinated her and had provided a role model for her as a teenager. Although Pam had accepted philosophically that Gianni was unfaithful to her, he had been reasonably discreet about it and had never before brought one of his women into any house that they shared. He had never rubbed her nose in it, so to speak, and now Pam was humiliated, deeply hurt, and furious.

Pamela's brother explained what happened next: 'Pam was very upset, naturally, and she flew at the girl. Gianni tried to prevent her and got his face slapped. There was a hell of a row.' Gianni's one thought was to get the girl out of the villa and he attempted to placate Pamela by saying he would take the girl home and they would discuss the matter when he got back. With Pamela shrieking at him, he somehow managed to get himself and the sobbing girl dressed and into his Lancia sports car to drive her to her parents' house at Cap Martin. He should not have driven: he had been drinking and after he had driven off Pam also saw the evidence on the bedside table that he had taken cocaine. Like Aly, Gianni was a recklessly fast driver even when sober. On this occasion, as he took the slight bend on the Corniche near the entrance to the Cap Roux tunnel he was going too fast and smashed into an unlit cart carrying some workers to the early-morning market at Nice.[10]

Back at La Léopolda, Pamela had taken a sleeping pill and cried herself to sleep. At about 3 a.m. she was woken by the telephone. It was a friend calling to tell her about the crash, and he said that Gianni had been taken to the hospital at Nice, very seriously injured, and was possibly already dead.

The friend who had phoned to give Pam the news had been at the same dinner party as Pam that evening, and he had come across the crash on his way home, shortly after it happened. The girl, Anne-Marie, received only scratches and bruising and she was scooped up and discreetly driven home; she slept late next morning, and it was years before her parents knew anything about the dramatic events of that night. The passengers in the truck received only minor injuries and were later well compensated by Gianni's lawyers. There was no police prosecution.

Pamela roused their chauffeur and rushed to Nice hospital to find Gianni alive but unconscious and in critical condition, his face a mask of blood from glass cuts and his jaw shattered.

He also had several broken ribs and his right leg had been crushed. It was considered doubtful the leg could be saved. He was about to be taken into the operating theatre when Pam arrived. She alerted them about the cocaine and that ruled out a general anaesthetic: the procedures to deal with the breaks and gashes had to be carried out under a local.

While Gianni weathered the first critical days Pam, who genuinely loved him, never left his side and it became clear he would need twenty-four-hour care for some time. Much as she hated to do so, she felt obliged to contact his sisters to discuss this. As soon as Gianni was able to be moved he was taken to a hospital in Florence, his head resting on Pam's lap for the whole journey. And it was Pam who held his hand and shielded his eyes while – again under a local anaesthetic because he had taken cocaine to dull the constant pain – gangrenous flesh was cut away from his damaged leg. An amputation was recommended, but Gianni refused; he would eventually recover, just as he insisted he would, but he walked with a marked limp for the remainder of his life.

During the two months he spent in intensive care at the hospital in Florence, Pam remained at his bedside, leaving him only to go to a nearby hotel to grab a few hours of sleep and to bathe and change clothes. When he was discharged and moved to his house in Turin, Pam went with him, and for another two months she nursed him devotedly, but by then the sisters were also sharing his care. By coincidence, news came that the papal annulment of her marriage to Randolph Churchill had finally been approved. There was nothing to stop Gianni marrying her, but following lengthy discussions Pam finally understood that it would never happen. His family was totally opposed to it – his sisters wished him to marry the Neapolitan princess Marella di Castagneto, the daughter of family friends and latterly regarded as one of the great beauties of the twentieth century.* Under normal circumstances Gianni would never have stayed in one place long enough for the sisters' harangues on the matter to have any serious effect on him. But following his accident he was a sitting duck and when Pam left them alone with him, their frequent insistence on the need for him to produce an heir, but importantly to marry the right sort of girl, began to take root.

Gianni and Pam still loved each other, but after five years of living together their love was no longer urgent enough for either to make huge sacrifices. Gianni accepted that he would have to marry and have a family, and he had been persuaded that despite her religious conversion Pamela was not marriage material. Pamela, nearing forty, could see no future in a relationship with Gianni if he married someone else, and she had no intention of waiting around while she lost her looks. They reached the only decision possible: it was time to part. Gianni's chauffeur drove them from Turin to the French border, where Pam had arranged to be met, and they were both in tears as Gianni limped back to his car and Pamela sped off towards La Léopolda to pack her belongings for the final time. They remained lifelong friends.

At a dinner party in Paris some months later, Pamela was seated next to one of Aly's polo-playing friends, Élie de Rothschild, whose wife had just had a baby. Nevertheless,

---

* Princess Marella Caracciola di Castagneto. Gianni eventually married Marella the following year when she became pregnant by him, and though Agnelli never refrained from womanising the marriage survived until his death from prostate cancer in January 2003.

before long they were an item. Unlike her relationships with Aly and Gianni – both of whom had been unattached – it was necessary to be discreet, even though most people in their circle knew about it. Their liaison was mainly conducted in northern France and they rarely appeared together in public, but word soon reached the Riviera, where the Duke of Windsor once asked his dinner partner Liliane de Rothschild if she knew which of the Rothschilds was having an affair with Pamela Churchill. 'It's my husband,' she replied coolly.

From Élie de Rothschild Pam learned about art and bloodstock. She had grown up with horses, had hunted throughout her childhood, and picked up an interest in bloodstock while involved with Aly, but now she improved that knowledge by closely following the horse-racing world in France and England. She impressed Winston by discussing with him the lineage of one of his own racehorses and the performance of its sire and dam. In her affair with Élie they saw each other only when he could manage to get away, so Pam spent her time in Paris visiting art galleries, the shops of high-end antique dealers and restoration workshops, learning about the things that she knew would interest him. It was initially so that she could keep up with Élie, but when it was added to her own innate taste and her background she developed a flair way beyond a mere passing interest. Her apartment, bought for her by Gianni, was known to be among the most beautiful and elegant in Paris, and Élie helped her to furnish it with pictures and tapestries and eighteenth-century French furniture. Her fresh-flower bill alone was over ten thousand dollars a year.

Pam occasionally popped up on the Riviera in the late Fifties, frequently as a guest at dinners while Winston was staying at La Capponcina or La Pausa, or aboard the *Christina*, but like Clementine she instinctively disliked Onassis, finding him vulgar and too unrefined for her tastes. Ari's arch-rival, the sophisticated and well-educated shipping tycoon Stavros Niarchos – who now owned La Croë, having bought it from the Windsors in 1953 – was far more Pam's style. Pam had a number of cruises on Stavros's 200ft three-masted sailing yacht, the *Creole*, and they too enjoyed an affair, but they parted friends and remained so for the rest of their lives: he died in April 1996, ten months before she did.

The end of her relationship with Niarchos also marked the end of Pam's time on the Riviera. Taking all the knowledge she had gained in the world of art, bloodstock and high finance, she sold up in Paris and London and moved to the United States. Though she did not know it, the most important part of her real life was just about to begin. No one would have been more surprised than Pam had she been told that she would one day return to France as the United States ambassador.

19

End of an Era

Some four months after the death of his father, Aly was contacted by the first President of Pakistan, Major-General Iskandar Mirza, who requested a meeting. As a result of their subsequent discussions, Aly was offered the post of permanent ambassador for Pakistan to the United Nations. At the time, having recently broken from India, Pakistan was suffering all the problems of a newly independent country with a much larger, unfriendly neighbour. What the country most needed was good representation on the world stage; someone able to ensure they got a hearing. Although Aly was an important name in the bloodstock and racing world, he was chiefly known for his endless pursuit of women, for marrying Rita Hayworth, and for his free-spending playboy image. Now he also carried the tag that his father had thought so little of him that he had been disinherited in favour of his own son. It was perhaps not the ideal CV for an ambassador, so it is not surprising that the rumoured appointment caused a good deal of supercilious comment masquerading as humour in the world press, and no less so in the diplomatic community. One politician wondered if Aly might appoint Marilyn Monroe and Ava Gardner to his team of advisers.*

It was widely noted that Aly was not a citizen of Pakistan, and as the *New York Times* reported, 'For most of the last twenty-five years Aly Khan has been busy building a name as a fabulously wealthy, hard riding, fast driving, restless man of the world with a liking for parties and beautiful women.'[1]

Yet his appointment was not entirely ridiculous – there were plenty of items on the credit side of the balance sheet. Aly knew almost everybody of influence on the world stage and was generally popular; if there was anyone he did not know and needed to know, he made it his business to get in touch with them and make friends. He was still regarded by many Ismailis in Pakistan as the man who by rights ought to have been the next Aga Khan; he had a reputation in that community for being able to resolve differences and was generally well thought of. One of his best wartime friends, Henry Cabot Lodge, Jr,† had been a former ambassador to the United Nations, and when Aly consulted him for advice, Lodge told him that he could do the ambassadorial job perfectly well provided he had a good team of advisers to back him.

A further advantage for a new country with very little in the way of a treasury was the fact that Aly asked for only one

---

* Before Ronald Reagan, this was regarded as amusing: the idea of a movie star becoming President of the United States was the stuff of a Hollywood screenplay.
† As well as serving as US ambassador to the UN Assembly, Henry Cabot Lodge was Senator for Massachusetts, and was Republican nominee for Vice-President in 1960.

rupee a month as salary, and could fund his own ambassadorial accommodation (a huge apartment overlooking the East River), his advisers, a fully staffed office and any amount of the necessary entertaining in New York and Washington. The Aga had removed Aly from succession to the title of Imam, but under Islamic law he could not – even had he wished to do so – disinherit Aly from a share in his assets, since all his legal heirs had to be treated equally. It is not known how much Aly received in his father's will for it took years to unravel the Aga's holdings, which had been distributed and squirreled away all over the world, but Aly was now regarded as one of the world's richest men.

Finally, Aly was totally cosmopolitan and multi-lingual, speaking English, Arabic, French, Italian and a number of Asiatic dialects. As one friend commented, 'When you see Aly in Karachi in Ismaili dress he looks like a Pakistani. In Paris he looks like a Frenchman. In Rome he could pass for any upper-class Italian. Even here in America Aly doesn't look foreign.'[2] What better attributes could there be for an ambassador?

He accepted the appointment with alacrity and it was publicly announced shortly after Karim was formally enthroned in Karachi as Aga Khan IV in January 1958. The secret knowledge of this forthcoming proclamation must have created a small warm place in Aly's heart as he watched the ceremony, for much as he loved his son and was proud of him, and proud for him, being passed over had been deeply humiliating. Aly had always felt a need to impress his father, hoping to receive some evidence of his father's love, and he had been emotionally shattered when his father had seemed to show him the ultimate rejection. The old Aga had served in the League of Nations, so this new appointment may well have seemed to Aly a form of inheritance, a small application of balm enabling him to hold up his head after the crushing blow of the will. While the initial press comment flared adversely about his appointment he went into hiding for two weeks at the home of the Pakistani Prime Minister, where Cabot Lodge was a fellow guest. Aly listened very seriously to every piece of advice they offered him; this was a lifeline thrown to him, a final chance to do something meaningful with his life, and he knew it.

One of the first things he did on arrival in New York was to have Pakistan House, an imposing mansion off Fifth Avenue, gutted and refurbished at his own expense. He then set up an office where he could house his secretariat and meet regularly with a team of advisers. When Aly stepped out of his Cadillac outside the UN Secretariat on a spring morning in March 1958, in morning dress and wearing his medals (the *Légion d'honneur* and *Croix de Guerre*) to present his credentials, it resembled a royal visit. Extra police had been called to control the press and television crews, and the crowds who gathered behind the barriers. Women employees who were blasé about well-known members of the UN leaned out of office windows to catch a glimpse of this notorious ladies' man who was also a prince.

As part of his policy of getting to know everyone, he threw a series of diplomatic receptions and parties. There was no shortage of such events, but Aly's were so elaborate that there was a black market in invitations among the blasé UN staff for there was no access without invitation, and plain-clothes guards screened each arrival. Although he was only required to attend the Assembly for a few months a year, Aly exceeded this minimum, commuting to France, Ireland and London for long weekends much as many of his peers went for long weekends in Connecticut.

After a short period, to the surprise of those who regarded his acceptance of the appointment as a mere whim, Aly was judged a success. He had thrown himself and his considerable energies into the role and, with a team of good advisers and Bettina to go home to every now and then, his lifestyle changed. There were still endless parties but now, as Elsa Maxwell noticed, there were fewer starlets. Instead, among the café society, the Hollywood greats and the New York elite there were sprinklings of diplomats and politicians. And instead of wooing young women Aly was more usually to be found in deep conversation with some aged ambassador, legislator or politician, such as the rich young Senator from Massachusetts, John F. Kennedy, or his brother-in-law Michael Canfield. Aly now considered such people important to his work, so they attended some of his gala New York events and he enjoyed visits to their Florida properties.

Aly had been friends with Michael Canfield and his wife for some time, having initially met them in New York.* In 1953 Canfield had married the socialite Lee Bouvier, sister of Jackie Bouvier, who married Jack Kennedy soon

---

* Michael Canfield was almost certainly the illegitimate son of George, Duke of Kent (who died in an air accident in 1942, an incident that is the subject of various conspiracy theories) by Violet Evans, a Canadian girl who was living in England. She had quickly married a cavalry officer to give her baby a name and prevent any scandal and there is some indication that financial help was given to the young couple by a royal source. The marriage did not last long; the child, born in 1926 and named Anthony, was subsequently adopted by rich American publisher Cas Canfield and his wife and renamed Michael. Michael was raised in New England, educated well and made financially secure by his adoptive parents.

afterwards; the two couples were the closest of friends. In July 1958 Jackie Kennedy was staying with her sister at the Canfields' rented town house in Rue du Bateau, a narrow cobbled street in the old walled town of Antibes. She was joined there in August by her husband, who had flown in from Sweden. At the time the Kennedy marriage was in deep trouble because of his frequent infidelities – more specifically Jack's current serious romance with a Swedish girl, Gunilla von Post – but also because of Jackie's free-spending habits. These problems were much discussed by their contemporaries, but although Jackie insisted to friends in Antibes that she had no intention of returning to her husband, several things prevented her from actually parting from him. First, their profound Catholic faith, and second his family's political ambitions. Old Joe Kennedy, with whom Jackie got on well, was vacationing nearby, in a rented villa at Cannes. He evidently refused to even discuss the possibility of a separation or divorce, knowing that it would prevent Jack ever running for President. Some years earlier it had been Joe Kennedy's intention to run himself, but his chances of contesting the nomination were quashed when his long-term affair with Gloria Swanson leaked into the press. The political baton then passed to his eldest son. But after Joe Jr's death in 1944, Jack became his family's best chance of achieving this ambition, and the old man made his position abundantly clear to both Jack and Jackie.

When some other guests of the Canfields were due to arrive to stay in the tiny rented house, it was intended that the Kennedys would move in with Joe. This was not a tempting prospect to the warring couple, especially as

Jackie's father, Black Jack Bouvier, had now showed up to stay with Joe Kennedy in order to take part in family crisis talks. So Jack and Jackie eagerly accepted Aly Khan's invitation to take over the Churchill suite at the Château de l'Horizon for as long as they wished. During the weeks they stayed there, they somehow resolved their differences and came to a working agreement to save their marriage. Aly was in New York that August to deliver his first speech at the UN. In his absence he gave the Kennedys the freedom of his Riviera home and staff, and encouraged them to invite their own friends to visit, which they duly did. The prolific playwright and former politician William Douglas-Home* and his wife Rachel joined them at the château. Douglas-Home, an early boyfriend of Kick Kennedy before the war, had known her brother Jack since they were at Harvard. In his autobiography Douglas-Home recalled his holiday with the Kennedys at l'Horizon and how something was always going on: a trip along the coast to Italy; a flight in a private plane to Venice for the day; dinners with the former wife of the Shah of Persia; gala parties and summer balls in Cannes; Gianni Agnelli zooming into lunch aboard his Riva powerboat to take Jackie, Lee and Rachel water-skiing; cruises on various superyachts. The pleasure was non-stop.

He also remembered how one night in September, soon after Aly returned to his villa he and all the house-guests at Château de l'Horizon dined aboard the *Christina*. Aly arranged this with Onassis after Jack Kennedy expressed a wish to meet his hero Winston Churchill. Winston, eighty-three years

---

* During the war William Douglas-Home had been court-martialled for disobeying an order to fire on civilians, and sentenced to a year in prison. Many years later he successfully fought to have this removed from his record on grounds of humanitarianism.

old now, was aboard the yacht for a few days after he and Clementine had celebrated their golden wedding anniversary at La Capponcina. Aly's party joined the yacht at Monte Carlo and Jack wore a white tuxedo, a garment much frowned upon by Winston, but Jackie, deeply tanned, dressed in a simple white A-line dress and speaking fluent French during dinner, charmed both Churchill and Onassis. Jack was disappointed that he seemed to make no impression on Churchill, and when he said so to Jackie as they disembarked, she relied crushingly: 'I think he thought you were a waiter.' Douglas-Home also recalled lying on a swimming raft one day at Eden Roc listening to a conversation between Michael Canfield and Jack:

Michael: I just can't understand why you want to be President.

Jack: Well, Mike, I guess it's just about the only thing I can do.

The Kennedy marriage would famously survive, but in the following year the Canfields would divorce: Lee to marry Prince Stanislaus Radziwill, and Michael the English aristocrat Laura Charteris.*

Aly's first speech to the United Nations Assembly in August 1958 was during a debate on the Middle East, a region about

---

* Laura's former husbands were Walter Long, 2nd Viscount Long, and William Ward, 3rd Earl of Dudley. She was also the long-term unrequited love of Randolph Churchill. In 1960 Laura and Michael Canfield lunched with her old friends the Duke and Duchess of Windsor, and noticed that the Duke could not take his eyes off Michael. When she asked him if anything was wrong, the Duke told her, 'Yes. I am certain your husband is my brother's son.' After Canfield's death Laura married, in 1972, the 10th Duke of Marlborough. Canfield's true parentage was later confirmed to her by sources close to the Royal Family.

which he was well qualified to speak. The *Washington Post* commented on the event: 'Prince Ali Khan, more commonly known as Aly, Ambassador Extraordinary and Plenipotentiary, Representative to the United Nations from Pakistan, stood up in the General Assembly and made his first speech. It was a momentous occasion, since the ambassador's previous public utterances had been largely limited to shouts of "Wine for everyone!" and "Where are the girls?"' It was inevitable that Aly could not expect to shrug off a lifetime of play overnight, but he enjoyed his new role and he worked hard at it. In a sense it was similar to his spell in the army: he was useful, busy and successful, and judged on his own performance. When the Pakistani government that had made him ambassador was suddenly overthrown in a coup, Aly worried that it meant the end of his time at the UN. He flew to Pakistan and the new government reconfirmed him in the post, for by this time he was accepted as a world diplomat, and was respected by his peers at the United Nations.

In the summer of 1959 one of the notable guests at Château de l'Horizon was Elizabeth Taylor. Recovering from the death of her husband Mike Todd, she was in Paris when she ran into Eddie Fisher, whose marriage to Debbie Reynolds was, he claimed, on the rocks. The two stars fell in love and Fisher scandalously divorced America's sweetheart to marry Elizabeth. In an attempt to escape the baying press they flew to Cannes, where they became virtual captives in the Carlton Hotel. Aly and Bettina had known both Elizabeth and Eddie when they were married to their former partners, and while passing the Carlton one day Bettina saw Elizabeth besieged by paparazzi on the steps of the hotel. She immediately invited them to come and stay at the villa, where they could be more private. The Château de l'Horizon had often shielded world-famous celebrities from such press attentions, and now it did so again.

Aly was not in France at the time, for he was deeply involved in a UN debate concerning Algeria and France. On 7 September he was rewarded for his work at the UN by being elected a vice-president of the General Assembly. Later he would serve as chairman of the Peace Observation Committee. In December that year the Algerian question was again raised and Aly, who by then had become something of a prime spokesman on the subject, cleverly avoided being accused of partisanship. It was tricky for him, as a lifelong resident of France, to fairly represent Pakistan's support for Algeria's case for independence without being critical of the French government, but, having given his objective opinion on the matter, he made his point by tactfully abstaining from the vote. Even so, there was much disparagement of him in French newspapers. He answered this calmly, stating that he had acted according to his conscience, and had served both Pakistan – 'my country' – and France, the country in which he made his home and which 'I love so much'.

He was able to do a good deal of work, garner support and canvass opinions at his renowned entertainments, and he threw an annual gala dinner in New York, much resembling his Bois de Boulogne summer ball. But the effect of all his entertaining and ambassadorial activity in his late forties was weight gain – enough to stop him riding in races. He was increasingly physically restless and one of the few outlets left now for his natural ebullience was driving too fast. Countless people told him, as his father had done, that he would kill himself; his response was usually that his time would be up when it was written, but in the meantime he would continue to try to get from life all he could. 'Death to him, as a Moslem,' Bettina wrote, 'was an ever present reality.'[3] With Bettina living mostly in France, Aly's womanising in the United States continued and his friends noticed that most of the women he was seen with around town were very young. It was as though he were trying to prove to himself that he was not ageing, and like most men in this not-unknown situation in mid-life he clearly did not realise how pathetic this appeared, nor how it affected the public perception of his work.

One explanation is that he had possibly been diagnosed with prostate cancer, and feared that the necessary operation might mean the end of his sexual activities. A friend who had had the operation, and with whom Aly had discussed the matter, told Aly's biographer that he had already noted how Aly frequently rubbed his abdomen – a recognisable symptom – and he also confided to Aly that following the surgery his sex life had ended.

During one of Aly's regular trips to Pakistan in 1959 the feelings between those who believed that Aly was the true Aga Khan (and with whom Aly had remained in constant touch) and those who supported Karim as their Imam, were evident. In Lahore a huge crowd of the former group turned out to welcome Aly and hundreds camped for days outside the house where he stayed simply to catch a glimpse of him and venerate him. The same thing had happened on visits to East Africa and Syria. In many ways these situations demonstrated the supreme wisdom of the old Aga: he knew that Aly would never do anything to harm Karim's imamship. But had Aly's love for his son not been stronger than his ambition, there was potential for a religious schism among the Ismailis, such as that which exists between Sunnis and Shias.

Following this trip to Pakistan Aly addressed a prestigious diplomatic assembly in Paris, eloquently making a case for Pakistan's potential to act as a link between West and East. That winter he commuted between New York, Paris and Cannes, keeping the small team of secretaries that he employed on UN work busier than ever, but always making time for major race meetings in France and England. His formal engagement to Bettina was announced at the same time he was named as Pakistan's ambassador to Argentina, a country he knew well and liked, and where he had many influential connections through his bloodstock dealings. It was another new challenge and he looked forward to meeting it.

By May 1960 Bettina was several months pregnant, and their wedding date was still a few weeks away. On the 12th they were in Paris for the races at Longchamp and that evening they were to dine with a group of old friends, among whom were Baron and Baroness Guy de Rothschild, Baron Élie de Rothschild, Porfirio 'Baby' Rubirosa and his wife, and Stavros Niarchos and his wife.

Because he had been working all evening, making telephone calls, organising his forthcoming summer ball, and dictating letters to a secretary, Aly was running late for the dinner engagement. Bettina had to remind him of the time. At 10 p.m. their hosts rang to ask where they were as they were holding dinner. Aly was still dictating to a secretary as they walked to the elevator. When they reached the garage

Aly decided to take his new car, a Lancia sports coupé he had bought only a few days earlier and had not yet driven. He told the chauffeur to get into the back seat so he could drive them home after the dinner. Aly took the wheel with Bettina beside him.

Publicity given to Aly's other exploits made many people forget that in the Thirties he was a well-known driver in practically all the big automobile races in France and Italy. In 1953 he was set to race his Alfa Romeo in the hazardous Mille Miglia until his father stepped in and forbade Aly to drive, using as an excuse that he had not sufficiently acquainted himself with the seven thousand death-dealing curves on the course, but even as recently as two years earlier Aly was still driving in some of the smaller races in Italy. He knew how to handle a car.

It was a dark night and raining as they drove along the Bois de Boulogne and through Paris. Aly, chatting to Bettina, was driving fast and confidently as he always did, breaking the speed limit for he knew the road well. They were almost at their destination as they approached a set of traffic lights near Saint-Cloud. A small car was driving slowly in front of them and Aly overtook it in order to make the lights before they changed, turning to make a complimentary remark about the car's handling to Bettina as he did so. In the gloom he evidently did not see a small Simca coming in the opposite direction and he smashed into it head on.

Bettina and the chauffeur suffered shock, concussion and facial injuries, as did the couple in the Simca, and Bettina would subsequently miscarry as a result of the trauma. Aly was taken unconscious to the Hôpital Foch in nearby Suresnes with severe head trauma. As he was being wheeled into the operating theatre his heart stopped and could not be restarted. He was forty-eight years old.

Inevitably, the crash caused world headlines: the sudden shocking death of a celebrity always makes news. Debo Devonshire remembered how all his friends thought it especially tragic that the Aly they had known, so full of life and laughter, had met his end on a rainy night in a Paris backstreet.

Following Islamic law Aly's fortune went almost entirely to his children, though Bettina received a $280,000 bequest. His wish was that his body should lie in Syria at Salamiyah, the site of his first personal triumph.

It was some twelve years earlier when Aly had flown to Syria in his green and red *Avenger* with his private pilot John Lancaster. They had driven off the main highway towards Salamiyah into the isolated area where the Ismailis live, thirty-odd miles south-east of the city of Hama in a lush farming area dotted with prehistoric tells, where it was not unusual to find irrigation provided by gigantic wooden water wheels, called *norias*, that had been in use since the Romans occupied the country. Large gatherings of very excited Ismaili Arabs had blocked the road, and having effectively stopped the car swarmed all over it.

Aly had been many times to Salamiyah since then, and he was always sure of a huge welcome. So it was at Salamiyah, he instructed, that his tomb was to be built. However, this had always been his plan for the distant future – he had not expected to die in his forties, and following his sudden death his wishes could not be effected immediately because of internal fighting in Syria. Until it proved possible to comply, it was decided by his sons that Aly's body would be buried temporarily under the small lawn outside his study at the

Château de l'Horizon. After the funeral in Paris, attended by Bettina and the Begum as well as the male members of the family, Aly's coffin was taken by train to Cannes, where it was solemnly interred at the Château de l'Horizon.

Aly's last wishes took a lot longer to fulfil than anyone envisaged and it would be another twelve years before the coffin was disinterred, in July 1972. An Air France passenger jet was privately chartered and flew Aly's remains to Damascus. At Salamiyah an exquisite small mausoleum had been built, and both his sons were in attendance as Aly's coffin was placed in the tomb.

The Château de l'Horizon was never the same after Aly's death. Karim used it occasionally, and there was a 'sensational' picture taken by paparazzi of the young Aga Khan asleep with his head on the lap of his current girlfriend. *Paris Match* spread the story across several pages, but it is simply a picture of a young man and young woman dressed in beach clothes, relaxing.

This was to be, however, the last story concerning the villa's residents, for soon afterwards Karim discovered his own Mediterranean bolthole. In 1962, while sailing off the northeast coast of Sardinia, he came across a thirty-five-mile stretch of isolated coast. It was how the French Riviera used to look in the Thirties: rocky outcrops with deserted sandy coves lapped by crystal turquoise waters. The best feature was the lack of tourists. Karim bought it and built there a marina playground resort for multi-millionaires. He called it the Costa Smeralda. The Château de l'Horizon was eventually sold to the King of Saudi Arabia and is still today owned by the Saudi royal family.

Maxine's world is long gone but each decade brings a new smart set to swirl between the stunning villas; richer and maybe not quite so captivating as those who used to people Maxine's terrace, in the days when the worst possible behaviour was to be boring. The allure of the area remains, and the resorts of Antibes, Juan-les-Pins and Cannes still flourish within a stone's throw of the old Château de l'Horizon. With its dazzling backdrops of blue sea and beaches crowded with serried ranks of cushioned sun-loungers and parasols under reliable sunshine, casinos, multi-million-dollar villas and fleets of superyachts, the region remains a symbol of wealth and success.

The unique quality of life to be found there, identified and cultivated by Maxine Elliott in 1930, has survived and against all odds the glamour and unique sense of *joie de vivre* somehow lives on.

Epilogue

I first heard of Maxine Elliott and her villa on the French Riviera when I was researching a previous book, *The Churchills*. It was obvious how Churchill's visits there often recharged him in the Thirties at times when the outlook for him was bleak. It occurred to me then that it was worth writing about: Maxine's friendship with Winston, her sybaritic spoiling of him and her uncritical admiration and belief in him quite possibly played a more important role in history than might initially seem, for it bolstered his confidence during the period he always referred to as the wilderness years, and his holidays at the Château de l'Horizon were highlights in his year.

While working on this book I flew to the South of France in 2013 to research archives there, hoping to find local information on the Château de l'Horizon.

The Cannes Municipal Archives had a file of information on the villa, which I was allowed to access, and the following day I arranged for a car and driver/guide to see and photograph the villa itself, and other properties in the area that are mentioned in this book. This was easier said than done for when I came to find the villa, despite knowing its precise location, it did not seem to be there. From the roadside, the building has always been protected by the high wall and gates that Maxine Elliott erected to shield it from the sound of passing trains. The height of that wall has now been raised and topped with protective wire, so that it is impossible to see over it.

I had been assured by the archivist at the Cannes Archives that the villa was still there, and by coincidence a few days before my long-planned departure for France I had seen an article in the American Express house magazine containing a photograph of the villa as it had looked in Maxine's day and in Aly's day, giving a brief *précis* of its history and stating that it still existed. My local guide, however, assured me that this could not be the villa I was seeking. 'This is the house of the Saudi King, Fahd,' he insisted. 'It has been there for many, many years. It is nothing like the picture you showed me. This cannot be the same place.' Since we couldn't see it anyway, I dropped the matter and concentrated on looking for the other houses in the area, such as the Aga Khan's Yakymour. I had a similar problem photographing the Château de la Croë, equally well-shielded by high walls and high security.

That evening I decided there were two ways in which to get the photos I wanted. Knowing that both properties fronted the sea I could hire a light aircraft and fly over them, or I could rent a boat and sail past. The latter option won on grounds of cost, and I was able to charter a small yacht with skipper for the day from Antibes Marina. Having sailed past the Château de la Croë on the Cap d'Antibes and taken photographs, we rounded the southerly point and eased sheets to lay a perfect course across the Golfe Juan with the Château de l'Horizon right on the bow. I had marked the position on a chart and we could see the building from a long way off, but as we got closer to the shore consternation set in. There was a building in the right place, but it looked nothing like the beautifully proportioned white art deco villa that I had researched. We reached the coast and sailed up and down for a mile in each direction, looking at other villas in case I had it wrong – there are not many, only three or four, well-spaced along that narrow stretch of rocky coastline. None even vaguely resembled the Château de l'Horizon. I took photographs of the building on the site anyway, a vast development painted pink and of no particular style, except that it could be described as vaguely Mediterranean.

That evening, when I returned to my hotel room I enlarged the photographs of the pink palace on my laptop screen and compared it with the old aerial photographs of the Château de l'Horizon. Immediately, I could see that part of the existing building encompassed what had been the old villa, which now accounts for perhaps a fifth of the entire new building. The shady pine trees that had once housed Maxine's artificial moon were gone from the terrace; the swimming pool wall towered some ten metres above the sea but no longer housed the water-chute built to accommodate Maxine's ample derrière – presumably the steps for swimmers to clamber back up to the terrace made it a security risk for the Saudi King, who, I now learned, had purchased the house from Karim Aga Khan in the early Eighties.

King Fahd made only one visit there before his death in 2005. His son, King Abdullah, is the present owner, but he owns another large palace in Cannes and rarely visits. I was told by local officials that in return for the town of Vallauris dropping a prosecution for major building work carried out on the Château de l'Horizon without the necessary planning permission, the King graciously agreed to pay for an extension of the Coastal Footpath – the *Littoral Méditerranée* – along the beach at the base of the wall housing his swimming pool.

Just as I was finishing this book in July 2015, a small furore erupted on the site, which made the UK national news. Because of an impending visit by the Saudi royal family to the villa, security guards had blocked access to the small public beach among the rocks to one side of the property. It was considered too dangerous for the royal family, although, arguably, for many decades personalities of equal importance mixed happily with such local residents as cared to venture across the rocks.

A petition deploring this closure of a public beach (used only by locals because of access difficulties) was signed by one hundred thousand local residents, but the King had approached the French President personally and the beach was closed for several days.

I smiled to think that the Château de l'Horizon is still making headlines.

Postscript

What happened to some of the major personalities in the book after 1960.

Rita Hayworth

After the collapse of her marriage to Aly Khan, Rita returned to Hollywood to star in a comeback picture, *Affair in Trinidad*, opposite Glenn Ford, with whom she had starred in her blockbuster, *Gilda*. Her constant rows with studio boss Harry Cohen caused her frequent suspension and the picture was late in production, but it was much publicised and ended up grossing a million dollars more than *Gilda*. She went on to star in a string of successful pictures alongside such stars as Charles Laughton, Stewart Granger, José Ferrer, Robert Mitchum and Jack Lemmon, but her career was badly affected by her tumultuous marriage to Dick Haymes.

Haymes was a singer with two previous wives, a hefty alimony bill and a massive outstanding tax bill. Rita paid off most of his debts and the pair married in Las Vegas in September 1953. Even her money was insufficient, and at the time Rita was fighting a custody battle with Aly Khan over Yasmin she and Haymes were also fending off – and sometimes hiding from – sheriff's deputies who had warrants to arrest Haymes for debts. When Haymes struck Rita in the face during a quarrel at a nightclub in Los Angeles, Rita walked out on the marriage. She was by then desperately short of money, so she returned to work in Hollywood and also did some television.

She married producer James Hill in 1958 and intended to retire, but this marriage was also unsuccessful and she filed for divorce three years later, citing extreme mental cruelty. There was plenty of supporting evidence for Hill had been witnessed by many, including Charlton Heston, heaping obscene abuse on Rita in public while she wept into her hands. Again she returned to making movies but years of personal problems and heavy drinking had prematurely aged her, and the intrusiveness of movie camera close-ups made her look older than her late thirties. In an interview for a German television programme in 1967 she was still beautiful and poised, but she noticeably struggled to remember some words. In her last movie, *The Wrath of God* (1972), her health and mental state was so poor that some scenes had to be shot a line at a time. There was a good deal of negative publicity when soon afterwards she was removed from a flight for drunken behaviour, and for some time afterwards she was reagarded as a hopeless drunk. Eventually, however, it was realised that her alcoholism had masked the symptoms of Alzheimer's disease.

Through these traumatic years, when she flew into violent

uncontrollable rages, Rita was cared for devotedly by her daughter Yasmin, who wrote of her enormous relief when Rita was finally diagnosed in 1980. Soon afterwards Rita's eldest daughter Rebecca (her child by Orson Welles) saw her mother for the first time in many years; she was not recognised, but after a while Rita began to understand who she was and sat with tears running down her face. Rita died in February 1987 at the age of sixty-eight, from complications arising from Alzheimer's.

Gene Tierney

Following her break-up with Aly Khan, Gene attempted suicide and was treated for severe depression; this included a series of electric shock treatments approved by her mother. Gene blamed the onset of this 'touch of insanity', as she later described it, on the life she had been leading in Hollywood and her personal relationships. In 1958 she returned to Hollywood, where she had been offered the lead role in *Holiday for Lovers*, but the stress was too much for her fragile mental health and she relapsed.

In 1958 Gene met the Texas oil baron W. Howard Lee, who was married to Hedy Lamarr. After his divorce, he and Gene married in 1960 and the couple lived quietly and happily in Houston, Texas until Lee's death in 1981. Gene suffered occasional bouts of depression for the remainder of her life, but in a television interview (still available on YouTube) said that as long as she lived a quiet life she was able to deal with the condition.

A heavy smoker, Gene died of emphysema in Houston in November 1991.

Daisy Fellowes

Daisy remained friends with Winston Churchill to the end of her life, and there are a number of friendly letters between them in the Churchill Papers, invariably signed with a drawing of a daisy flower in place of her name. They continued to meet on the Riviera when Winston was holidaying there, but never in England since Clementine deprecated Daisy and her lifestyle.

After Reggie Fellowes died in 1953, the sixty-three-year-old Daisy suffered a series of depressions and several times attempted suicide (Daisy's mother had committed suicide when Daisy was a young child). In the late Fifties Daisy left the Riviera for good and moved into her vast Parisian mansion on the rue de Lille where she died, aged seventy-two, in 1962.

She is still known for her fabulous collection of bespoke jewels, created for her – often to her own design – by the great jewellers such as Cartier, Van Cleef & Arpels, Lacloche, Boucheron, and Mauboussin, which perfectly captured the style of between-the-wars Modernism. It was arguably among the best collections of fine jewels in the world and when a piece occasionally reaches the salerooms today it can easily generate as much excitement in the press as one of the pieces owned by Daisy's friend the Duchess of Windsor.

Pamela Digby Churchill

After her relationships with Gianni Agnelli and Élie de Rothschild failed, Pam travelled to America, where she made her home. Just a few days before Aly Khan's death in May 1960, Pam married the Broadway impresario and producer Leland Hayward, whose greatest hit was *The Sound of Music*. Until Leland's death in 1971 the couple lived in great luxury at his country estate, called Haywire after his early Broadway production. It was a happy marriage and Pam ensured that everything revolved around her husband – even to the detriment of his children. During Leland's lifetime Pam's relationship with her stepchildren was cordial enough, but following his death their association became extremely acrimonious and Pam's stepdaughter wrote a bitter memoir, titled *Haywire*, which openly accused Pam of robbing Leland's children of valuable items left by their father.

In 1971 Pam met up with her first real love, Averell Harriman, now aged seventy-nine and, like Pam, recently widowed. Pam and Averell took up their old relationship and were married six months later, at which point she became a United States citizen. Again, the marriage was happy and again there were problems when the children of Averell's previous marriage felt ousted by Pam, which created deep antagonism. Following Averell's death in 1986 Pam became embroiled for years in bitter legal arguments over his will. She had been left sixty-five million dollars and Harriman's children accused her of wasting thirty million dollars of their trust fund in ill-advised investments, leaving them only three million.

During her marriage to Harriman Pam had become active in Washington society, and in particular within the upper echelons of the Democratic Party. She became a mover and shaker in her own right, founding and running successful fund-raising campaigns and a political action committee called Democrats for the 80s (and later Democrats for the 90s). She was named the National Democratic Club's Woman of the Year in 1980 and in 1993, and for her help in his presidential campaign – it was said he never would have succeeded without Pam's stamp of approval – President Bill Clinton sent her to Paris as United States ambassador. She was a stunning success.

On 3 February 1997, while swimming in the pool at the Ritz, Paris, she suffered a brain haemorrhage and died two days later.

President Clinton sent Air Force One to collect Pam's body from Paris, and she was received in Washington with full military honours. The *New York Times* said her funeral 'was the closest thing to a state funeral Washington has seen in years'. No previous American ambassador had ever been so honoured.

It was Pam's misfortune to have two hostile biographers. The first biography began as a cooperative venture: Pam was to supply the information and documentary materials, and the professional biographer was to do the writing. Some months into the project Pam's brother Eddie and her sister Sheila persuaded her to pull out as they believed it would reflect unfavourably on her position. She cancelled her agreement and the biographer went on to write an unauthorised biography of Pam anyway, in a context which could not be described as sympathetic. The second biography, perhaps taking its cue from the first, was also an unflattering portrait, concentrating on Pam's numerous love affairs and the deeply subjective evidence of her disaffected stepchildren – the equivalent of writing a biography of Kennedy via his bedroom conquests, as told by the lovers' husbands and children.

Men were indeed important milestones in Pam's life, and she learned much from most of them about art, wine and music – all this she regarded as part of her education. But apart from her indisputable abilities as a courtesan she was a success above the ordinary in her own right. Ask any Parisian about Pam's contemporary achievements as ambassador and you will more often than not receive a glowing commendation. In Washington she was revered as a political hostess by Democrats and highly respected, albeit grudgingly, by Republicans. Her former lovers remained good friends and were welcomed by her family years after the love affairs had ended.

Elsa Maxwell

In October 1956 Elsa met Maria Callas. She was surprised that Callas wanted to see her, for she had just written an unfavourable review of the diva's debut at the New York Met. The two women became close friends, but for Elsa it was more than a friendship: she became infatuated with Callas and followed her on tours, bombarding the singer with love letters ('the greatest love one human being can feel for another' she wrote in one of them) and telephone calls. Elsa could never resist playing Cupid, however, and just as she had once introduced Aly Khan to Rita Hayworth in one of the era's great fated romances, she topped it when, at a Greek ball that she threw at the Hotel Danieli in Venice, she introduced Maria Callas to Ari Onassis. Both were in reasonably happy long-term marriages at the time – Callas to Giovanni Meneghini and Onassis to Tina. It was a doomed meeting which would eventually ruin both their lives, as well as those of their partners.

Over the next months, as Maria cancelled appearance after appearance, earning a reputation for being impossible to work with, Elsa escorted her around Paris where they dined with some of the Rothschilds, attended the races as Aly's guest, took tea with the Windsors and attended every important party going – seldom getting to bed until 4 a.m. Later Elsa told Joan Sutherland that she blamed herself for the decline of Maria Callas's voice by introducing her to the world of jet-setters.

It was in the spring of 1959 that Onassis invited Callas and her husband to join him and Tina, along with Winston and Clementine, on a cruise aboard the *Christina*. Elsa was in Monte Carlo and dined with the party before the yacht departed, but she was not invited to sail with them on that occasion. The rest is history.

In 1961, while dancing the twist with Onassis, Elsa suffered a mild stroke which left her very lame. Nevertheless, as she recovered her career went from strength to strength as she became a major personality on late-night television chat shows whenever she was in the USA. Her series of books were all brought back into print and sold well on the back of her new popularity.

Despite her decline in health she was still partying in the late summer of 1963, still visiting old friends such as Princess Grace of Monaco on a birthday trip to the Riviera, still pulling strings and conducting introductions in the Ritz Bar in Paris, still organising and acting the *grande dame* at events such as the April in Paris charity ball in New York, which she had helped to found, though in October 1963 she attended it in a wheelchair. A week later she was admitted to hospital having suffered a heart attack and she died there two days later. Her lifelong friend Dickie Fellowes-Gordon was her sole heir. Elsa left only ten thousand dollars, and Dickie outlived Elsa by twenty-eight years. She gradually sold off her assets including the house in France, and she died in distressed circumstances in London in 1991, aged one hundred.

Elsie de Wolfe

In June 1939 Elsie, aged seventy-two and dressed in her shorts and conical hat, was doing handstands on Maxine's terrace while she and her friends waited to see how Maxine would fare following her stroke. A few weeks later, on the night of 1 July 1939, Elsie threw her second annual Circus Ball at her beloved Villa Trianon in Versailles. From 10 p.m. until breakfast was served at 5 a.m., seven hundred guests, including Coco Chanel, Elsa Schiaparelli and the Windsors, partied at what proved to be the last great soirée of the pre-war Paris social season, and indeed of the era. She had built a ballroom in the garden for the occasion and the garden entertainments featured a circus ring among trees that were softly uplit to provide a magical atmosphere. Beautifully dressed and bejewelled guests, seated on gilded chairs and wearing fur wraps to keep off the damp of a summer night, watched clowns, acrobats and the famous grey Lipizzaner stallions of the Spanish Riding School of Vienna perform. Inside the exquisite house vast containers filled with ice kept hundreds of bottles of champagne at the correct temperature, and the salons were trimmed with great garlands of flowers and massive floral arrangements by Constance Spry. Elsie had a simple aim: perfection – and it was generally conceded that she achieved it.

As the Germans swept into France the fortunate few who were able to do so made their escape. Elsie and her husband Charles Mendl headed for California, where she renovated a crumbling mansion in Beverly Hills and somehow contrived with the aid of friends to rescue a stool that had belonged to Marie Antoinette and had been left behind at Villa Trianon. Since the villa was occupied by Nazis at the time this was quite a feat. When the stool arrived in California Elsie spent a morning moving it around the room so that it could get air and sun following the traumas it had suffered on its journey.

Elsie's American citizenship, which had been lost by her marriage to Charles, was restored by special act of Congress, but as soon as the war ended she could not wait to get back to Paris and her beloved Villa Trianon. She found it in a poor state after five years of occupation by German High Command, followed by a brief spell housing General Eisenhower and his staff. Despite her increasing frailty (she was by now in her eighties) she spent four years renovating her house to return it to its former state, and she died there in 1950. At her specific request no funeral was held as she said she preferred her friends to remember her 'in their hearts'.

Charles had retired as a diplomat before they fled to California in 1939, but in an unlikely turn of events found work in Hollywood playing the role of an archetypal British aristocrat in several films including *Notorious* in 1946 and *Ivy* in 1947. He died on 15 February 1958 in Paris.

The Duke and Duchess of Windsor

Wallis was never accepted by the Royal Family. In 1945, after they returned from the Bahamas to France, the Duke wrote a best-selling autobiography, titled *A King's Story*, which was published in 1951. Perhaps encouraged by the success of this, Wallis also wrote her autobiography, *The Heart Has Its Reasons* (1956), though Diana Mosley told me the book said more about the ghost writer than about Wallis herself, or the vibrant personality of the woman who captured a king. Since then, an entire literary industry has evolved about this couple whose story continues to enthral millions of readers.

After they sold La Croë they settled in a beautifully converted ancient mill house near Paris, although as they aged they told close friends they wished they had opted for the more kindly climate of the Riviera. The Duke of Windsor died in Paris on 28 May 1972 of throat cancer. His body was flown to England in an RAF aircraft for the funeral and interment at Frogmore, in the private burial ground of the Royal Family. Wallis flew to London for the funeral accompanied by Winston Churchill's daughter Mary. Wallis was no longer afraid of flying for, as she told Mary, she had nothing now to live for.

Wallis stayed at Buckingham Palace and was driven by Prince Charles to Windsor on the eve of the Duke's funeral to see her husband's body lying in state at St George's chapel. The authorities had underestimated the amount of interest in the occasion: more than sixty thousand people came to pay their respects. Apart from one short private day visit to view her husband's grave in 1974, using an airplane loaned to her by the Queen, the Duchess remained in

Paris, becoming increasingly frail and withdrawn from her friends. She ended her life being cared for by her lawyer, almost a prisoner in her own bedroom. For some years prior to her death on 24 April 1986 even her friends were refused entry to her house on the grounds that Wallis was too ill to receive them. She was buried alongside the Duke at Frogmore.

Prince Karim, Aga Khan IV

In 1969 Karim married Sally Croker-Poole, a former British model, who became Begum and took the name Princess Salimah Aga Khan. During a twenty-five-year marriage they had one daughter and two sons. His eldest child from that first marriage is Princess Zahra, but it is Prince Karim's first son, Prince Rahim, who is expected to succeed his father to the title as leader of the Ismailis. However, the Aga Khan has refused to reveal his intentions in this respect, which – he announced – will be revealed after his death.

Despite the fact that he does not rule over any geographic territory the Aga Khan was in 2015 listed by *Forbes* magazine as one of the world's ten richest royals, with an estimated net worth of eight hundred million dollars. This includes hundreds of racehorses, a number of stud farms, an exclusive yacht club and hotel on Sardinia, a private island in the Bahamas, two private jets, a superyacht and several large estates, including his principal home in northern France. His exchequer benefited hugely when the French President Nicolas Sarkozy ruled that the Aga Khan – who is a British subject – would not have to pay any direct taxes, stamp duty and wealth tax to France.

He is founder and chairman of the Aga Khan Development Network, one of the largest private development networks in the world, whose laudable aims are the global improvement of the environment, health, education, architecture, culture, microfinance, rural development, disaster reduction, the promotion of private-sector enterprise and the revitalisation of historic cities.

Source Notes

Full details of the publications cited in the text are provided in the Bibliography.

Abbreviations used in the notes
CHUR – Churchill Papers, Churchill College, Cambridge
CHAR – Chartwell Papers, Churchill College Library, Cambridge
WSC – Sir Winston S. Churchill
CSC – Clementine Spencer Churchill
ME – Maxine Elliott
DFR – Diana Forbes-Robertson

Introduction

1 *Daily Mail*, 12 October 2013.

PART ONE

In this sketch of Maxine's early life, I have drawn mainly on the biography *My Aunt Maxine: The Story of Maxine Elliott* by Diana Forbes-Robertson, *Blossom: A Biography of Mrs F.G. Miles* by Jean M. Fostekew, the Diana Forbes-Robertson Collection on Maxine Elliott in Special Collections, Raymond H. Fogler Library, University of Maine, the Churchill Archives at Churchill College, Cambridge, and British and American newspaper reports at Colindale Newspaper Library (now at Boston Spa, West Yorkshire) that are too numerous to mention.

Chapter 1

1 Rockland, Maine, Town Birth Register.
2 Comment by Constance Collier, quoted in DFR: *My Aunt Maxine*, p. 165.

Chapter 2

1 Quoted in DFR: *My Aunt Maxine*, p. 88.
2 Nat C. Goodwin: *Nat Goodwin's Book*, p. 217.
3 Sundry entries in DFR's research notes, Special Collections. Raymond H. Fogler Library, University of Maine.
4 DFR: *My Aunt Maxine*, p. 193.
4 ME, undated letter to Constance Collier (*c*. 1907), noted in DFR's research notebook, Special Collections, Raymond H. Fogler Library, University of Maine.
5 Unidentified newspaper cutting in DFR research papers, Special Collections. Raymond H. Fogler Library, University of Maine.

Chapter 3

1 CHUR. WSC to CSC, 25 June 1911.
2 See Robert Philip: 'Matinee idol of tennis who lived and died for adventure', *Daily Telegraph* website, 20 June 2005. Also A. Wallis Myers: *Captain Anthony Wilding*, p. 5.
3 Ibid., pp. 227, 237, 248.
4 'People in the Limelight', *Dundee Evening Telegraph*, 7 November 1913.
5 A. Wallis Myers: *Captain Anthony Wilding*, pp. 262–3.
6 Ibid., p. 286.

Chapter 4

1 Martin Gilbert: *The Wilderness Years*, p. 600.
2 DFR: *My Aunt Maxine*, p. 259.
3 Ibid., p. 263.
4 Elsa Maxwell on ME, quoted in Sam Stagg: *Inventing Elsa Maxwell*, p. 70.
5 Diana Vreeland, introduction to Jane S. Smith: *Elsie de Wolfe*.

6 Elsa Maxwell: *R.S.V.P.*, p. 138.
7 Ibid., pp. 164–5.
8 DFR: *My Aunt Maxine*, p. 263.

PART TWO

Chapter 5

1   Emrys Williams: *Bodyguard*, p. 134.
2   Vincent Sheean: *Between the Thunder and the Sun*, p. 30.
3   Ibid., p. 41.
4   Ibid., p. 68.
5   *Daily Express*, 3 September 1933, p. 5.
6   Victor Steibel, quoted in Chris Montague, 'Cara's VERY naughty aunty!', *Daily Mail*, 19 July 2013, pp. 7–8.
7   Leonard Mosley: *Castlerosse*, p. 80.
8   Ibid., p. 71.
9   Ibid., p. 82.
10 Excerpts from Noël Coward: *Private Lives: An Intimate Comedy in Three Acts* (Heinemann) 1930.
11 Diana Mosley: *A Life of Contrasts*, p. 89.
12 DFR: *My Aunt Maxine*, p. 263.

Chapter 6

1   Churchill College Cambridge, Ref. CSC 2/247. WSC to CSC, 16 August 1934.
2   Author's interview with Lady Soames, 9 September 2009.
3   Phyllis Moir: *I Was Winston Churchill's Private Secretary*, p. 61.
4   WSC addl volume, 17 August 1933, p. 862.
5   Vincent Sheean: *Between the Thunder and the Sun*, p. 42.
6   Consuelo Vanderbilt Balsan: *The Glitter and the Gold*, p. 217.
7   Vincent Sheean: *Between the Thunder and the Sun*, pp. 47–8.
8   Michael Bloch: *Wallis and Edward*, p. 130.
9   Ibid., p. 131.
10 Private interviews given to the author during research for this book,

and also *The Churchills*: Hugo Vickers interview; the late Diana Mosley interview; anonymous source.

11 Review by A.C. Black of *Whites, the First 300 Years* by Anthony Lejeune, *Spectator*, 9 July 1993.
12 Mary Soames: *Speaking for Themselves*, pp. 37–8.
13 Vincent Sheean: *Between the Thunder and the Sun*, p. 48.
14 CHAR 1/299/77. Doris Castlerosse to WSC, 9 July 1937.

Chapter 7

1   'King's Holiday in France', *Hull Daily Mail*, 25 July 1936.
2   CHAR 1/299/77. Doris Castlerosse to WSC, 9 July 1937.
3   Churchill College Cambridge, CSCT2 (2b). WSC to CSC, 13 September 1936.
4   *Churchill Correspondence*, December 1936, p. 493.
5   Michael Bloch: *Wallis and Edward*, p. 253.
6   Michael Bloch: *The Secret File of the Duke of Windsor*, p. 126.
7   CHAR 1/299.
8   CHUR 1/300. WSC to ME, 4 July 1937
9   *Churchill Papers*, vol. 12, p. 871.
10 Michael Bloch: *The Secret File of the Duke of Windsor*, p. 123.
11 Vincent Sheean, *Between the Thunder and the Sun*, p. 62.
12 Spencer-Churchill Papers, Churchill College Cambridge. WSC to CSC, 18 January 1938.
13 Vincent Sheean: *Between the Thunder and the Sun*, pp. 65–6.
14 Ibid.
15 DFR: *My Aunt Maxine*, p. 278.
16 Spencer-Churchill Papers, Churchill College Cambridge. WSC to CSC, 18 January 1938.
17 Forsch Collection, Dartmouth College Library, MS 788-23(2). WSC to ME, 8 February 1938.
18 CHAR 1/323/24-25. Clare Sheridan to WSC, 5 March 1938.
19 Diana Wells Hood: *Working for the Windsors*, p. 49.
20 Michael Bloch: *The Duke of Windsor's War*, pp. 97–100.
21 Debo, Dowager Duchess of Devonshire, to author. The Dowager Duchess had this information from the Windsor's

housekeeper, who later came to work at Chatsworth.

22 Debo, Dowager Duchess of Devonshire, to author.

23 James Lees-Milne: *Harold Nicolson*, pp. 106–7.

24 Spencer-Churchill Papers, Churchill College, Cambridge, folio 5. WSC to CSC, 10 January 1938.

Chapter 8

1   Harold Nicolson: *Diaries and Letters 1930–39*, p. 351.

2   Ibid., p. 352.

3   Maxine Block and E. Mary Trow (eds), *Current Biography 1942* (H.W. Wilson) 1942, p. 155.

4   CHAR 1/324/16.

5   *Churchill Correspondence*, December 1938, p. 1330.

6   Spencer-Churchill Papers, Churchill College, Cambridge. WSC to CSC, 8 January 1939.

7   Vincent Sheean: *Between the Thunder and the Sun*, pp. 149–50.

8   Mary S. Lovell, *The Mitford Girls*, p. 348.

9   CHAR 1/344/14-17. WSC to CSC, 18 January 1939.

10 CHAR 1/343/55-56. Daisy Fellowes to WSC, 12 February 1939.

11 CHAR 1/343. ME to WSC, 27 January 1939.

12 CHAR 1/343/61-62. ME to WSC, 10 February 1939.

13 CHAR 1/343/34-36. ME to WSC, 1 February 1939.

14 DFR: *My Aunt Maxine*, p. 282.

15 CHAR 1/343/129-30. ME to WSC, 20 June 1939.

16 CHAR/2/365/4-5. ME to WSC, 6 July 1939.

17 Duchess of Windsor: *The Heart Has Its Reasons*, p. 319

18 Noël Coward: *Future Indefinite*, p. 321.

19 Ibid.

Chapter 9

1   CHAR 2/394. ME to WSC, 18 February 1940.

2   Ibid.

3   W. Somerset Maugham: *Strictly Personal*, p. 11.

4   CHAR 2/394. Dr Brès to WSC, 5 March 1940.

5   CHAR 2/394, WSC to Dr Brès, 15 March 1940.

PART THREE

Chapter 10

1 Quoted in Anne de Courcy: *The Viceroy's Daughters*, p. 308.
2 Duchess of Windsor: *The Heart Has Its Reasons*, p. 332.
3 Andrew Barrow: *Gossip*, p. 105.
4 Jacques Cygler of Cannes in private conversation with author, May 2013.

Chapter 11

1 CHAR 20/1978/171. Air Chief Marshal Sir Arthur Harris to WSC, 22 March 1945.
2 Charles J.V. Murphy: 'The New Riviera', *Life*, 10 November 1947, p. 150.
3 Ibid., p. 146.
4 Ibid., p. 149.
5 Ibid., p. 150.
6 Duff Cooper and John Julius Norwich: *Duff Cooper Diaries*, p. 402. Entry for 15 February 1945.
7 Hugo Vickers: *Cecil Beaton*, pp. 325–6.
8 Emrys Williams: *Bodyguard*, p. 135.

Chapter 12

1 Emrys Williams: *Bodyguard* p. 134.
2 Ibid., p. 135.
3 Debo Devonshire to her mother, 7 June 1953. Reproduced by kind permission of The Mitford Archive at Chatsworth.
4 The Aga Khan: *The Memoirs of Aga Khan*, p. 87.
5 Speech given by the Aga Khan III to the All India Conference (in his Presidential Address), Delhi, 1904. For full text see www. ismailignoses.com.
6 India Office Archives, private files: Aga Khan III. A number of letters make it clear that the Aga's requests to make him a ruling prince were disregarded because his son was 'not a very desirable person', 13 February 1934.

7 Lancaster quoted in Leonard Slater: *Aly*, p. [to come].
8 Charlotte Mosley (ed.): *The Letters of Nancy Mitford*, p. 263. 29 June 1948.

Chapter 13

1 Elsa Maxwell: *I Married the World*, p. 240.
2 Emrys Williams: *Bodyguard*, p. 139.
3 Ibid., pp. 140–1.
4 Ibid., p. 142.
5 Ibid., pp. 150–1.
6 Ibid., p. 152.
7 Ibid., p. 153.
8 Ibid., p. 157.

Chapter 14

1 Mary S. Lovell: *The Churchills*, p. 500.
2 Author's conversation with Lord Digby at Minterne, 2009.

Chapter 15

1 The Aga Khan: *The Memoirs of Aga Khan*, p. 313.

Chapter 16

1 Emrys Williams: *Bodyguard*, p. 186.
2 Deborah Devonshire: *Wait for Me!*, p. 165.
3 Ibid., p. 167.
4 Lady Soames in conversation with author, 9 September 2009. See also her biography *Clementine Churchill*, p. 306.
5 Michael Wardell, *Churchill's Dagger*, short memoir of the 1949 holiday. Churchill Centre and online.
6 Anne Sebba: *That Woman*. Donahue's story is detailed in this sympathetic biography of Wallis.
7 Anne Sebba, private correspondence with author.
8 Ibid., 3 October 2013.

9 Quoted in Christopher Wilson, 'The night that Edward confronted Wallis over her gay lover', *Mail on Sunday*, 20 September 2014.

Chapter 17

1 Anthony Montague Browne: *Long Sunset*, p. 224.
2 Statement issued through Rita's Paris attorney, Maître Suzanne Blum. Quoted in Leonard Slater: *Aly*, p. 185.
3 Leonard Slater: *Aly*, p. 186.
4 All quotations from letters written by Debo Devonshire printed by kind permission of The Mitford Archive at Chatsworth.
5 Author's interviews and private correspondence with 'Heather Manchester'.
6 Leonard Slater: *Aly*, p. 191.
7 Justine Picardie: *Coco Chanel*, p. 165.
8 Anthony Montague Browne: *Long Sunset*, p. 216.
9 Mary Soames, private correspondence with author.
10 Lord Moran: *Churchill*, p. 693.
11 Anthony Montague Browne: *Long Sunset*, p. 220.
12 Mary Soames: *Speaking for Themselves*, p. 604.
13 Ibid., p. 601.
14 Anthony Montague Browne: *Long Sunset*, p. 221.
15 Noël Coward: *Diaries*, p. 323.
16 Ibid., p. 220.
17 Mary Soames: *Speaking for Themselves*, p. 601.
18 Lord Moran: *Churchill*, p. 767.
19 Robert Boothby: *Recollections of a Rebel*, p. 65.

Chapter 18

1 Quoted in Leonard Slater: *Aly*, p. 225.
2 Ibid., p.226
3 Ibid., p. 218.
4 Author's conversation with Lady Soames, 9 September 2009.
5 Martin Gilbert: *Never Despair*, p. 1238.
6 Anthony Montague Brown: *Long Sunset*, p. 242.
7 Martin Gilbert (ed.): *Winston Churchill and Emery Reves*, pp. 385–6.

8 Martin Gilbert: *Never Despair*, p. 1317
9 See Mary S. Lovell: *A Scandalous Life: The Biography of Jane Digby* (Richard Cohen Books) 1995.
10 Account of the accident and aftermath provided by Lord Digby in conversation with the author, November 2009.

Chapter 19

1 'Playboy to Statesman: Aly Khan', *New York Times*, 7 February 1958, p. 4.
2 Joe D. Brown: 'Aly Khan: Sporting Prince', *Sports Illustrated*, 23 March 1959.
3 Bettina: *Bettina*, p. 240.

Bibliography

All books published in the UK unless otherwise noted.

Aga Khan, The: *The Memoirs of Aga Khan: World Enough and Time* (Cassell & Co.) 1954

Balsan, Consuelo Vanderbilt: *The Glitter and the Gold* (Heinemann) 1953

Barrow, Andrew: *Gossip, 1920–1970* (Pan) 1978

Beaton, Cecil: *The Wandering Years: Diaries, 1922–1939* (Weidenfeld & Nicolson) 1961

Bettina (trans. Marguerite Barnett): *Bettina: An Autobiography* (Michael Joseph) 1965

Bloch, Michael: *The Duke of Windsor's War: From Europe to the Bahamas, 1939–1945* (Weidenfeld & Nicolson) 1982

—— *Wallis and Edward: Letters 1931–1937: The Intimate Correspondence of the Duke and Duchess of Windsor* (Weidenfeld & Nicolson) 1986

—— *The Secret File of the Duke of Windsor: The Private Papers 1937–1972* (Corgi) 1989

Boothby, Robert: *Recollections of a Rebel* (Hutchinson) 1978

Bose, Mihir: *The Aga Khans* (Windmill Press) 1984

Cooper, Duff and John Julius Norwich: *The Duff Cooper Diaries, 1915–1951* (Weidenfeld & Nicolson) 2005

Coward, Noël: *Future Indefinite* (Heinemann) 1954

—— *The Noël Coward Diaries* (Weidenfeld & Nicolson) 1982

—— *Autobiography* (Methuen) 1986

—— *The Letters of Noël Coward* (Methuen) 1986

Coudert, Thierry: *Café Society: Socialites, Patrons and Artists 1920–1960* (Flammarion, Paris) 2010

de Courcy, Anne: *The Viceroy's Daughters: The Lives of the Curzon Sisters* (Weidenfeld & Nicolson) 2000

Devonshire, Deborah, Duchess of: *Wait for Me! Memoirs of the Youngest Mitford Sister* (John Murray) 2010

Edwards, Anne: *Throne of Gold: The Lives of the Aga Khans* (HarperCollins) 1995

Emerson, Maureen: *Escape to Provence* (Chapter and Verse) 2008

Forbes-Robertson, Diana: *My Aunt Maxine: The Story of Maxine Elliott* (Viking, New York) 1964

Fostekew, Jean M.: *Blossom: A Biography of Mrs F.G. Miles* (Cirrus Associates) 1998

Gilbert, Martin: *Winston S. Churchill: The Wilderness Years* (Macmillan) 1981

—— *Winston S. Churchill: Never Despair* (Macmillan) 1988

Gilbert, Martin (ed.): *Winston Churchill and Emery Reves: Correspondence 1937–1964* (University of Texas Press, Austin) 1997

Goodwin, Nat: *Nat Goodwin's Book* (Gorham Press, Boston) 1914

Higham, Charles: *Mrs Simpson: Secret Lives of the Duchess of Windsor* (Pan, New York) 1988

Hood, Diana Wells: *Working for the Windsors* (Allan Wingate) 1937

Jackson, Stanley: *The Aga Khan: Prince, Prophet and Sportsman* (Odhams Press) 1952

Leaming, Barbara: *If This was Happiness: A Biography of Rita Hayworth* (Ballantyne, New York) 1989

Lees-Milne, James: *Harold Nicolson: A Biography* (Chatto & Windus) 2 vols 1980–1

Leslie, Anita: *Edwardians in Love* (Hutchinson) 1972

—— *Cousin Randolph* (Hutchinson) 1985

Lovell, Mary S.: *The Mitford Girls: The Biography of an Extraordinary Family* (Little, Brown) 2001

—— *The Churchills: A Family at the Heart of History – from the Duke of Marlborough to Winston Churchill* (Little, Brown) 2011

Maugham, W. Somerset: *Strictly Personal* (Heinemann) 1942

Maxwell, Elsa: *R.S.V.P.: Elsa Maxwell's Own Story* (Little, Brown, Boston) 1954

—— *I Married the World* (Heinemann) 1955

—— *The Celebrity Circus* (W.H. Allen) 1964

Moir, Phyllis: *I Was Winston Churchill's Private Secretary* (Angus & Robertson) 1941

Montague Browne, Anthony: *Long Sunset: Memoirs of Winston Churchill's Last Private Secretary* (Cassell) 1966

Moran, Lord (Charles McMoran Wilson Moran): *Churchill: The Struggle for Survival 1945–60* (Constable) 1966

Mosley, Charlotte (ed.): *Love from Nancy: The Letters of Nancy Mitford* (Sceptre) 1994

—— *The Letters of Nancy Mitford and Evelyn Waugh* (Hodder & Stoughton) 1996

Mosley, Diana: *A Life of Contrasts: The Autobiography of Diana Mosley* (Hamish Hamilton) 1977

—— *The Duchess of Windsor* (Gibson Square Books) 2003

Mosley, Leonard: *Castlerosse* (Arthur Baker Ltd) 1956

Myers, A. Wallis: *Captain Anthony Wilding* (Hodder & Stoughton) 1916

Nicolson, Harold: *Diaries and Letters 1930–39* (Collins) 1966

Picardie, Justine: *Coco Chanel: The Legend and the Life* (HarperCollins) 2010

Quinn, Edward: *Riviera Cocktail* (teNeues) 2011

Ring, Jim: *Riviera: The Rise and Rise of the Côte d'Azur* (Faber and Faber) 2011

Sebba, Anne: *That Woman: The Live of Wallis Simpson, Duchess of Windsor* (Weidenfeld & Nicolson) 2011

Sheean, Vincent: *Between the Thunder and the Sun* (Macmillan) 1943

Slater, Leonard: *Aly: A Biography* (W.H. Allen) 1966

Smith, Jane S.: *Elsie de Wolfe: A Life in the High Style* (Atheneum, New York) 1982

Smith, Sally Bedell: *Reflected Glory: The Life of Pamela Churchill Harriman* (Touchstone, New York) 1997

Soames, Mary: *Clementine Churchill* (Cassell) 1979

—— *Speaking for Themselves: The Personal Letters of Winston and Clementine Churchill* (Doubleday) 1998

—— *A Daughter's Tale: The Memoir of Winston and Clementine Churchill's Youngest Child* (Doubleday) 2011

Staggs, Sam: *Inventing Elsa Maxwell: How and Irrepressible Nobody Conquered High Society, Hollywood, the Press, and the World* (St Martin's Press, New York) 2012

Thompson, W.H.: *I Was Churchill's Shadow* (Christopher Johnson) 1951

Tomkins, Calvin: *Living Well is the Best Revenge* (MoMA, New York) 2007

Vickers, Hugo: *Cecil Beaton: The Authorized Biography* (Weidenfeld & Nicolson) 1985

Williams, Emrys: *Bodyguard: My Twenty Years as Aly Khan's Shadow* (Golden Pegasus Books) 1960

Windsor, Wallis Warfield, Duchess of: *The Heart Has Its Reasons: The Memoirs of the Duchess of Windsor* (Michael Joseph) 1956

Young, Kenneth: *Churchill and Beaverbrook: A Study in Friendship and Politics* (Eyre and Spottiswoode) 1966

Ziegler, Philip: *Diana Cooper* (Alfred A. Knopf, New York) 1982

Acknowledgements

I owe a debt of gratitude to many people who helped in one way or another during the research or production of this book, and the following list is not conclusive. I hope, though, that I have contacted everyone personally to thank them appropriately, including those who for one reason or another wished to remain anonymous.

Anne Biffin, Kate Bower (Ian Brodie Ltd), Sophie Bridges (Churchill College, Cambridge), Judith Brown, Marie Brunell (Archives Municipal de Cannes-Montrose), Desiree Butterfield-Nagy (Fogler Library, University of Maine), Jacques Cygler, the late Duchess of Devonshire, Lord Digby, Mel Johnson (University of Maine), Barbara Kroger (Rauner Library, Dartmouth College, New Hampshire), Helen Marchant, the late Diana Mosley (notes from various interviews), Richard Pike (Curtis Brown), Maureen Rivett, the late Heather Rubin, Anne Sebba, Jane Turner, Barry Singer (Chartwell Booksellers), Hugo Vickers, Kay Williams (Chartwell NT). A special thank you to Hussein Hinnawi of Damascus, who was able to discover for me that Prince

Aly Khan's mausoleum is undamaged by the civil war in Syria.

No book is produced by the author alone. I should also like to thank the 'backroom boys' at Little, Brown, who have been such a massive support – especially when I experienced a bout of ill health which put back publication by over a year. Thank you, everyone, for standing by me.

Commissioning editor: Richard Beswick
Editor: Zoe Gullen
Picture researcher: Linda Silverman
Production: Marie Hrynczak
Jacket designer: Bekki Guyatt
Proofreader: Steve Gove
Indexer: Mark Wells

And finally, thank you to my literary agent, Louise Chinn Ducas, who is an unfailing prop and stay; a friend through thick and thin.

Index

411

Credits

Churchill Archives/Curtis Brown: 35, 36, 37
© National Portrait Gallery, London: 38
Everett/REX/Shutterstock: 40
Nafsger/Bundesarchiv: 42
© John Frost Newspapers/Alamy Stock Photo: 43
Time Life Pictures/Getty Images: 44
John Swope/Getty Images: 46
British Pathé: 47
Coburn/Columbia/REX/Shutterstock: 49
Robert Coburn Sr/Getty Images: 50
© TopFoto: 51
© Pictorial Press Ltd/Alamy Stock Photo: 52
Nat Farbman/Getty Images: 53
Topfoto.co.uk: 55
Mondadori Portfolio/Getty Images: 56
RDA/Getty Images: 57

Author's Note

I am deeply grateful to those copyright owners who have kindly allowed me to quote from various publications and publish images. I have exhaustively attempted to find the copyright holders of all quotations and images used, but in a few cases it has not been possible as the publishers no longer exist and the authors/owners are presumed dead because of the passage of time and copyright holders cannot be traced. Please do not hesitate to contact the author c/o the publishers if this book affects a copyright held by you and it will be corrected in any future editions.

To buy any of our books and to find out
more about Abacus and Little, Brown, our authors
and titles, as well as events and book clubs,
visit our website

www.littlebrown.co.uk

and follow us on Twitter

@AbacusBooks
@LittleBrownUK

To order any Abacus titles p & p free in the UK,
please contact our mail order supplier on:

+ 44 (0)1832 737525

Customers not based in the UK should contact
the same number for appropriate postage
and packing costs.